Court Procedures and Housing Cases – a practitioner's guide

Rita Parmar and Michael Parry

edited by John Thorne

Published in 2002
by Shelter, 88 Old Street, London EC1V 9HU.
020 7505 2043
Registered company 1038133
Registered charity 263710

ISBN 1903595 01-0

Edited by John Thorne, Shelter
Design and layout by Janine Roberts, Shelter
Printed by Russell Press
Distribution by Turnaround 020 8829 3000

Authors

Rita Parmar and Michael Parry are both qualified and experienced solicitors specialising in housing law. They form an integral part of Shelter's Legal team. The team is at the forefront of giving legal advice to those in housing need, writing legal publications, drafting amendments to proposed housing legislation and seeking to positively influence the development of housing law.

Acknowledgements

Our thanks to the following for their valuable input: Adele McCully, Diane Astin, Jayesh Roshi, Jill Howard, John Gallagher, Kim Sartori, Russell Campbell, Sally Morshead, Steve Povey and Shelter Publishing.

Thanks are due also to the other members of Shelter's Legal team for the additional work taken on by each of them during the writing of this book.

Michael would also like to thank Vicky for her patience, encouragement and good humour throughout.

Rita would like to give special thanks to Uma Joshi, Geeta Parmar, Jassy Parmar, Bal Lionnel, Tushar Bala and Rob Wilkins for their constant encouragement and support.

Rita Parmar
Michael Parry

Dedication

I would like to dedicate this book to my mother, Marianne Parry.
Michael

For my family.
Rita

Shelter

Shelter's vision is that everyone should be able to live in a decent and secure home that they can afford within a socially mixed neighbourhood where people feel safe, can work and fulfil their potential. Shelter is Britain's largest homelessness charity, with a network of over 50 housing aid centres and projects providing advocacy and advice at a local level for people in housing need. The start of Shelterline in 1998 marked the launch of Britain's first 24-hour free national housing advice line; the telephone number is 0808 800 4444. The start of Shelternet marked the launch of the UK's first website solely for people to get information about their housing problems; the address is www.shelternet.org.uk. Every year Shelter's services help well over 100,000 people.

For further information about Shelter, please contact:

Shelter, 88 Old Street, London, EC1V 9HU tel. 020 7505 2043 www.shelter.org.uk

Contents

Part I

Part II

Introduction

On 26th April 1999 the Civil Procedure Rules (CPR) came into force and fundamentally changed the landscape of civil litigation in England and Wales. Based on the aims and objectives outlined by Lord Woolf in his report 'Access to Justice', published in July 1996, the new rules represented the greatest single reform of civil procedure in England and Wales. The guiding principle behind the reforms, enshrined in the overriding objective, was that the new system should, as far as possible, ensure that cases are dealt with justly. Lord Woolf's concerns that the system of civil litigation was expensive, slow and inaccessible to litigants saw an attempt to simplify and streamline court procedure. In doing so it was hoped that civil actions would progress through the courts more quickly, efficiently and cheaply.

The main aim of this book is to provide specialist housing practitioners of varying experience with an accessible and practical guide to the CPR within the framework of housing litigation.

The book falls into two main parts. The first part takes the reader through the typical stages involved in a civil action. It starts with pre-action matters continuing through each stage to the final hearing and beyond to the methods used for enforcing judgments. In the final three chapters of Part One, separate consideration is given to certain types of claims which have their own set of rules; namely, possession claims, homelessness appeals in the county court, and judicial review claims.

The second part of the book contains a series of case studies on the main types of claims likely to be encountered by housing practitioners. The case studies are intended to give the reader practical examples of how cases may progress, with examples of the documents involved.

The book as a whole is written predominantly in the context of county court claims to reflect the high proportion of housing cases that are pursued there. The exception to this is the chapter on judicial review claims that are brought and dealt with in the High Court.

A word of caution should be added here. The contents of the book reflect the CPR – and also housing legislation – as at May 2002. However, it would be wrong to believe that the process of reform of civil procedure is at an end. Lord Woolf's idea of a single set of rules for all civil cases in the High Court and in the county courts is yet to be fully realised, with a number of the former rules being preserved in the CPR schedules. For this reason and for the purposes of "fine tuning", substantial amendments have been made since the implementation of the Rules. Practitioners should therefore keep abreast of changes to the Rules made from time to time and which may affect the content of this book. Many advisers will be familiar with the *Civil Court Practice*, better known as *the Green Book* produced and periodically updated by Butterworths. In addition, the Stationery Office produces a three-volume folder version in looseleaf allowing regular updates to be made with ease. The current Rules may also be accessed on the internet via the Lord Chancellor's website at www.lcd.gov.uk.

Michael Parry
Rita Parmar

May 2002

Foreword by Jan Luba QC

Resolving housing disputes forms a significant "chunk" of the work of the civil courts in England and Wales. Our 200-plus local county courts get through over 200,000 claims for possession of residential property each year, together with a significant number of other housing disputes about disrepair, deposits, illegal eviction, homelessness and the like. The High Court and Court of Appeal then hear a steady stream of appeals generated by a proportion of those cases. The judicial review jurisdiction of the Administrative Court has long had "housing" as its second most frequent category of work.

But behind the bald statistics is the real personal dimension of each and every housing dispute, particularly for the occupiers of housing and the homeless. Most ordinary citizens see the civil court process as daunting and uncertain. Their concerns are all the greater when the matter in dispute is something so sensitive as access to, or enjoyment of, a "home". In the most part they are unwilling participants in the court process either as defendants or, less commonly, as claimants seeking hesitantly to assert their (none too extensive) rights when all else has failed.

Those consumers of housing and housing services who become involved in court-based housing disputes have long been troubled by not only the complexity of housing law itself, but by the often obscure and unwieldy procedures of the civil courts. Now, as a result in significant part of the representations made by housing advisers and specialist housing lawyers, a gradual process of change is underway.

In relation to *housing law* itself, the Law Commission has recently embarked on a process of simplification, reform and codification. In Spring 2002 it published the first of a series of consultation papers intended to produce real improvements in the accessibility and clarity of housing law. Hopefully, we will now not have to look too far into the future to see housing law collapsed into a single tome in place of the present six volumes of the *Encyclopaedia of Housing Law & Practice*.

On the *procedure* side much is also happening. The reformed Civil Procedure Rules (1-51) introduced in 1999 have bedded-in. Problems in shoe-horning housing cases into the new regime have been in large part resolved by subsequent modification to the Rules. Witness the more recent introduction of CPR 52 (Appeals), CPR 54 (Judicial Review) and CPR 55 (Possession). The process is not yet concluded but there is much to welcome in the changes that have been wrought.

The challenge for the adviser of a party involved in a housing dispute is to be able to master not only the substantive housing law in play but also the procedural rules, so as to achieve the best possible outcome for the client. And there's the rub. Given the plethora of both substantive law and civil court procedural rules, the adviser needs a veritable library of materials on the shelf in the office and a very large bag to transport them all to court.

That is where *Court Procedures and Housing Cases – A Practitioner's Guide* fulfils a real unmet need. In a single volume it provides the basic material to which every housing adviser, taking or defending a housing case, needs ready access. In Part 1 it outlines, in clear and straightforward language, not only the general practices and procedures of the courts in handling civil claims, but the ways in which those rules are applied (and often modified) in the main categories of housing cases. In Part 2, the reader is offered a step-by-step guide to the handling of the most common forms of housing dispute in the civil courts (possession, disrepair, homelessness and the like). Through the use of case studies which embrace the very latest references to new legislation, rules and protocols, the reader is taken on a carefully guided journey through a relevant sample slice of housing litigation – with many valuable tips offered along the way.

I am flattered to have been invited to write the foreword to such a useful work. My only sadness is that no such material was available, those many years ago, when I started to become involved in advocacy in housing cases. Now, thanks to the work of these authors and the input of their many similarly-skilled colleagues at Shelter, the next generation of housing advisers will be spared the exercise of both "reinventing the wheel" and weightlifting their books to court. I am delighted to commend this work.

Jan Luba QC
Housing Team
2 Garden Court Chambers
London
May 2002

Editor's note

For the ease of the reader, a number of style points have been used in the writing of this book. A reference to a specific civil procedure rule is indicated by the letters CPR, and then the number of the rule. A reference to a paragraph number in a Practice Direction is indicated by the letters CPR, the letters PD, the number of the Part and then "para" and the paragraph number. So, CPR 15.3 means Rule 15.3 of the Civil Procedure Rules, CPR PD 52 para 15.3 means paragraph 15.3 of the Practice Direction supplementing Part 52 of the Civil Procedure Rules.

Where relevant, cross-references are made to other parts of the book for further information. These references are to a paragraph number or to a page number, depending on which is the most useful.

A term that is highlighted in bold means it is defined in the glossary. A term is not in bold every time it is stated. This is because either the term is defined in its particular context, or it has been in bold already in that section.

References have been included to Practice Directions as they carry the same importance as the Rules themselves. However, case law which predates the introduction of the CPR is not binding, but persuasive, as the overriding objective is of paramount importance.

John Thorne

Glossary

Acknowledgement of service A form (N9) which is sent to the court by the defendant to acknowledge receipt of the claim form and particulars of claim.

Adjournment An order by the court that proceedings are put off to a certain day in the future or indefinitely with permission to the parties to restore the matter. Adjournments are often made on terms, eg. that a defendant pays current rent plus an amount towards arrears.

Affidavit A written statement sworn before a person authorised to administer oaths.

Aggravated damages Additional damages which the court may award as compensation for the defendant's objectionable behaviour.

Allocation The process by which the court assigns a case to one of the three case management tracks.

Alternative dispute resolution Collective description of methods of resolving disputes otherwise than through the normal court system.

Attorney-General The principal law officer of the Crown and head of the Bar of England and Wales.

Authorised litigator As defined in the Courts and Legal Services Act 1990.

Bankruptcy The situation whereby a person has been declared bankrupt following insolvency proceedings brought by that person her/himself or another party. On the making of a bankruptcy order the bankrupt's estate vests in a trustee in bankruptcy or the Official Receiver. The order continues until the bankruptcy is discharged.

Case management conference A court hearing sometimes held in multi-track cases at the allocation stage or after. The purpose of the conference is to enable the court to assess how a case is progressing, to encourage the parties to agree on as many matters as possible and to lay down future directions for the conduct of the case.

Case management directions In exercise of its case management powers, the court will usually give directions to provide a timetable for the parties to follow in relation to the future conduct of the case.

Chambers A judge's offices where hearings which are not open to the public are held. The hearing is referred to as being held "in chambers".

Charging order An order which imposes a charge on the property of a judgment debtor to secure payment of a debt.

Child A person under the age of 18 years.

Circuit judge Judge appointed by the Crown to serve in the High Court or the county court in one of the six circuits of the Court Service in England and Wales.

Clear days Where the court rules specify that an act must be done by reference to an event, the day on which the period begins and the day on which the event occurs are not included.

CLS funding *See* Public funding.

Committal proceedings Proceedings for contempt of court brought against a party who has breached a court judgment or order which included a penal notice, eg. an injunction. A person in breach may be sent to prison for a period not exceeding two years or may be fined.

Consent judgment or consent order A judgment or order, the terms of which are agreed by all the parties to the proceedings.

Contempt of court A disregard for the authority of courts of justice, punishable by imprisonment of the offender or a fine.

Contributory negligence Where a person contributes to the events which lead to an accident or other occurrence to her/himself albeit that the accident or occurrence is partly or mainly due to the negligence of another.

Damages A sum of money awarded by the court as compensation to the claimant.

Declaration A ruling of a judge or a court on a question of law.

Default judgment/judgment in default A claimant may obtain judgment in default, otherwise known as "default judgment", where the defendant has failed to file an acknowledgment of service or a defence within the time specified by the CPR.

Detailed assessment The procedure by which the amount of costs incurred in a case is decided by a costs officer in accordance with Part 47.

Directions hearing A hearing at which the court considers which case management directions to make for the future conduct of the case.

Disbursements Payments made by a solicitor on behalf of the client and incurred in the course of litigation, eg. experts' fees, counsel's fees, court fees.

Disclosure The revealing of information, generally documents, that may serve as evidence in a trial, by one party to the other in advance of the trial.

District judge Judges appointed to serve in a county court with more limited jurisdiction to hear cases than circuit judges. Confusingly, district judges are also appointed to serve in District Registries of the High Court.

Evidence in chief The evidence given by a witness for the party who called her/him.

Exemplary damages Damages given principally in respect of tortious acts where the defendant has calculated that the profit to be made from the wrongdoing exceeds the risk of damages. Damages will exceed the amount required to compensate the claimant for the loss or injury suffered by her/him.

Filing In relation to a document, this means delivering it, by post or otherwise, to the court office.

Freezing injunction Previously known as a "Mareva" injunction, a form of interim injunction, available in the High Court, restraining a party in proceedings from removing or otherwise dealing with assets located within the jurisdiction of the court.

General Civil Contract Contract between suppliers and the Legal Services Commission for the provision of advice and assistance under the legal help and help at court schemes.

Hearsay evidence Evidence of an oral or written statement made to the person giving evidence which is used to establish the truth of certain facts, ie. where no first-hand evidence of facts is available.

Help at court One of the levels of service provided under the Community Legal Service. Help at court enables legal representation for particular hearings.

Indemnity basis Method of assessment of costs whereby issues of proportionality are not considered. Any doubts as to whether costs were reasonably incurred or were reasonable in amount are resolved in favour of the receiving party.

Injunction A court order prohibiting a person from doing something (restraining) or requiring a person to do something (mandatory). Injunctions may be granted either during the course of proceedings (interlocutory or interim) or as a final order.

Insolvency An inability to pay debts that may lead to insolvency (bankruptcy) proceedings.

Interim application An application for an order or for directions made during the course of proceedings prior to the full hearing of the case.

Interim costs order Costs order made during the course of proceedings.

Interim declaration A ruling of a judge or a court on a question of law made during the course of proceedings.

Interim or interlocutory injunction An injunction order made during the course of proceedings, or, in certain situations, before proceedings are begun.

Interim payment Where it is clear that the claimant will be at least partially successful in a claim, the court may order the defendant to make a payment on account of any damages or other sum which s/he will be liable to pay on final judgment in the proceedings.

Interim remedy An order granting a remedy to a party during the course of proceedings.

Jointly and severally liable A situation, such as that of joint tenants, whereby two or more parties share a single liability. This means each party can be held liable to pay the whole of a judgment debt or damages.

Judgment creditor A person who has obtained or is entitled to enforce a judgment or order.

Judgment debt A debt due under a judgment or order.

Judgment debtor A person against whom a judgment or order is made where the judgment or order remains unsatisfied.

Judgment in default *See* Default judgment.

Jurisdiction The authority of a court to deal with matters brought before it. In the context of the CPR, the court's jurisdiction, unless otherwise stated, refers to England and Wales and any part of the territorial waters of the United Kingdom adjoining England and Wales.

Lay adviser A person who is not legally qualified but who is assisting a party to proceedings. In fast track and multi-track cases lay advisers may represent that party at court only with the express permission of the court. Certain non-legally qualified persons may represent a party, for example local authority officers in respect of possession actions involving local authority housing (section 60(2) of the County Courts Act 1984). Lay advisers may represent a party in cases which are allocated to the small claims track (Lay Representatives Order 1992 SI 1992/1966).

Legal aid Replaced by Community Legal Service funding in April 2000, legal aid provided a system of public funding for those persons eligible under the scheme. Legal aid was divided into two main schemes: advice and assistance (replaced by Legal Help); civil legal aid (replaced by Legal Representation).

Legal help One of the levels of service provided under the Community Legal Service. Legal Help enables the provision of initial advice and assistance to those persons eligible under the scheme.

Legal representation Legal representation is a form of public funding under the Community Legal Service. It is divided into two levels of service: investigative help, for cases which require detailed investigation before a party is in a position to contemplate commencing legal action; full representation, to enable the party to be represented in an action.

Legal representative A barrister or a solicitor, solicitor's employee or other authorised litigator instructed to act for a party in relation to a claim.

Legal Services Commission The body entrusted with administration of the Community Legal Service. It replaced the Legal Aid Board which administered the Legal Aid scheme.

Letter before action A letter written by a potential claimant to put another party on notice of her/his intention to commence proceedings and allow the other party an opportunity to change her/his decision or otherwise reach a settlement of the proposed claim.

Litigant in person A party who is not represented by a solicitor.

Litigation friend A person who conducts proceedings, whether as a claimant or a defendant, on behalf of a "child" or a "patient" as defined by the CPR. ("Child" and "patient" are also defined in the glossary.)

Mortgagor A debtor who creates a mortgage, usually by way of a legal charge on the property, as security for the loan.

Mortgagee A creditor in whose favour a mortgage is created.

Patient A person who by reason of mental disorder within the meaning of the Mental Health Act 1983 is incapable of managing and administering her/his own affairs.

Paying party The party who must pay the other party's costs.

Penal notice A notice endorsed on an injunction that warns the person required to obey the injunction of the consequences of non-compliance with the order.

Practice direction The CPR are supplemented by practice directions which must be adhered to. In essence, the practice directions provide the flesh on the bones of the CPR.

Pre-action protocol Statements of understanding between legal practitioners and others about pre-action practice which are approved by a relevant practice direction.

Pre-trial review A court hearing held prior to the final hearing of a multi-track case. The main aims of pre-trial reviews are for the court to assess how a case is progressing and to foster a possible settlement in the case, to achieve an agreement with regard to the issues to be resolved at trial and to set a programme and budget for the trial.

Privilege The right of a party to refuse to disclose a document, produce a document or to refuse to answer questions on the ground of some special interest recognised by law, eg. confidential communications between a party and her/his legal adviser with regard to the issue before the court.

Provisional damages An award of damages in a personal injuries case that allows the claimant to apply for further damages in the future should s/he develop a serious disease or suffer a deterioration in her/his physical or mental condition.

Public funding A term used commonly to refer to Legal Services Commission funding under the Community Legal Service.

Purge A person who is held in custody for contempt of court following committal may make an application for an early discharge from custody if s/he can show that s/he has atoned or wishes to atone for the contempt of court.

Receiving party The party that is getting her/his costs paid by the other side.

Return date Where an interim order is made without notice of the application having been given to the other party, the court will include within the order a return date for a further hearing to enable the respondent to be present and contest the application.

Rights of audience The right of a person to appear before a court to represent a party in proceedings.

Search order Previously known as an "Anton Pillar" order, a form of interim injunction, available in the High Court, allowing a person to search and take possession of another person's property following an application made without notice.

Set aside Cancelling a judgment, order or a step taken by a party in the proceedings.

Standard basis Method of assessment of costs whereby the court will only allow costs that are proportionate to the matter in issue. Additionally, any doubt as to reasonability and proportionality will be resolved in favour of the paying party.

Standard of proof The degree of certainty that the evidence of the claimant must provide to establish the facts sufficiently for liability to fall on the other party. In civil cases the standard of proof is on a balance of probability. In committal proceedings arising from a breach of an order made in a civil action, the criminal standard of proof of beyond reasonable doubt is required.

Statement of case A concise but complete statement of the nature of a party's case. The following are all statements of case which must be verified by a statement of truth: a claim form, particulars of claim (where separate from claim form), a defence, a Part 20 claim, a reply to a defence, any further information given in relation to any of these documents, whether provided voluntarily or by court order.

Statement of truth A statement by a party putting forward a document or by the maker of a witness statement that s/he believes that the facts stated in the document are true.

Statement of value Where a claim is for money the claimant must include in the claim form a statement of value which is an assessment of the amount which s/he expects to recover from the defendant. This helps the court to allocate the case to the appropriate track and determines the amount of the court fee.

Stay A stay imposes a halt to the proceedings save for taking any steps allowed by the CPR or the terms of the stay.

Strike out The court's power to strike out written material – so that it may no longer be relied upon in the proceedings – or even the whole action.

Summary assessment The procedure by which the court decides the sum of money to be paid under a costs order at the time the order is made.

Summary judgment Judgment at an early stage of proceedings to either party where a claim or a defence has no real prospects of success and where there is no other compelling reason for dealing with the matter at trial.

Third party debt order Where a person, or more usually a financial institution, owes money to a judgment debtor – for example money held in a bank account – the court may make a third party debt order requiring that person or institution (the third party) to pay the judgment creditor monies up to the level of the outstanding judgment debt.

Tort A civil wrong which is actionable by the person affected but which is independent of a claim in contract or a crime, eg. negligence, nuisance, trespass to person or land.

Track Defended cases are allocated to one of the three case management tracks: the small claims track, the fast track or the multi-track.

Trial bundle The bundle of documents usually prepared and filed by the claimant before the trial which, broadly, contains all the documents relevant to the case. The CPR specify the documents which should be included in a trial bundle.

Undertaking A promise made to another party or to the court. A breach of an undertaking made to the court may amount to a contempt of court.

Vexatious In the context of a claim the term means one brought purely to annoy or oppress another party.

Waiver The abandonment of a right by one party so that afterwards s/he is stopped from claiming it.

Warned date Where the court has not listed a hearing for an exact date but is able to "warn" the parties as to when it is likely to be. Usually the court will indicate that the hearing will be held during the course of a particular week, otherwise known as the trial window.

Warrant An order issued by the court giving court officers (in the form of bailiffs) the authority to put the terms of the judgment into effect.

Warrant of delivery A warrant that allows the court bailiffs to seize goods owned by the claimant and/or payment of their monetary value and/or other goods where a judgment requires the return of goods owned by the claimant.

Warrant of execution A warrant that entitles a court bailiff to seize goods owned by the judgment debtor in order that they may be sold to satisfy a judgment debt and court costs. Certain goods necessary for basic domestic needs or used in the judgment debtor's employment are protected and should not be removed.

Warrant of possession A warrant used for the enforcement of a possession order and exercised by a court bailiff who may evict anyone found on the premises whether or not they were parties to the possession proceedings.

Winding up Bringing the activities of a company to an end, often on the ground that the company is unable to meet its financial liabilities.

Without prejudice Where negotiations are undertaken with a view to settlement and are conducted "without prejudice", this means that the circumstances in which the content of these negotiations may be revealed to the court are very restricted. Commonly, negotiations are made "without prejudice except as to costs", which means that the content of the negotiations may only be revealed to the court when the dispute in the case has been resolved and the court considers the question of costs.

Witness statement A written statement of the oral evidence which the witness intends to provide on any issues of fact to be decided by the court.

Witness summons A document issued by the court requiring a witness to either attend court to give evidence or produce documents to the court.

List of Court Rules

County Court Rules

List of CPR forms

References in bold indicate an example of the form.

Title of Parts

Below is the title of the Parts of the Civil Procedure Rules referred to in the book.

1   Overriding Objective
2   Application and Interpretation of the Rules
3   The Court's Case Management Powers
6   Service of Documents
7   How to start Proceedings – The Claim Form
8   Alternative Procedure for Claims
9   Responding to Particulars of Claim – General
10   Acknowledgement of Service
12   Default Judgement
13   Setting Aside or Varying Default Judgement
14   Admissions
15   Defence and Reply
16   Statements of Case
17   Amendments to Statements of Case
18   Further Information
19   Addition and Substitution of Parties
20   Counterclaims and other Additional Claims
21   Children and Patients
22   Statements of Truth
23   General Rules about Applications for Court Orders
24   Summary Judgement
25   Interim Remedies and Security for Costs
26   Case Management
27   The Small Claims Track
28   The Fast Track
29   The Multi-track
30   Transfer
31   Disclosure and Inspection of Documents
32   Evidence
33   Miscellaneous Rules about Evidence
34   Depositions and Court Attendance by Witnesses
35   Experts and Assessors
36   Offers to Settle and Payments into Court
38   Discontinuance
39   Miscellaneous Provisions Relating to Hearings
40   Judgments, Orders, Sale of Land Etc.
41   Provisional Damages
44   General Rules about Costs
45   Fixed Costs

List of cases

List of abbreviations

AEO   Attachment of Earnings Order
CCR   County Court Rules
CLS   Community Legal Service
CPR   Civil Procedure Rules
LSC   Legal Services Commission
PD   Practice Direction

Tables of Part 7 and Part 8

Part 7 – Defended claim

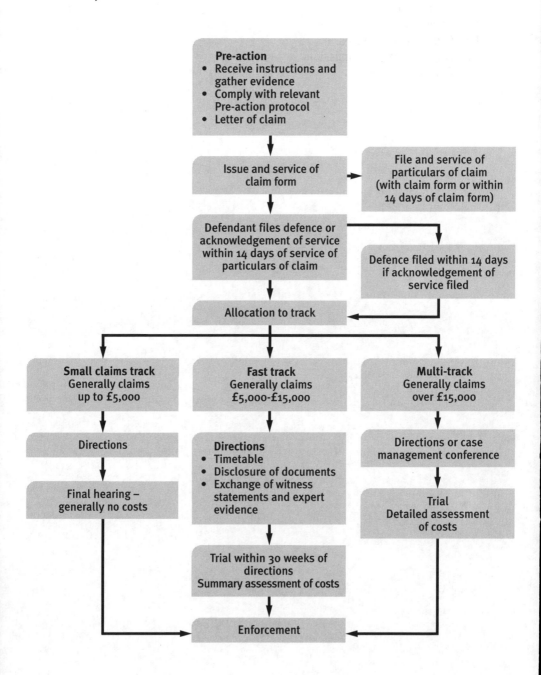

Part 8 – Defended claim

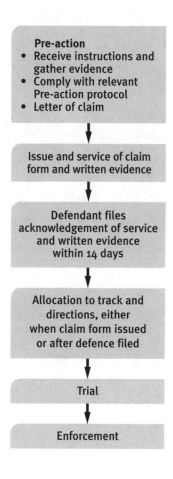

Pre-action
- Receive instructions and gather evidence
- Comply with relevant Pre-action protocol
- Letter of claim

Issue and service of claim form and written evidence

Defendant files acknowledgement of service and written evidence within 14 days

Allocation to track and directions, either when claim form issued or after defence filed

Trial

Enforcement

The overriding objective

CPR 1.1(2)

CPR 1 deals with the overriding objective that the courts must pursue in managing civil cases. The overriding objective is to deal with cases justly. This includes, so far as is practicable:

- ensuring that the parties are on an equal footing

- saving expense

- dealing with the case in ways that are proportionate to:
  - the amount of money involved
  - the importance of the case
  - the complexity of the issues
  - the financial position of each party

- ensuring that the case is dealt with expeditiously and fairly

- allotting to the case an appropriate share of the court's resources, while taking into account the need to allot resources to other cases.

These are examined in more detail below.

1.1 Dealing with cases justly

CPR 1.1 means that the main concern of the court is doing justice. Generally, a litigant should not be prevented from bringing or defending a case if there has been a breach of the rules, in view of the court's paramount obligation to decide cases on their merits.

An example of such a breach might be where a party does not serve court papers within the time specified for service. In *Jones v Telford and Wrekin District Council (1999)*[1] the Court of Appeal allowed an extension of time for service of the particulars of claim where the claimant's solicitors had caused the delay. This was because they had been unable to obtain psychiatric reports for service with the particulars in a personal injury claim. In personal injury claims, the medical evidence must be served with the particulars of claim. In this case, the claimant's solicitors had obtained other medical evidence. However, they did not feel that this was enough and so wanted a psychiatric report as well. This took a long time to acquire; therefore an extension of time was needed. The defendant's solicitors did not think that this should be allowed. The court allowed the extension, with some hesitation, but held that failure to get medical evidence would not usually be a good reason for not serving proceedings within time. The extension of time was allowed largely

---

1   Jones v Telford and Wrekin District Council (1999), noted at *Times* 29 July, CA

because the court believed it should not lose sight of the fact that its primary concern was doing justice.

The courts are increasingly willing to apply the overriding objective. Cases are briefly listed below, showing the actions that the courts are now likely to take to ensure that cases are dealt with justly.

In *Habib Bank Ltd v Abbey-Pearl,*[2] the Court of Appeal held that the lower court was correct in striking out a statement of claim because the supporting evidence was limited and stale, and the claimant had not complied with the court timetable and directions.

The claims were also struck out in *Lord v Carnell*[3] and *Zimbler v Miller.*[4] In the first case, this was because the claimant had twice failed to sign the statement of truth; even after the court had ordered costs sanctions. In the second case, the claimant had embellished the claim – which should have been allocated to the small claims track (see page 80) – and had failed to progress it.

The court decided in *Biguzzi v Rank Leisure*[5] that costs penalties were preferable to a strike out for late service of documents.

The court ordered the defendant to pay a significant sum into court in *Sithole v Thor Chemical Holdings*[6] because he had persistently failed to comply with court orders.

CPR 17.4(3)

In *Gregson v Channel Four TV,*[7] the court decided that amending the name of a defendant after the limitation period had expired was 'just and fair as the mistake was only re the exact name and no-one had been misled'.

1.2   Equal footing

The court cannot prevent a party from instructing solicitors or barristers of its choice, even where one party could not afford solicitors and barristers as expensive as those being used by the other.[8]

In *McPhilemy v Times Newspapers Ltd,*[9] Lord Woolf, one of the judges in this case, said that if a party wished the court to restrain the activities of another party with the object of achieving greater equality, then that party should show that s/he was conducting the proceedings with a desire to limit expense as far as practicable.

1.3   Saving expense

Parties should try where possible to settle cases, thereby saving expense. The courts have a power to award costs on an indemnity basis and

CPR 36.21

enhanced interest (see page 188) where a reasonable offer to settle

2   Habib Bank Ltd v Abbey-Pearl [2001] All ER D 185, CA
3   Lord v Carnell [2000] WL 191857, CA
4   Zimbler v Miller [2000] WL 38148892, CA
5   Biguzzi v Rank Leisure [1999], noted at *Times* 5 October
6   Sithole v Thor Chemical Holdings [2000] WL 1421183, CA
7   Gregson v Channel Four TV [2000], noted at *Times* 11 August, CA
8   Maltez v Lewis [1999] 21 LS Gaz Ref: 39, Neuberger J.
9   McPhilemy v Times Newspapers Ltd [1999] 3 All ER 775, Lord Woolf MR, CA

has been rejected (see paragraph 5.5).[10] Pre-action protocols have also been developed (see paragraph 2.1) to ensure, as far as practicable, that litigation is a last resort.

1.4   Dealing with cases expeditiously and fairly

The court, in furthering the overriding objective, should deal with cases in a fair and efficient way. For example, in *Keene v Martin*,[11] the claimant had started proceedings using the procedure set out in Part 8 of the CPR (see paragraph 3.1) which, on the facts, was not the appropriate one for the case. However, the Court of Appeal allowed the case to go on as an ordinary chancery action, rather than strike it out, because this was more cost effective than making the claimant start again by issuing fresh proceedings.

1.5   Allotting an appropriate share of the court's resources

The court should not spend too long on any one case as this would be unfair to the progress of other cases. For example, it would not be a good use of the court's resources to consider the merits of an appeal against an **injunction** granted during the proceedings (see Chapter 9), when the trial date was less than a month away and the issue would be resolved then.[12]

Another example is found in the case of *Adoko v Jemal*.[13] The claimant here wanted to amend an appeal notice. At the hearing for this, he had failed to supply a bundle of the relevant material as the court had specifically required. The court wasted over an hour trying to sort out the bundle. It was decided that this was not an appropriate use of the court's time and that no more of the court's resources should be allocated to a case conducted in this way. The court did not allow the amendment of the notice and the appeal, as it stood, was dismissed as it was inadequate.

In *Vass v Pank*,[14] the Court of Appeal refused permission to appeal because the costs of taking the case would have been disproportionate to the amount of the claim.

Every other provision in the CPR is subsidiary to the objective of dealing with cases justly. Consequently, if the court considers that another provision prevents it from dealing with a case justly, then the overriding objective will prevail.

CPR 1.3   It is the duty of all parties to assist the court to further the overriding objective. This includes co-operating with each other and the court as much as possible throughout the proceedings.

CPR 1.4   In furthering the overriding objective, the court has a duty to actively manage cases. In doing so, the court should:

---

10 Little v George Little & Co (1999), noted at
    Times 17 November
11 Keene v Martin (1999), noted at *Times* 11 November

12 SBJ Stephenson Ltd v Mandy [1999] NLD 30 June, CA
13 Adoko v Jemal (1999), noted at *Times* 8 July, CA
14 Vass v Pank (2000), 14 November, CA

- encourage the parties to co-operate with each other in the conduct of the proceedings

- identify the issues at an early stage

- decide promptly which issues need full investigation and trial, and accordingly deal with other issues at an early stage

- decide the order in which issues are to be resolved

- encourage the parties to use an **alternative dispute resolution** procedure if the court considers that appropriate, and facilitate the use of such a procedure

- help the parties to settle the whole or part of the case

- fix timetables or otherwise control the progress of the case

- consider whether the likely benefits of taking a particular step justify the cost of taking it

- deal with as many aspects of the case as it can on the same occasion

- deal with the case without the parties needing to attend at court

- make use of technology

- give directions to ensure that the trial of a case proceeds quickly and efficiently.

The court's powers of case management are dealt with further in Chapter 6.

2

Before starting court action

Where a party is considering taking court action, there are certain steps which must be taken before proceedings are started. The main considerations to bear in mind are dealt with below.

2.1 Pre-action protocols

Pre-action protocols are rules and procedures that parties must comply with before starting court proceedings. There are specific pre-action protocols for certain areas of law. Those particularly relevant to housing law are the judicial review pre-action protocol and the pre-action protocol for housing disrepair cases. These are dealt with in Chapter 16 and Case Study 4 respectively. The pre-action protocol for personal injury claims should also be followed in housing law cases that include claims for personal injury in their entirety and not just the personal injury element of the claim.[1] For example, where a housing disrepair claim includes a claim for personal injury, the protocol should be applied to the whole case and not just the personal injury element. This protocol is not examined here as personal injury is outside the scope of this book.

In addition to the above, there is also to be a general pre-action protocol to be used in cases not covered by one of the specific pre-action protocols. It is not yet certain when this will be introduced.[2]

Generally, the aims of pre-action protocols are:

• to encourage the exchange of early and full information about the prospective legal claim

• to enable parties to avoid litigation by agreeing a settlement of the claim before commencement of proceedings. Once parties have exchanged information, they may be able to assess the strengths of the case and therefore agree a settlement. It is easier, quicker and cheaper to reach an agreement than start court proceedings

• to support the efficient management of proceedings where litigation cannot be avoided.

Pre-action protocols generally require a letter before action to be written (see page 11).

Where pre-action protocols exist and are not followed, the court has the power to order parties who have unreasonably failed to comply with the protocol to pay costs or be subject to other sanctions. Case law suggests that the courts are willing to use this power and apply sanctions where parties have disregarded the protocols:

CPR 44.14

---

1 Pre-action protocol for Personal Injury Claims para 2.2   2 details of the draft protocol can be found on the Lord Chancellor's Department website; www.lcd.gov.uk

- In *Jimaale v London Buses Ltd,*[3] the court struck out the claim because of non-compliance with the pre-action protocol for personal injury. This was held to be an abuse of process. The claimant had waited nearly three years, after instructing solicitors, to issue the claim. As a result, the defendant had been severely prejudiced in that the claim could not identify the bus or driver.

- In a building claim,[4] the defendant had appointed an expert to try to settle the case. The claimant knew this but still issued proceedings. The claimant was held to be unco-operative and in breach of the draft construction protocol. The court ordered the claimant to pay the defendant's costs on an indemnity basis (see page 188).

Where parties have complied with the protocols, the courts have reacted positively. In *Amin v Hussain,*[5] the claimant forgot to mention the personal injury element of a road traffic accident in his pleadings. The court allowed him to set aside judgment in default of a defence (see Chapter 5) to amend the claim, because there was no prejudice as he had informed the defendant of the injuries in the letter of claim.

Legal representatives should make sure that they comply with the protocols. Additionally, they should apply for sanctions when others have not complied with the protocols.

Where no protocol applies

A general pre-action protocol is due to be introduced in cases not covered by one of the specific pre-action protocols. Until it is introduced, the following is relevant where no protocol applies.

The overriding objective should still be followed where there is no protocol to follow (see Chapter 1). Parties will be expected to co-operate fully with one another. This includes disclosing documents (see Chapter 7) before court action has started and undertaking negotiations to settle the claim. Claimants should:

- write a full letter of claim

- allow a set time for the defendant to admit or deny liability and make offers to settle where applicable

- reply to reasonable requests for information

- be willing to negotiate a settlement

- send a final warning letter before issuing the claim

- only issue the claim once the time allowed for the defendant to reply as above has expired.

3   Jimaale v London Buses Ltd [2000] 28 February, CL
4   Thomas Construction v Hyland & Power [2000]
    8 March, TCC
5   Amin v Hussain (2000), CL

The courts have ordered parties to pay costs on an indemnity basis (see page 188) where they have not followed the overriding objective (see Chapter 1). For example, this happened in *Taylor v D Coach Hire*[6] when the defendant waited until after the claim had been issued to negotiate.

2.2 Public funding

For many parties, whether they can afford the costs of court proceedings will be a major consideration in deciding to start court action. Those on low incomes may be entitled to help with the costs from the Legal Services Commission. The process of applying for public funding is outside the scope of this book and is not examined here. The effect of not taking certain steps before starting court action is considered here.

The Legal Services Commission has published The Funding Code, which gives guidance on when it is likely to grant public funding to an applicant. Relevant points arising from the guidance are noted below.

Where a party is applying for public funding to bring proceedings, the application may be refused unless the other party has been notified of the potential case and given an opportunity to respond and put matters right. This notification will generally be in the form of a letter before action (see below), which should always be sent.[7]

However, a letter before action need not be written where it is impracticable, eg. where the case is genuinely urgent or where any delay would cause serious prejudice to the party's case. A genuinely urgent case might be where a party has been unlawfully evicted and has nowhere else to stay.[8]

In addition to the above, the guidance sets out when public funding would be granted in different areas of housing law. In particular, there are certain steps that need to be completed prior to starting court action in housing disrepair cases before public funding will be granted.[9] These steps are not considered here but are set out in The Funding Code. **Legal representatives** are strongly advised to refer to The Funding Code when applying for public funding.

2.3 Letters before action

In areas of law where pre-action protocols do not exist, a party wishing to start court action should still inform the other party of her/his intention to do so. This is usually done in the form of a letter before action.

6   Taylor v D Coach Hire (2000), CL
7   R v Horsham District Council ex parte Wenman (1994) 4 All ER 68, and para 3C-202 of *The Funding Code: Decision Making Guidance* published by the Legal

Services Commission
8   para 3C-202 of *The Funding Code: Decision Making Guidance* published by the Legal Services Commission
9   para 3C-217 ibid.

The purpose of a letter before action is:

• to put the other party on notice of the claimant's intention to commence court proceedings

• to allow the other party a final chance to change her/his decision or reach a settlement.

CPR 44.14

A party runs the risk of being penalised in costs if s/he commences proceedings without sending a letter before action, where there was sufficient time to send one and wait for a reply. The courts may decide that it was unnecessary to start court action and order the party to pay the other party's costs, as well as her/his own costs. This could happen where a party starts proceedings without having sent a letter before action, and the other party, who was unaware of the complaint until receiving the claim form, agrees to the requests set out in the claim form.

A letter before action should not be sent unless the party proposes to take the action threatened. This is particularly important where advisers challenge the decisions of certain organisations or people regularly, eg. a local authority. If letters before action are sent to the local authority on a regular basis without the action threatened being actually taken, the local authority might begin to disregard them. As a result, in future cases, a party might be required to actually start court action before the local authority will take her/him seriously. This would defeat the purpose of a letter before action.

Examples of letters before action can be found in Case Studies 1, 5 and 6 (see pages 262, 378 and 400 respectively).

Style

A legal representative writing the letter before action on behalf of a party normally writes in the first person plural, ie. "we". However this is not essential and an adviser may wish to use "I". S/he should inform the other party that s/he is writing on behalf of her/his client. There is no need for detailed allegations, points of law or evidence, but there is often a need to set out the basic factual background and to outline any legal points that support the client's case.

A party writing her/his own letter before action should write in the first person, ie. "I".

Contents

The following points are a simple guide to what a letter before action should include.

1. Confirm your role

- We are advising John Jones who we understand is an assured tenant of 1 Acacia Gardens.

- I was an assured shorthold tenant of 20 Acacia Gardens.

2. If necessary, confirm the other party's role

- We understand that you are the landlord of 1 Acacia Gardens.

3. Set out allegations of fact

- Mr Jones informs us that on 11 May 2002, while he was at work, you attended the property and changed the locks.

- I left 20 Acacia Gardens on 20 June 2002 at the end of my six-month assured shorthold tenancy but, despite the accommodation being in the same condition as when I moved in and there being no rent outstanding, I have still not received my deposit of £500 back from you.

4. Set out the legal position

- Pursuant to the Protection from Eviction Act 1977, Mr Jones cannot be lawfully evicted without a court order.

- I am entitled to this money as it legally belongs to me.

5. The ultimatum

The ultimatum invites the other party to respond to a notice of proposed litigation. The response does not necessarily have to execute all the requests made within the time given by the ultimatum, as this may be an unrealistic deadline for certain cases. For example, in a disrepair case, the landlord may respond to the letter before action by putting forward proposals for when the repairs are to take place.

Different cases call for different lengths of time to allow the other party to respond to a letter before action. For example, where a party is going to be homeless that day, it would be reasonable to give the other party notice of 24 hours, or even until the end of the day, of the intention to start court proceedings. However, in other cases, eg. minor disrepair, 14 days would be sufficient notice. Fourteen days is the normal response period allowed where the case is not urgent.

- Unless we receive confirmation by 4pm tomorrow that Mr Jones will be reinstated to the property immediately, our client has been advised to apply to the county court forthwith for an injunction ordering his reinstatement.

- Unless I hear from you within 14 days, I will have no option but to start court proceedings to claim my deposit money back.

6. The finale

- We trust this course of action will not prove necessary and look forward to hearing from you as requested. Should court proceedings become necessary, we will be applying for our costs of the litigation to be paid by you.

- I would prefer not to take this course of action and hope to hear from you as requested. If I need to go to court to claim my deposit money back, I will be applying for my costs to be paid by you.

It is advisable to add a sentence informing the proposed defendant that, if proceedings are issued, s/he may also be liable for the costs of the proceedings.

Who to send the letter to

In cases involving a local authority, the letter before action should be addressed to the housing officer or the person who last made a decision on the case, unless the local authority has specified who to send any such letter to. It is also good procedure to copy this letter to the legal department of the local authority, as it is likely to end up there. The same applies to other organisations such as housing associations.

Where the other party is a private landlord, the letter should be addressed to her/him. If the landlord has agents acting on her/his behalf, the letter should still be addressed to the landlord but the address for service might be that of the agents, unless the landlord has given her/his address.

2.4   Negotiations

Once a letter before action has been written, negotiations between the parties to try to reach a settlement might start. The purpose of negotiations could be:

- to avoid the risk of not being successful in the litigation

- to avoid the inevitable delay in reaching a resolution

- to avoid the stress of litigation.

These are just a few reasons why a party may wish to negotiate a settlement. The ultimate aim of negotiations is to reach a settlement that all parties are happy with.

During negotiations, the defendant usually makes an offer accompanied by details of terms in the claimant's case. If the defendant's points are fair, the claimant might want to consider accepting the offer. If the claimant thinks otherwise, s/he would write to the defendant asking for an increased offer and responding to the points made. This would continue until a settlement is reached or until it becomes necessary to start court proceedings.

Negotiations can take place by way of "without prejudice" communications. These are discussed further in paragraph 7.6. If "without prejudice" communications take place, they cannot be used in court proceedings should negotiations fail to produce a settlement.

An additional consideration is whether a party is willing to put her/his offer in line with the procedure set out in Part 36. Basically, a Part 36 offer is where a party puts her/his offer in writing and sends it to the court. There could be costs implications if the other party does not accept the offer and is awarded no more than the offer at the final hearing. Part 36 offers are examined in detail in paragraph 5.5.

If none of the above actions results in a settlement of the claim, it will be necessary to start court action. The following chapters deal with the various stages in a court case. Throughout the case, all parties should bear in mind the possibility of a settlement. Negotiations should take place whenever possible throughout court proceedings as these are likely to further the overriding objective of the CPR.

Chapter 3: **Beginning a county court action**

3

Beginning a county court action

The CPR have simplified the process by which actions are commenced in the county court, not least in reducing the number and range of originating forms. However, important differences remain, in particular in relation to the documents that must be filed at court to commence certain types of proceedings.

This chapter examines how general civil claims are commenced in a county court. The processes involved will be outlined in relation to Part 7 CPR claims, followed by a look at the alternative method for claims within Part 8.

The CPR provide a separate procedure for bringing possession claims. This is in Part 55 which was introduced in October 2001. Separate consideration is given to Part 55 in Chapter 14.

Separate attention is also given in Chapters 15 and 16 to the specialist procedures involved in bringing statutory homelessness appeals in the county court, and claims for judicial review in the High Court.

3.1   Part 7 or Part 8 claim?

An initial consideration for a claimant is whether the claim should be brought under Part 7 or under the alternative procedure in Part 8. The alternative procedure in Part 8 is designed primarily to be used where the claim does not involve a substantial dispute on the facts. It should also be used where a rule or practice direction requires. The types of housing claim which should be brought using the Part 8 procedure are stated later in this chapter.

The Part 8 procedure involves significant departures from the standard procedure adopted for Part 7 claims. For this reason, separate sections of this chapter and Chapter 4 are devoted to Part 8 claims. An overview of both procedures is provided in the tables of Part 7 and Part 8 (see pages XL and XLI).

3.2   How to start proceedings – Part 7 CPR

The first matter for consideration is where to commence the proposed action.

High Court or county court?

A decision should be made as to whether the proposed action is one suitable for issue in the county court or whether it would be more appropriate for the matter to be commenced in the High Court.

Legislation, the rules and practice directions provide that certain types of claim, such as judicial review, must be brought in the High Court.[1] Other claims, for example statutory homelessness appeals, must be commenced in a county court.[2] In addition, the rules and practice directions provide that certain claims should normally be brought in either the High Court or a county court, but allow departures from the usual rules in specified circumstances. Thus, possession claims will normally be brought in the county court in which the land is situated unless there are exceptional circumstances to justify starting the claim in the High Court.[3]

Generally, an action cannot be commenced in the High Court unless the value of the claim is greater than £15,000. However, where the action includes a claim for damages for personal injuries, the value of the claim must be £50,000 or more to be brought in the High Court.[4]

Where the value of the claim meets these thresholds then, generally, the claimant has a choice of issuing in the High Court or a county court.

However, claims should be brought in the High Court and not the county court if due to:

CPR PD 7 para 2.4

(1) *the financial value of the claim and the amount in dispute, and/or*

(2) *the complexity of the facts, legal issues, remedies or procedures involved, and/or*

(3) *the importance of the outcome of the claim to the public in general*

the claimant believes that the claim ought to be dealt with by a High Court Judge.

Effectively this means that, if the trial of the matter should take place in the High Court, then this is where the action should be started. In the absence of any wider importance to the general public or particular complexity, claims for less than £50,000 are likely to be heard in a county court and should consequently be started there.

A claim brought in the High Court may be transferred to the county court, or vice versa, if this is appropriate having regard to certain criteria outlined later in this chapter. A party may face consequences as to costs for starting a claim in an inappropriate court.

The value of the claim is assessed by reference to the amount that the claimant *'can reasonably be expected to recover'*. In assessing this amount, any anticipated awards of costs and interest (other than interest due under a contract, which will form part of the damages) should be excluded.[5]

Another matter to consider is the Human Rights Act 1998. If the claimant alleges that her/his human rights have been breached, the normal rules

1   section 31 Supreme Court Act 1981; CPR PD 54 para 2.1   4   CPR PD 7 para 2.1-2.2
2   section 204(1) Housing Act 1996   5   High Court and County Courts Jurisdiction Order 1991
3   CPR PD 55 paras 1.1-1.4   (SI 1991 No.724), para 9 (as amended)

apply. A county court must construe legislation as far as possible so as to ensure compatibility with Convention Rights, and itself act compatibly with Convention Rights.[6] Where, however, a declaration of incompatibility is sought, the claim should be brought in the High Court.[7]

Which county court?

Generally, the claim can be brought in any county court in England and Wales. The court has no jurisdiction to refuse to accept a claim on the ground that it should be brought in a different county court.[8] However, the claimant should have regard to a number of matters when deciding in which county court to bring the claim.

All claims for the recovery of land must be brought in the court for the district in which the land is situated (see Chapter 14).

For other types of claim, if a defence is filed, the matter is likely to be transferred and heard in the defendant's local court. In fact, where the claim is for a specified amount of money and a defence is filed, the case is automatically transferred to the defendant's local court under CPR 26.2.

Therefore, if the claimant wants a speedy outcome to the proceedings, it would be prudent to issue the claim in the defendant's local court, particularly where it is anticipated that the defendant will defend the claim. An outline of the provisions relating to the transfer of claims to other courts is provided below.

The claimant should also have regard to the fact that a number of methods for enforcing a judgement in her/his favour may be pursued only in the defendant's home court. Therefore, it may be sensible to bring an undefended claim there so as to avoid the need for transfer after judgment has been obtained.

Transfer

An application may be made by either party for transfer of a claim between a county court and the High Court, or between different county courts. Equally a court may make such an order of its own volition.[9] The criteria which the court must have regard to when CPR 30.3 considering an order for the transfer of a claim include:

- the financial value of the claim and how much of the claim is actually in dispute

- the convenience or fairness to each party for the hearings, including the trial, to be heard in another court

- the complexity or otherwise of the facts, legal issues, procedures and remedies involved in the case

6 section 6(1) Human Rights Act 1998
7 section 4(5) Human Rights Act 1998
8 Gwynedd County Council v Grunshaw (1999) 149 NLJ 1286
9 see generally CPR 30

- the availability of a judge with specialism in the particular type of claim

- the importance of the outcome of the claim to the wider public

- whether the facilities available at the court are inadequate due to any disabilities of a party or witness

- the likelihood of the court having to consider whether to make a declaration of incompatibility under section 4 of the Human Rights Act 1998.

The claim form

An action is started when the court issues the claim form in accordance with a request by the claimant. However, for the purposes of the Limitation Act 1980 and other statutes, the proceedings are brought when the claim form is lodged and not when the court issues the claim.[10] This may be crucial where tight deadlines are involved, for example the 21-day time limit for bringing a statutory homelessness appeal.

For general litigation matters the practice Form N1 should be used, but it should be noted that for certain actions, including Part 8 claims (see page 35), possession claims (see Chapter 14) and statutory appeals (see Chapter 15), specialist forms must be used. Examples of a completed Form N1 are given in Case Studies 4, 5 and 6 (see pages 354, 381 and 402 respectively).

Content of claim form

The claim form must be completed so as to meet the requirements of Part 16 CPR, to include:

- the names and addresses of each party. These should be complete and accurate to avoid encountering any future difficulties with the claim

- a concise statement of the nature of the claim. This should be included in the section of the claim form, 'Brief details of the claim'

- the remedy sought by the claimant. If a particular remedy sought is not included, the court might still grant the remedy, but this is a discretionary power.

Human Rights Act 1998

The claim form includes a question on whether the claim includes an issue under the Act. The claimant should bear in mind the words of Lord Woolf in *Daniel v Walker*, where he said that, 'judges should be robust in resisting inappropriate attempts to introduce arguments based on the Human Rights Act 1998'.[11]

Statement of value

CPR 16.3 Where the claim is for money, a "statement of value" must be included which requires the claimant to assess what amount s/he expects to recover from the defendant. This information will assist the court in deciding which track to allocate the case to (see page 80).

If an exact amount, such as a debt, can be specified as a fixed amount, then this should be provided. Often the claimant will be unable to specify a fixed amount. This is invariably the case in disrepair claims; a rough estimate of damages sought is all that may be given. In such actions, the claimant should make a statement that s/he expects to recover:

• not more than £5,000, or

• between £5,001 and £15,000, or

• more than £15,000.

If the claimant is unable to state how much is expected, then a statement should be made to this effect.

Where the claim is for personal injuries, the claimant must state whether the amount expected in respect of pain, suffering and loss of amenity is above or below £1,000.

Similarly, where the claim is for housing disrepair of residential premises and the tenant is seeking an order that the landlord carry out repairs, the claimant must state whether the estimated costs of the repairs or other work is above or below £1,000.

Statement of truth

The statement of truth is an innovation of the CPR. It is a simple statement signed by the party submitting a document within proceedings that s/he believes the facts stated in the document are true.

The form of the statement of truth is:[12]

[I believe] [the claimant believes] that the facts stated in [this claim form] [these particulars of claim] [this witness statement] are true.

A statement of truth must be included in each of the following:

CPR 22.1(1) • statements of case. This includes: the claim form, particulars of claim (where not included in a claim form), defence, counterclaim form, reply to defence, further information given under CPR 18.1 and any document amending any of the aforementioned; and

• **witness statements**.

---

12 CPR PD 22 paras 2.1-2.3

Who signs?

CPR 22.1(6)

The statement of truth can be verified, ie. signed, by the party, her/his legal representative, or litigation friend. However, witness statements must always be signed by the witness.

CPR 2.3(1)

"Legal representative" is limited to include only barristers, solicitors (or employees of a solicitors' firm) and authorised litigators instructed to act for a party to a claim.

"Litigation friend" refers to someone entitled under the Rules to act for a **child** or **patient** (see Part 21 CPR), and should not be confused with **lay adviser,** otherwise known as a McKenzie friend. Lay advisers cannot sign statements of truth.

Where the statement of truth is signed by a legal representative, it should refer to the belief of the client that the facts are true and not to the belief of the legal representative. It should be signed in her/his own name, and state the capacity in which s/he signs and the name of the firm as appropriate.[13]

In doing so, the court assumes that the representative has explained to the client the nature of the statement of truth, and the consequences to the client if subsequently it appears that the client did not honestly believe the truth of the facts. It is also taken to mean that the client has authorised the representative to sign.[14] For the avoidance of doubt, it is wise to include the following statement immediately after the statement of truth:

I am duly authorised by the claimant to sign this statement.

False statements

CPR 32.14

If a party makes, or causes to be made, a false statement, which is verified by a statement of truth, without an honest belief in its truth, s/he may face proceedings for contempt of court. Proceedings for contempt of court can be brought by another party or by the **Attorney-General**. If a party wishes to bring contempt proceedings then s/he must obtain the permission of the court. In considering whether to allow proceedings for contempt, the court will have regard to the overriding objective and the concept of proportionality[15] (see Chapter 1).

CPR 22.2

If a statement of truth is not included in a statement of case, then the document remains effective; however, it may be struck out by the court. In any event the party cannot rely on the statement of case as evidence of any matters set out in it. Most court forms now include a pre-printed statement of truth. However, some older forms still in use for certain types of claim do not and in this case it must be added to the form.

13 CPR PD 22 para 3.7
14 CPR PD 22 para 3.8

15 CPR 1(1-1.2); Malager Ltd v R E Leach Engineering (2000), noted at *Times* 17 February

Issuing the claim

The claimant or her/his representative should send or take the following to the court for issue of the claim:

- copies of the claim form. There should be a copy each for the court, the defendant and the claimant

- copies (as above) of any other documents in support of claim, eg. particulars of claim, **witness statements**

- the prescribed fee based on the value and/or type of the claim. These are updated regularly and practitioners should check in the most recent **fees guide**, produced by the Court Service, or alternatively telephone the appropriate court. Cheques are payable to HMPG (the abbreviation for Her Majesty's Paymaster General), regardless of which court is issuing the claim.

Claimants with limited means, but without legal funding, should ask the court for Form EX160 – Application for a fee exemption or remission – and send or take evidence of means, including proof of welfare benefits if appropriate.

It is also advisable to include a covering letter asking for the issue of the claim, particularly where the form is posted rather than taken in person to the court. If the claim is one which needs to be lodged urgently, it may be sensible to take it to the court for personal issue. If this is not practicable, sending by recorded or special delivery should be considered. If a time limit must be complied with, then it is essential to telephone the court to check that the claim has been received.

On receipt, the court should issue the claim by sealing – ie. stamping – the claim form and the particulars of claim (if filed at the same time) with the court seal, and allocate a claim number to it. The court will then send the claimant or her/his representatives a notice of issue confirming the claim number, issue date, and payment of fee. If service was effected by the court, then the notice will also confirm the date of service.

Particulars of claim

The particulars of claim are the claimant's written statement of case. It sets out the type of claim being made and outlines the relief or remedy sought by the claimant from the defendant. The particulars of claim should expand upon the nature of the claim provided on the first page of the claim form. This should enable the defendant to understand the nature of the claim against her/him and respond accordingly.

The particulars of claim may be set out on the claim form itself or in a separate document. In most cases, it will be necessary to draft them in a separate document for the simple reason that the claim form allows little room for including the particulars. Particulars for simple debt claims, such as recovery of rent deposits, can usually be incorporated in full on the claim form (for an example see Case Study 6, page 402).

Content of particulars of claim

CPR 16.4(1) sets out the information to be included in the particulars of claim:

- 'a concise statement of facts' – although it is concise, the claimant should provide sufficient detail of facts which s/he seeks to rely on in the claim

- if the claimant is seeking interest, a statement to that effect with certain specified details (see CPR 16.4(2))

- if the claimant is seeking **aggravated damages** or **exemplary damages**, a statement to that effect and her/his grounds for claiming them; eg. in cases of harassment/illegal eviction

- if the claimant is seeking **provisional damages**, a statement to that effect and her/his grounds for claiming them; this is for personal injury claims only

- 'such other matters as may be set out in a practice direction'.

Additional information required for certain claims

The Practice Direction to Part 16 provides a list of additional information required in certain types of cases. Of most interest to housing practitioners are the following types of claim.

PERSONAL INJURY CLAIM

A housing-related personal injury claim may be injuries or health problems caused by housing disrepair. The particulars of claim must contain:[16]

- the claimant's date of birth

- brief details of the claimant's personal injuries

- a schedule giving details of past and future expenses and losses claimed; this needs to be attached to the particulars of claim

- any report of a medical practitioner which the claimant is seeking to rely upon; this needs to be attached or served with the particulars of claim.

16 CPR PD 16 paras 4.1-4.4

In a **provisional damages** claim the claimant must also state:

- that s/he seeks an award of provisional damages under either section 32A of the Supreme Court Act 1981 or section 52 of the County Courts Act 1984

- that there is a chance in the future that the claimant will develop a serious disease or a deterioration in her/his physical or mental condition. In such cases, details need to be given of the anticipated disease or deterioration (see also Part 41 CPR).

CLAIM BASED UPON A WRITTEN AGREEMENT

The written agreement may be a tenancy or mortgage agreement.

The claimant should attach or serve the following with the particulars of claim:[17]

- a copy of the contract or documents that make up the agreement. The originals should be made available at the hearing

- any conditions incorporated into the contract. For example, a lender may have standard terms referred to in the mortgage agreement.

CLAIMS BASED ON AN ORAL AGREEMENT OR CONDUCT

This may relate to an unwritten tenancy arising from an agreement reached verbally, or by reference to the conduct of the landlord and tenant.

The claimant should set out in the particulars of claim the contractual words or conduct. The claimant should include appropriate details of who said or did what and where.[18] Clearly this will depend on the circumstances of the particular claim. It is suggested that it is not necessary to provide extensive details of discussions relating to matters which may not be in dispute, for example a description of the property and the fact that a tenancy was granted. More detail may be required where the matter discussed is crucial to the case, such as the level of rent or the provision of furniture in the property.

ADDITIONAL INFORMATION REQUIRED WHERE CLAIMANT SEEKS TO RELY ON CERTAIN MATTERS

Often the claimant will wish to rely on specific types of evidence or information in support of the claim. In such a situation s/he must set out appropriate details in the particulars of claim:[19]

- Criminal convictions which the claimant seeks to rely on under section 11 of the Civil Evidence Act 1968, eg. conviction for assault relating to harassment/illegal eviction of a tenant. Details should

17 CPR PD 16 para 8.3
18 CPR PD 16 para 8.4
19 CPR PD 16 paras 9.1-9.2

include the type of conviction, the court which convicted and the issue that the conviction relates to.

• Allegations of fraud, illegality, misrepresentation, unsoundness of mind or undue influence, breaches of trust, wilful default, notice or knowledge of a fact, and facts relating to mitigation of loss or damage.[20]

Specific additional information is required for possession claims. This is discussed on page 207.

Where the claimant chooses to serve the particulars of claim separately from the claim form, the particulars must also include the:[21]

• name of court in which claim is brought

• claim number

• title of proceedings

• claimant's address for service.

Joinder

The CPR do not use the term "joinder". This is presumably in an attempt to modernise the language used in proceedings. The term refers to the act of joining different claims or parties within the same proceedings.

Claims

CPR 7.3

CPR 1.1

The claimant may use one claim form to start different claims if these can all be conveniently dealt with within the same proceedings. In fact, the claimant should always give serious consideration to joining separate claims where this would further the overriding objective (ie. saving expense and dealing with claims expeditiously).

This may occur where separate claims relate to the same circumstances, for example claims against a landlord for disrepair alleging breach of section 11 of the Landlord and Tenant Act 1985, and breach of an express term of the tenancy. Alternatively, a claimant may join separate claims for debts owed by the defendant into a single claim.

Parties

CPR 19.1

CPR 19.3

Any number of claimants or defendants may be joined as parties to a claim. An example of this is where joint landlords bring a claim for possession and rent arrears against joint tenants. Where there is more than one person who is jointly entitled to the remedy sought, then both must be parties unless the court orders otherwise. Thus, in the example

---

20 CPR PD 16 paras 9.1-9.2   21 CPR PD 16 para 3.8

of possession proceedings above, both landlords must be claimants unless the court allows one to pursue the claim alone.

CPR 19.4

Once the claim form has been served, it is necessary to obtain the court's permission to remove, add or substitute a party. An application may be made by an existing party or a person who wishes to become a party.

Although the CPR do not make it clear, an application will usually only succeed where there has been a genuine mistake or a relevant change of circumstances.[22] A relevant change of circumstances could include a situation where a party dies and it is necessary to join the estate as a party. Another example is where a landlord sells a property and the new landlord must be joined in order to seek an order for remedial works to be undertaken by her/him.

CPR 19.4(5)-(6)

If a party is removed, added or substituted the order must be served on all parties and anyone else affected by the order. The court may also give **directions** such as the filing and serving of the claim form or other document on any new defendants.

Amendments to statements of case

CPR 17.1

A party may amend a statement of case at any time before it has been served on any other party. Statements of case include the claim form, particulars of claim, defence, counterclaim form, reply to defence and

see CPR 2.3

further information given under CPR 18.1.

CPR 17.1(2)

If the statement of case has been served then it may be amended only:

• if all the other parties give written consent, or

• with the court's permission.

If the parties agree to an amendment of one party's statement of case, they may also wish to agree directions allowing amendments to be made to the other party's statements of case in order that appropriate responses can be made to the changes.

Applications for amendments should be made without delay, particularly where the trial is imminent. However, late amendments may be permitted where the circumstances and the interests of justice demand.[23]

CPR 22.1(2)

An amended statement of case must be verified by a statement of truth.

A party who proposes to amend her/his statement of case should be prepared for the likelihood that s/he may be required to explain inconsistencies between the original and the amended statement of case. The credibility of the party may be damaged significantly by such inconsistencies.

---

22 International Distillers & Vintners Ltd v Hillebrand (UK) Ltd [2000], noted at *Times* 25 January

23 Chilton v Surrey CC [2000] 1 CL 40, & Charlesworth v Relay Roads Ltd [1999], noted at *Times* 31 August

Calculation of time

Before looking at the rules relating to service, it is important to consider how time is calculated when a party has to do a certain act, such as serving a claim form or filing a defence. These rules apply to any act required under the rules, any practice direction, or judgment or order of the court.

CPR 2.8(1)

The basic rule is that any period of time expressed as a number of days will be a period of clear days. In all situations, this means that the day on which the period begins is not counted.

CPR 2.8(2)-(3)

Example

Harpal serves a claim form without particulars of claim on 1 May. He is required to serve the particulars within 14 days. He must effect service by 15 May.

On occasions an act is required to be done by reference to an event such as the trial date. In these situations the day on which the event takes place is not counted.

CPR 2.8(3)

Example

Harpal must file a trial bundle for his claim. This must be done not more than seven days and not less than three days before the start of the trial. The trial is listed for 30 November. The earliest date on which he can file the bundle is 22 November; the latest date is 26 November.

If the period specified for doing an act is five days or less, the following days are not included in the calculation:

CPR 2.8(4)

• a Saturday or Sunday, or

• a Bank Holiday, Christmas Day or Good Friday.

Example

Harpal must serve notice of an application at least three days before the hearing. The hearing is listed for Monday 20 August. He must serve the notice of application by Tuesday 14 August.

It is important to remember that if the time specified is more than five days, then these days – Saturday, Sunday, Bank Holiday, Christmas Day and Good Friday – are not excluded. However, if the date for doing an act falls on a day on which the court office is closed, then the requirement will be met if it is done on the next day on which the office is open.

CPR 2.8(5)

As far as practicable, any court order or judgment that imposes a time limit by which an act must be done should specify the calendar date for

CPR 2.9

compliance. Indeed, any document prepared by the parties to an action should refer to specific calendar dates. This would apply, for example, where the parties file a consent order with the court.

Service of documents

Part 6 of the CPR provides general rules for the service of documents within proceedings and also particular rules relating to the service of claims forms.

Who serves?

Normally, all documents issued within proceedings will be served by the court. The court chooses the method of service, which will invariably be by first class post.

CPR 6.3

However, the court will not effect service in the following circumstances, when:

- a court order, rule or practice direction specifies otherwise. For example, where the court makes an injunction order following an application made without notice, the applicant will, invariably, give an undertaking to serve the injunction order by personal service

- a party notifies the court that s/he wishes to serve the document her/himself. The urgent nature of some applications, such as those for the suspension of warrants for possession, means that it will often not be possible to list the hearing so as to give the other side the proper period of notice. In such cases the party making the application should try to ensure that the other party has as much notice as possible. This may necessitate informing the court that s/he will serve the application documentation and effecting personal service or service by fax. If service is simply impracticable owing to the urgent nature of the case, the party making the application should, at the very least, give consideration to giving the other party notice of the hearing by telephone

- the court has failed to serve the document and has sent a notice of non-service.

Address for service

All parties are required to give an address for service within the court's **jurisdiction**. Where a party has a solicitor acting for her/him, the address for service is the business address of the solicitor. The only exceptions to this are if the document in question is the claim form – in which case it can be served on the legal representative only if s/he is authorised to accept service – or the method used is personal service (see page 32).

Methods of service

Documents may be served by using a variety of methods. Service by facsimile (fax), document exchange (DX) and other electronic means (eg. email) are available only in certain specified circumstances.

The date on which service is deemed to have taken place for each method is specified in CPR 6.7. For each type of service, except personal service, it should be remembered that as the deemed dates for service are all periods of less than five days, then Saturdays, Sundays, Bank Holidays, Christmas Day and Good Friday are all excluded.

CPR 2.8(4)

PERSONAL SERVICE

Where the document is to be served on an individual, then the document can be served by leaving it with that individual.

This method should not be used where a solicitor is authorised to accept service on behalf of that party, and has notified the party in writing of this. In this situation the document must be served on the solicitor unless personal service is required by a statutory provision, rule, practice direction or court order.

CPR 6.4

In *Nanglegan v Royal Free Hospital NHS Trust,* service on a party who had given appropriate notification authorising a solicitor to accept service was not effective.[24]

Where the party to be served is a company or partnership, special rules apply as to whom to serve and the address for service.[25] Similarly, there are special rules for service on a **child** or **patient**.

CPR 6.6

Since May 2000, where a document is served before 5pm on a **business day**, service is deemed to have taken place on that day. Where service takes place after 5pm or on a non-business day (Saturday, Sunday or a Bank Holiday, which includes Christmas Day and Good Friday), it is treated as having taken place on the next business day.

FIRST CLASS POST

When service is by first class post, it is deemed to have taken place on the second day after the day on which the document was posted. Thus, a document posted on Friday 16 July will be deemed to have been served on Tuesday 20 July.

DELIVERING TO OR LEAVING AT A PERMITTED ADDRESS

When service is by delivery to or leaving at a permitted address, it is deemed to have taken place on the day after the document is left or delivered at the permitted address.

24 Nanglegan v Royal Free Hospital NHS Trust (2001)   25 ibid. & CPR PD 6 paras 4.1-4.2 & 6.1-6.2
   All ER D 147

BY FACSIMILE (FAX)

Service can only be effected by facsimile (fax) where the party on whom the document is to be served, or her/his **legal representative**, has indicated in writing that s/he is willing to accept service by fax and has provided a fax number to be used. In any event, if the party to be served is acting by a legal representative, then the fax must be sent to the legal representative's business address.

Where a document is to be served on the legal representatives of a party, a fax number set out on their writing paper is sufficient indication that the party is willing to accept service by fax. Whether a party is acting in person or by legal representatives, a fax number set out on a statement of case or response to a claim filed at court is also sufficient indication.[26]

If the fax is transmitted before 4pm on a **business day**, service is deemed to have taken place on that day, or otherwise on the next business day. Where the date of service is important, it is essential to check after sending the fax that it has actually been received by the party or her/his representatives.

DOCUMENT EXCHANGE (DX)

Service by document exchange (DX) may be used where the party has given an address for service which includes a numbered box at a DX, or this appears on the writing paper of the party to be served or that of her/his **legal representative**. In any event DX may not be used where the other party has indicated their unwillingness to be served by this method.[27]

Service by DX is effective on the second day after the document is left at the exchange.

OTHER ELECTRONIC MEANS (eg. EMAIL)

CPR PD 6 para 3.3

Service by this method may take place only where:

- the party serving and the party to be served are both acting by legal representatives, and

- the document is served at the business address of the legal representative, and

- the legal representative to be served has expressly indicated in writing that s/he will accept service in this manner and has provided her/his email address, ISDN or other electronic number.

Service is effective on the second day following transmission.

---

26 CPR PD 6 paras 3.1-3.2   27 CPR PD 6 paras 2.1-2.2

Service of claim forms

CPR 7.5 (2)

Once the claim form has been issued, the claimant has four months in which to effect service on the defendant, unless the claim form is to be served outside of the court's **jurisdiction**, in which event s/he has six months.[28]

Normally, the claimant will issue a claim and the court will serve it on the defendant shortly afterwards. On occasions, however, the claimant must issue a claim to meet a relevant limitation period before s/he has had time to properly investigate a claim and prepare full particulars of claim. The four-month period allows the claimant to issue and then properly prepare the case before service of the claim. In this situation the claimant should notify the court that s/he wishes to serve the claim, and then delay service until such time that s/he is in a position to serve the particulars of claim. If the claimant does not notify the court, then the court will normally serve the claim form and the claimant would be required to serve the particulars of claim within 14 days.

Although the court has the discretion to extend the time limit for service of the claim form, the court will make such an order only where the claimant has acted promptly and the court has been unable to effect service, or the claimant has taken all reasonable steps to effect service.[29]

CPR 7.4

Where the particulars of claim are not included in the claim form, then they must be served on the defendant within 14 days of the date of service of the claim form. In any event the particulars of claim must be served within the four-month period from date of issue of the claim.

CPR 6.14(1)

If the court serves the claim form, it must send the claimant a notice which will include the date of deemed service.

CPR 6.10

If the claimant serves the claim form, s/he must file a certificate of service – Form N215 – at court within seven days. The certificate must state that the document has not been returned undelivered and should also confirm the date of posting/personal service or delivery.

CPR 6.14(2)

Failure to file a certificate of service will prevent the claimant from obtaining judgment in default (see paragraph 5.3).

CPR 6.15

If a contract specifies an alternative method for service in the event of a claim being issued in relation to that contract, the form may be served in this manner.

Alternative method for service

CPR 6.8

The court may authorise service by another method where it is satisfied that there is a good reason to do so. This is most likely to occur where it is impracticable to effect service; perhaps because it is proving difficult

---

28 CPR 7.5(3). For rules relating to service out of jurisdiction see CPR 6.17-6.31 and PD 6B

29 CPR 7.6; also see Amerada Hess v C W Rowe [2000] 144 SJ 146 and Vinos v Marks & Spencer plc [2000], noted at *Independent* 17 July

to locate a party or they are deliberately evading service. Alternative forms of service may include placing advertisements in newspapers or service on a party's insurers.[30]

An application may be made to the court for an order for a specified alternative method of service. The application should be supported by evidence stating the reasons for the application and the steps taken to effect service by the usual methods (see paragraph 9.1).[31]

3.3   Part 8 – alternative procedure for claims

The CPR provide an alternative procedure for commencing certain types of claim. These types of claim fall into two main categories:

• claims where there is unlikely to be a substantial dispute on the facts, or

CPR 8.1
• where a rule or practice direction requires or allows the claimant to use this procedure (see below).

Unless another form is specified for certain types of proceedings, the claimant is required to use the general Part 8 claim form, Form N208. If the claimant uses the wrong form, then the court is not likely to strike out the claim if the defendant is aware of the mistake and has not been misled.[32]

Contents of claim form

The contents of the claim form when using the alternative procedure are different from those required for Part 7 claims. Thus Part 16, which outlines the required content of statements of case, does not apply to
CPR 8.9
Part 8 claims.

Part 8 claim forms must include the following:

• a statement that Part 8 applies to the claim

• the question the claimant wants the court to decide or the remedy sought, and the legal basis for the claim

• if a claim is made under any enactment, what that enactment is

• if the claimant or defendant is sued in a representative capacity, what that capacity is.

As for other claims, a statement of truth must be included.

Filing and serving written evidence

An important difference from the Part 7 claim procedure lies in the requirement that when the Part 8 procedure is used, the claimant must file

---

30 Abbey National plc v Frost, Solicitors'
  Indemnity Fund intervening [1999] 2 All ER 206

31 CPR 6.8(2) & PD 6 para 9.1
32 Hannigan v Hannigan (2000) 2 FCR 650, CA

CPR 8.5(1)-(2) with the claim form any written evidence on which s/he intends to rely. This evidence must also be served on the defendant along with the claim form.

The importance of this requirement is illustrated in CPR 8.6. This provides that the claimant cannot rely on written evidence unless it was served on the defendant with the claim form or permission is obtained from the court. In practice it is often possible to obtain the permission of the court at a **directions hearing**.

Service of claim form and written evidence

The rules relating to service are the same as those outlined earlier in relation to Part 7 claims.

Part 8 procedure and housing claims

Clearly, it will be appropriate for some housing-related actions to be brought as Part 8 claims. Examples of the types of claim this may apply to are claims for a **declaration** as to whether a tenancy is a protected tenancy, a clause in a tenancy agreement is an unfair term or, in the case of an assured or secure tenancy, where the issue is one of law and the facts are largely not in dispute. However, if the claimant is in doubt as to whether the defendant will dispute certain alleged facts, a quicker outcome to the case may be achieved by using the Part 7 procedure.

Possession claims

Prior to the introduction of Part 55 in October 2001, claims for the recovery of possession of land in the county court had to be brought using the Part 8 procedure, though specialist claim forms for possession were retained. Advisers may therefore come across ongoing landlord and tenant or mortgage possession claims commenced using the procedure. This may occur where repayment terms have been agreed between the parties, and the proceedings have been adjourned with the claimant given liberty to restore in the event that the terms are not met by the defendant.

As discussed in Chapter 14, the vast majority of possession claims after October 2001 should be brought in accordance with Part 55. Specifically excluded from this Part, however, are possession claims where the claimant is seeking an interim possession order against trespassers. Such claims should be pursued using the Part 8 procedure and Part II of Order 24 CCR Or24 r10 of the County Court Rules 1981 retained by Schedule 2 of the CPR.

Certain landlord and tenant claims – Part 56 CPR

In addition, Part 56 specifies certain types of actions referred to as "landlord and tenant claims", which should be brought using the Part 8 procedure as modified by Part 56. These include:[33]

33 CPR 56 and CPR PD 56

- claims for new business tenancies under section 24 of the Landlord and Tenant Act 1954

- claims for compensation for improvements for business tenancies under Part 1 of the Landlord and Tenant Act 1927

- claims for acquisition orders under section 28 of the Landlord and Tenant Act 1987

- claims for orders varying leases under sections 36, 38 or 40 of the Landlord and Tenant Act 1987

- certain claims under the Access to Neighbouring Land Act 1992, the Chancel Repairs Act 1932, the Leasehold Reform Act 1967, and the Leasehold Reform, Housing and Urban Development Act 1993.

Claims in the "Schedule Rules" and other claims

Certain claims must be brought using the former County Court Rules or Rules of the Supreme Court, and/or the claim forms preserved by virtue of Schedules 1 and 2 of the CPR. These preserved rules are referred to as the "Schedule Rules". The Practice Direction to Part 8 modifies the procedure to be used for such claims, though claimants should first comply with the special provisions applied by the Schedule Rules or any Act of Parliament to each particular type of claim.

In relation to housing-related claims, these include:[34]

CCR Or31 r4(1)
- enforcement of a charging order by sale

- certain actions under the Agricultural Holdings Act 1986[35]

CCR Or49 r6B(1)
- applications by local authorities for injunctions for anti-social behaviour under section 152 of the Housing Act 1996

- claims for damages for harassment under section 3 of the Protection from Harassment Act 1997.[36]

Where a claim form is listed against a particular type of claim in Table 2 in Practice Direction 8B, this form must be used by the claimant to commence the claim. All other claims require the use of the Part 8 claim form.[37]

Fixed date

On issue of the claim, the court may fix a date for the hearing and will provide a notice of the hearing to the parties. For certain types of Part 8 claim, the court should always list the matter for a hearing on issue.[38] This includes a claim against trespassers in which the claimant applies for an interim possession order under Order 24 of the CCR 1981.[39]

---

34 CPR PD 8B see section B.1 & Table 2
35 CCR Or44 r1(1) & r3(1)
36 CPR PD 8B Section B para B.1(2)(b)

37 CPR PD 8B Section B para B.8
38 CPR PD 8A para 4.1;PD 8B Section B para B.9
39 see CPR PD 8B Section B; claims listed in Table 2

The claim form must be served not less than 21 days before the hearing date. This is to enable the defendant to consider her/his options and respond accordingly.[40]

If the claimant is to serve the claim form, s/he must provide notice of the hearing date at the same time.

4

Responding to a county court action

The emphasis within the CPR on the speedy resolution of cases is illustrated by the requirements on defendants to act quickly once served with a claim form and particulars of claim. This chapter outlines the possible courses of action available to defendants in responding to an action. It also examines situations when further statements of case need to be prepared (ie. reply and defence to counterclaim and the provision of further information).

How the defendant responds to a claim depends on whether it is brought under Part 7 or Part 8 of the CPR. This chapter contains a separate section highlighting the different procedure to be followed where the claim has been brought under Part 8. Examples of the types of claim brought under Parts 7 and 8 respectively are outlined in the preceding chapter.

In addition, an overview of the procedure for both Part 7 and Part 8 claims is given in the tables of Part 7 and Part 8 (see pages XL and XLI).

Responding to possession claims is dealt with in Chapter 14, while the procedure in relation to statutory homelessness appeals and judicial review is contained in Chapters 15 and 16 respectively.

4.1   Part 7 claims – response by defendant

CPR 7.8

When the court or the claimant serve the **particulars of claim** on the defendant, they must include a response pack containing each of the following:

- an acknowledgement of service with information to the defendant about responding to the claim – Form N9

- an admission form – N9A (if the claim is for a specified amount) or N9C (if the claim is for an unspecified amount or a non-money claim)

- a defence and counterclaim form – N9B (specified amount; see page 406 for an example of a completed Form N9B) or N9D (unspecified amount or non-money claim)

- notes for the defendant on replying to the claim form – Form N1C. This form provides detailed notes designed to help the defendant to respond to the claim. It also gives information on time limits for responding.

CPR 9.2

The defendant has three possible responses and the forms enclosed with the particulars reflect these. S/he may file one of the following:

- an acknowledgement of service

- a defence

- an admission.

CPR 9.1(2)

It is important to note that the defendant need not respond at all to the claim until service of the particulars of claim. Thus, for the purpose of the time limits discussed in the forthcoming sections, time does not begin to run where the claim form only is served. Often the claim form will be accompanied by the particulars of claim and time will begin to run.

Acknowledgement of service

An acknowledgement of service is simply a form that the defendant completes and sends to the court, thereby acknowledging receipt of the claim form and particulars. The form also requires the defendant to indicate whether s/he intends to defend all or part of the claim, or wishes to contest the jurisdiction of the court.

There are two main situations where it is appropriate for a defendant to file an acknowledgement of service.

• S/he wants to dispute the jurisdiction of the court. In this situation, the defendant must file the acknowledgement of service and then apply for an order in accordance with Part 11 of the CPR.

• If s/he cannot file a defence within the specified time; this is usually 14 days.

CPR 10.3(1)

CPR 15.4(1)

The defendant has 14 days from service of the particulars of claim to file an acknowledgement of service at court. By doing so, the time for service of the defence is extended by 14 days. This means that if an acknowledgement of service is filed in time, the defendant has 28 days from service of the particulars of claim in which to file a defence.

An adviser may wish to file an acknowledgement of service where time is needed to take detailed instructions from the defendant before drafting the defence, or further information is required from other sources.

Content of acknowledgement of service

The acknowledgement of service is contained on the bottom of the Form N9.

The acknowledgement of service must be signed by the defendant or her/his **legal representative** and include the defendant's address for service. Where the legal representative has signed the form, the address must be her/his business address. Otherwise, the address for service is the defendant's residence or place of business.[1]

Children and **patients** may acknowledge service only by their **litigation friend**, or her/his legal representative, unless the court orders otherwise.[2]

Special rules apply where the defendant is a company or a partnership.[3]

---

1   CPR 10.5 & PD 10 paras 3.1-3.2   3   CPR PD 15 paras 4.2-4.4
2   CPR PD 15 para 4.5

Service of the acknowledgement of service

CPR 10.4

Once the court receives the acknowledgement of service it must notify the claimant in writing. This is not the case for Part 8 claims where the defendant must serve a copy of the acknowledgement of service on every claimant (see page 53).

Defence

The provisions stating the procedure for defending the claim are contained in Part 15 of the CPR. Part 15 does not apply where the claimant has used the Part 8 procedure for claims (see page 52).

CPR 15.4

If the defendant wishes to defend a claim, then s/he must file a defence:

• 14 days after the particulars of claim is served; or

• if an acknowledgement of service is filed, 28 days after the particulars of claim is served.

If there is insufficient time in which to file a defence, the defendant may wish to seek the agreement of the claimant for an extension to the period allowed for filing a defence. This can be done without an application to the court, but the time can only be extended by up to 28 days. In the event that such an agreement is reached, the court must

CPR 15.5

be notified in writing by the defendant.

If an extension of more than 28 days is sought, or the claimant does not agree to an extension, then the defendant can apply to the court. The court may extend the time limits by using its case management

CPR 3.1

powers (see paragraph 6.1).

Advisers for the defendant should always consider asking the claimant for an extension where the defence cannot be filed in time. If a claimant unreasonably refuses to agree to an extension, the court may award the costs incurred in making the application against her/him.

On the other hand, where the claimant has followed a relevant **pre-action protocol** or the defendant has delayed taking action, the court may be reluctant to order a lengthy extension. It would be rare for the court not to grant any extension having regard to the overriding principle.

If the defendant fails to file a defence, then the claimant may be able to

CPR 15.3

apply for **judgment in default** (see paragraph 5.3).

Service of the defence

CPR 15.6 provides that a copy of the defence must be served on every other party to the action, but gives little else by way of guidance on when service is to be effected and whether it is done by the court or the defendant. In any event, it is good practice, and therefore advisable for the defendant, to serve the defence as soon as is practicable after filing.

The rules as to methods of service outlined on page 32 apply to service of a defence. So, where a solicitor is acting for the claimant or other party to be served, the address for service is the business address of her/his solicitor.

CPR 6.5

Contents of the defence

It is crucial to draft the defence in the manner prescribed in the CPR. It is not sufficient for the defendant merely to state that s/he contests the claim and no more than that. CPR 16.5 provides the fundamental requirements for defences, which must include a statement by the defendant as to which allegations in the particulars of claim s/he:

• admits

• denies

• is unable to admit or deny, but which s/he requires the claimant to prove.

Wherever the defendant denies an allegation, s/he must give reasons for doing so. This entails providing her/his own version of events where it differs from that of the claimant.

CPR 16.5(1)-(2)

In most cases, the clearest way to do this is to deal with each paragraph of the particulars of claim in turn, stating matters which are admitted, denied or "not admitted" and which the claimant is required to prove.

It is important to be accurate about what is being denied. For example, the claimant may have suffered loss and injury arising from a particular incident which s/he alleges are the defendant's actions. In many instances it will not be appropriate for the defendant to deny that these losses and injuries have taken place, as distinct from denying that the cause of the loss and damage was the defendant's conduct. It may be that the losses and injuries occurred as the result of the conduct of another person. In this situation the defendant will usually deny the breach but "not admit" the losses and injuries, so that the claimant must prove them even if the breach and causation is proved.

Where the defendant makes an admission on certain matters in the particulars of claim, the claimant will not have to prove the point at trial. For example, there may be no disagreement on the date and type of tenancy entered into by the parties, in which case this should be reflected in the defence.

If the defendant does not deal with a particular allegation in this way, but within the defence has set out the nature of her/his case on the matter, the claimant will be required to prove the allegation. However, if the defendant has simply failed to deal with the allegation then s/he will be taken to have admitted it. One exception to this is where the claim includes a money claim, eg. rent arrears, return of deposit and damages for disrepair. In such cases, the claimant is required to prove any allegation relating to money unless expressly admitted by the defendant.

CPR 16.5(5)

CPR 16.5 (4)

Other contents of defence

In addition to those matters described above, the defence must include:

• A statement of truth as follows:[4]
'[I believe][the defendant believes] that the facts stated in the defence are true'

(See page 23 for further information relating to statements of truth.)

• An address for service if the defendant did not file an acknowledgement of service.

CPR 16.5(8)

• Where the claim is for personal injuries, certain other information specified by the Practice Direction to Part 16.[5]

In addition the defendant may include any of the following in the defence:

• any point of law on which a defence and/or counterclaim is based

• the names of any witnesses s/he proposes to call

• a copy of any document necessary to support the defence and/or counterclaim, eg. an expert's report. This may be attached to the defence or served with it as a separate document.[6]

Claimant's reply to defence

The claimant can, if s/he wishes, file and serve a reply to the defence. This will be appropriate where the defence refers to matters not addressed in the particulars of claim. If the claimant chooses not to file a reply, this does not mean s/he has admitted any matter contained in the defence. If the claimant does file a reply, but does not deal with matters raised in the defence, the defendant will still be required to prove the matter at trial.

CPR 16.7(1)

CPR 16.7(2)

If a reply is filed, it must be filed and served at the same time as the allocation questionnaire. The reply must contain a statement of truth.

CPR 15.8

---

4   CPR PD 16 paras 12.1-22.3
5   CPR PD 16 paras 13.1-13.2
6   CPR PD 16 paras 14.1-14.3

In practice, replies are more usual where the defendant has filed a counterclaim and the claimant has to file a defence to the counterclaim (see page 50).

Admissions

As an alternative to filing an acknowledgement of service or defence, the defendant may file an admission to admit the truth of the whole or part of the other party's case. The appropriate admission form should be included in the response pack as referred to earlier (see page 41). However, the defendant may simply give notice of an admission by letter.

CPR 14.1(2)

An admission should be returned or filed 14 days after service of the particulars of claim. Where the particulars of claim are included on the claim form then this will be 14 days from service of the claim form. However, as long as the claimant has not obtained judgment in default (see paragraph 5.3), the defendant may return or file the admission after the 14-day time limit. It is then treated as though it had been made within the time limit.

CPR 14.2

Claims for specified amount of money

Where the admission relates to a claim for a specified amount of money, the procedure to be followed depends on whether the admission relates to the whole of the claim, or just part of it.

ADMISSION OF WHOLE OF CLAIM

The defendant returns the admission form N9A to the claimant. The form includes a section for the defendant to either offer to pay the amount in full by a specified date, or offer to pay the amount by monthly instalments. It also gives the defendant the opportunity to provide details of income and expenditure.

CPR 14.4 & 14.9

The claimant may obtain judgment by filing a request at court (Form N225), and may accept or reject the defendant's proposals for payment by a certain date or by instalments. If s/he accepts, then the court will enter judgment.

If the claimant rejects the defendant's proposals for payment, then the court will decide the time and rate of payment. If the amount outstanding, including any costs, is not more than £50,000, then a court officer may make the decision and there will not be a hearing. In any event, the decision may be made by a judge who may make an order without a hearing.

CPR 14.10 & 14.11

ADMISSION OF PART OF CLAIM

The defendant completes admission form N9A as above, but indicates in the appropriate box that only part of the claim is admitted. S/he must then file the form at court rather than returning it to the claimant directly.

CPR 14.5

The court will then serve a notice on the claimant (Form N225A) and will attach a copy of the N9A form returned by the defendant. The form requires the claimant to return the notice to the court indicating that:

• s/he accepts the amount admitted in satisfaction of the claim, or

• s/he does not accept the amount admitted and wants the proceedings to continue, or

• s/he accepts the amount admitted but not the defendant's proposals for payment.

The claimant should return the notice to the court within 14 days of service on her/him. If the claimant does not return the notice within this period, then the claim is **stayed** until s/he does.

If the claimant accepts the amount admitted and the proposals for payment, then the court will enter judgment on those terms.

CPR 14.10 & 14.11

If s/he accepts the amount admitted but not the defendant's proposals for payment, then the court will decide the time and rate of payment as described above and judgment is entered.

If the defendant has not made any proposals for payment, the claimant may specify in the request for judgment:

• the date by which the whole of the judgment debt is to be paid, or

• the time and rate at which the debt is to be paid by instalments.

On receipt of the request, the court will enter judgment for the amount admitted which is:

• to be paid by the date or at the rate specified by the claimant in the request for judgment, or

• to be paid immediately if the claimant has not specified the date or rate for repayment.

If the claimant rejects the amount admitted, then the case will continue as a defended action.

Claims for unspecified amount of money

Where the admission relates to a claim for an unspecified amount of money, the procedure to be followed depends on whether the admission accepts liability for the whole of the claim, or the defendant accepts liability and offers a sum in satisfaction of the claim.

ADMISSION OF WHOLE OF CLAIM

CPR 14.6

The defendant admits the claim by filing the admission form N9C. The court will serve a copy of the admission on the claimant. The claimant may then file a request for judgment at court (Form N226).

Normally the court will enter judgment and list the matter for a **disposal hearing** to assess damages and costs. The court may give **directions** specifying what each party needs to do before the hearing. Alternatively the court may ask the parties to complete an **allocation questionnaire,** following which the court will **allocate** the claim **to track** and give

CPR 14.8 & 12.3   directions in the same way as it would for a defended claim.

If the claimant fails to file the request for judgment within 14 days of service, then the claim is **stayed** until s/he does so.

ADMISSION OF LIABILITY TO PAY CLAIM – DEFENDANT OFFERS SUM IN SATISFACTION OF CLAIM

The defendant files Form N9C and indicates on the form that s/he wishes to offer an amount in full satisfaction of the claim. The court

CPR 14.7   serves a copy of the admission form on the claimant.

If the claimant accepts the amount offered and proposals for payment, s/he will request, and the court will enter, judgment accordingly.

If the claimant accepts the amount offered, but not the proposals for payment, the court will decide the time and rate of payment as above.

If the claimant does not accept the amount offered, s/he may obtain judgment and the amount will be decided by the court as above.

Time and rate of payments – re-determination

Either party may apply for the decision on the time and rate for

CPR 14.7   payment to be re-determined where:

- it was determined by a court officer, or

- it was determined by a judge without a hearing.

An application must be made within 14 days of service of the determination in accordance with the Part 23 procedure (see paragraph 9.1).

Variation

Where there is a change of circumstances since the date of the decision, then either party may apply to vary the time and rate of payment. Thus, if the defendant has a sudden drop in income, for example as a result of losing employment, it may be appropriate to seek a variation.[7]

Counterclaims and other Part 20 claims

Part 20 of the CPR governs the procedure to be used where the defendant wishes to bring a counterclaim against the claimant, or against the claimant and some other person. This commonly arises where a landlord seeks possession against a tenant for rent arrears and the tenant counterclaims

CPR 20.2(1)(a)   for disrepair, or perhaps for harassment.

7   CPR PD 14 paras 6.1-6.2

The procedure is also used where the defendant wishes to bring a claim against another person, whether or not they are already a party to the proceedings. The defendant could in this way seek a contribution or an indemnity to the main claim. For example, where a claim is brought against a landlord for disrepair, the landlord may wish to bring a related claim against building contractors for their failure to remedy the alleged disrepair. In this way the building contractors would become "third parties" to the proceedings. Indeed, the third party, once joined, may wish to bring other parties, for example, building sub-contractors.[8]

This section looks at the situation where a defendant counterclaims against the claimant. For the procedure in other situations, see Part 20 of the CPR.

How to make a counterclaim against the claimant

The defendant may counterclaim against the claimant by filing particulars of counterclaim when s/he files the defence. The defendant does not need the permission of the court to do this where the claim is brought under Part 7. The defence and counterclaim should normally form one document:[9] the counterclaim follows on from the defence as illustrated on page 406.

CPR 20.4(2)

If, however, the defendant decides to make a counterclaim after filing the defence, s/he must apply to the court for permission to do so.

As outlined below, in Part 8 claims the defendant can bring a counterclaim only with the permission of the court.

How Part 20 claims are treated

CPR 20.3

Part 20 claims are treated in the same way as other claims (eg. as regards to the content of particulars, issue and method of service) with a few exceptions:

- The provisions for **case management** relating to **allocation to track** under Part 26 of the CPR are applied according to the nature of the initial claim.

CPR 20.8

- Part 20 claims have their own rules about service of the particulars of claim (see below).

Service of counterclaim

CPR 20.8

In a situation where a counterclaim may be made without the court's permission, it must be served on every other party with the defence. If the court has given permission for a counterclaim to be made, it will give **directions** regarding service.

---

8   CPR 20.2(1)(b)-(c)   9   CPR PD 20 para 6.1

Claimant's reply and defence to counterclaim

The claimant does not have to return an acknowledgement of service; however, s/he must file a defence within 14 days.[10] If s/he is unable to do so, then there is the possibility of agreeing an extension of up to 28 days, as referred to above. A failure to defend a counterclaim may allow the defendant to enter judgment in default against the claimant in respect of the counterclaim (see paragraph 5.3).

CPR 20.3(3)(a)

Further information

On occasions a party, or indeed the court, may want to ask another party to provide more information in relation to the case. Part 18 applies and CPR 18.1(1) states:

The court may at any time order a party to:

(a) clarify any matter which is in dispute in the proceedings; or

(b) give additional information in relation to any such matter.

However, the CPR provide a procedure for further information to be given voluntarily without the need to make an application.

Preliminary requests

The Practice Direction to Part 18 outlines the procedure to be used by a party seeking further clarification or information.[11] In all cases the requesting party should serve a written request on the other party to allow the other party to respond voluntarily.

The request should be sufficiently concise and confined to those matters that are reasonably pertinent and proportionate to the case. As far as practicable, such requests should be made in a single document rather than as a series of requests.[12] If the request for information is brief and the reply is likely to be brief, a request can be made by letter. So as to distinguish the letter from other routine letters written in the course of a case, a request by letter should:

• specify that it constitutes a request made under Part 18

• not deal with any other matter than the request.

A request for information may also be made in a separate document. Whether in letter or separate document form, the request must:

• be headed with the name of the court and the claim number

• state in the heading that it is a request made under Part 18, and set out the parties in the case and the date on which it is made

10 CPR 20.4(3) & 20.3(3)(a)
11 PD 18 paras 1.1-4.2

12 Burt v Montagu Welt [1999], Legal Action April 2000, CA

- set out in separate numbered paragraphs each request for clarification or information
- where the request relates to a document, identify that document and, if appropriate, specify the particular paragraphs or words to which it relates
- specify the date by which the party expects the other party to respond. This should allow the latter a reasonable period, the length of which will depend on the nature of the clarification or information requested.

Requests not made in letter form may be set out so as to include the numbered paragraphs referred to above on the left-hand side of the document, thereby allowing the responses to be included next to them on the right. Where this is done, the requesting party should provide an extra copy for the responding party to complete.

RESPONDING TO A REQUEST

Responses to requests must be in writing, dated and signed by the party or her/his **legal representative**. The response may be in letter form if the request itself was by letter. Unless the request is in the format which allows the response to be included on the same document, the response must also:

- be headed with the name of the court, the title and number of the claim
- identify itself in the heading as a response to the request
- repeat the exact text of each paragraph of the request and under each set out the appropriate response
- refer to and attach a copy of any document not already given to the requesting party which forms part of the response.

OBJECTIONS TO REQUEST

A party may object to a request by another party for further information. If so, s/he should set out, in a letter or other document, the reasons for the objection. If the objection relates only to the time given for responding to the request, s/he should give a date by which she anticipates being able to do so.

STATEMENT OF TRUTH

Responses to requests made under Part 18 are statements of case and as such must include a statement of truth (see page 23).

SERVICE

The responding party must serve on the requesting party and every other party, and file at the court, a copy of both the request and her/his response.

Application for further information

If a request for further information has been refused or not responded to, an application to the court can be made. A party should always make a written request before making an application; failure to do so may result in adverse costs consequences for that party.

An application is made in accordance with Part 23 (see paragraph 9.1), with the modifications set out in Part 18 which are outlined below.[13]

In addition to the usual information required in the application notice, the requesting party should:

- Set out or attach the wording of the order s/he seeks, specifying those matters on which further clarification or information is sought.

- If a request for the information to be provided voluntarily has not been made, give an explanation for this.

- If any kind of response has been made by the other party, provide a description of this response. This may be included on either the application notice or any evidence in support, such as a witness statement.

Where a request has been made to the other party, the application notice need not be served on the other party, provided:

- 14 days have elapsed, and

- the time for compliance with the request has expired.

The court may deal with the application without a hearing. In any event, an order made by the court must be served on every party to the claim.

Clearly, a party asked to provide further information voluntarily should refuse only where there is a legitimate reason, for example, where the information requested is simply not available. An unreasonable refusal or failure to provide a response is likely to lead, at the very least, to an award of costs against her/him, in respect of the application.

4.2   Part 8 claims – response by defendant

On the issue of a Part 8 claim, the court may list the matter for a hearing. The claim form and the written evidence in support of the claim must be served on the defendant not less than 21 days before the hearing date. The defendant must also be served with the notice of the hearing.

Where the claim is brought using the Part 8 procedure, the defendant is not required to file a defence and the provisions of Part 15 of the CPR do not apply.

CPR 15.1

---

13 CPR PD 18 paras 5.1-5.8

Acknowledgement of service

The defendant must file an acknowledgement of service at court not more than 14 days from service of the claim on her/him. S/he must then serve the acknowledgement of service on the claimant and any

CPR 8.3(1)
CPR PD 8 para 3.2

other party to the action. This should be on Form N210; however, an acknowledgement may also be given by letter.

The defendant should indicate on the acknowledgement of service whether s/he contests the claim and any remedy which s/he seeks not already set out on the claim form. Otherwise the contents of the

CPR 8.3(2)-(3)

acknowledgement of service are as for Part 7 claims (see above).

If the defendant fails to file an acknowledgement of service within the 14 days allowed, then s/he may attend the hearing but can take part in

CPR 8.4

the hearing only if s/he is permitted by the court. However, failure to file the acknowledgement of service does not allow the claimant to

CPR 8.1(5)

apply for **judgment in default**.

For certain types of Part 8 claim, the defendant does not have to serve an acknowledgement of service. This includes a claim against trespassers in which the claimant applies for an interim possession order under Order 24 of the CCR 1981.[14]

Written evidence

If the defendant wishes to rely on any written evidence (eg. **witness statements**), then s/he must file and serve this evidence when filing the

CPR 8.5(3)-(4)
CPR 8.6

acknowledgement of service. Any written evidence not filed and served by either party may not be relied on unless permitted by the court.

It is possible for the parties to agree to an extension of the time to file and serve evidence, but not for longer than an additional 14 days. If agreed, the defendant must file evidence of the agreement (ie. letters

CPR PD 8 para 5.6

between the parties) when filing the acknowledgement of service.

If the parties cannot agree to extend the time then the party seeking the extension may apply to the court. The advisable course of action is for the party to file and serve the evidence as soon as possible. The party seeking to rely on the evidence filed late may seek the permission of the court at any subsequent hearing; this includes the trial of the matter. Either party may also apply to the court for permission to file and serve additional evidence.[15]

The claimant then has 14 days from service of the defendant's written

CPR 8.5(5)-(6)

evidence to file and serve any written evidence in reply.

---

14 CPR PD 8B Section B; claims listed in table 2.   15 CPR 8.6 & PD 8 para 5.6

Listing the claim

If the court has not already listed the matter for hearing, it will give **directions** for the disposal of the case as soon as practicable after the defendant has filed an acknowledgement of service, or after the time limit for acknowledging the claim has expired.[16] In practice, the claim will be listed for a hearing at an early date. At this hearing the court may dispose of the matter, or, more probably, where the claim is contested, give directions for the future management of the case.

Counterclaims and other Part 20 claims

CPR 8.7

Any party who wishes to bring a Part 20 claim must apply for the court's permission to do so.

Defendant objects to use of Part 8 procedure

The defendant may object to use of the Part 8 procedure where s/he does not accept that a rule or practice direction requires its use, or because s/he contends that there is a substantial dispute of fact (see paragraph 3.3).

CPR 8.8 & 8.1(3)

The defendant indicates her/his contention, providing reasons, when filing the acknowledgement of service. On receipt of the acknowledgement of service and written evidence in support, the court will usually list the matter for a hearing. The court may order that the claim continue as a Part 8 claim, or that it continue as though the claimant had not used the Part 8 procedure. In either case, as before, the court will give directions for the future conduct of the case.

Allocation

Part 8 claims, other than those listed in Table 8B of the Practice Direction, are treated as allocated to the **multi-track**. However, this does not prevent the court giving directions similar to those normally given in fast-track cases. For claims listed in Table 8B, these may be allocated to track when the court gives case management directions following the filing of a defence. The normal rules as to the scope of each track apply.[17]

5

Bringing proceedings to an end

This chapter looks at the ways in which proceedings can be brought to an end or halted prematurely. This can be by order of a court or by action taken by one or more of the parties. One of the underlying aims of the CPR is to reduce costs and filter out unnecessary litigation; this is in evidence in each of the procedures and processes described in this chapter.

5.1 Striking out

The court may strike out a statement of case in certain situations. This process is described on page 74 as one of the sanctions the court can apply in exercise of its **case management** powers.

Striking out is closely related to summary judgment, described below. Striking out is concerned with disposing of statements of case which are patently hopeless; where, for example, they reveal no basis in law. Clearly, in many cases, there will be an overlap with summary judgment. An application for striking out may be accompanied by an application for summary judgment in the alternative.

5.2 Summary judgment

CPR 24.2

Summary judgment can be employed to give judgment at an early stage of proceedings to either party where a claim or a defence has no real prospects of success and where there is no other compelling reason for dealing with the matter at trial.

It follows that summary judgment should not be given where there is a compelling reason, such as it is in the public interest that the matter proceeds to trial. Another compelling reason for proceeding might be where a party is temporarily unable to provide valuable evidence in support of her/his statement of case, for example where an important document is held by someone else.

The CPR have changed the scope of summary judgment. Prior to 1999 it was available only against defendants who could defeat an application by showing that there was a triable issue regardless of the strength of the defence. Summary judgment may now be obtained where, although there is a triable issue, the case is weak and has no real prospect of success.

Types of proceedings

CPR 24.3

Summary judgment is available in:

• any type of proceedings against a claimant, and

• any type of proceedings against a defendant, except possession proceedings against a tenant or mortgagor of residential premises.

Procedure

An application may be made by either party in accordance with the general rules relating to applications in Part 23 of the CPR (see paragraph 9.1). Alternatively, the court, in exercise of its **case management** powers, may itself direct that a summary judgment application be heard; indeed in some cases the court may make an order for summary judgment without a hearing.

CPR 3.3(4)

An application may be based on:[1]

- a point of law (including an issue relating to the construction of a document), or

- the evidence (or lack of it) reasonably expected to be available at trial, or

- a combination of the above.

When to make an application

A claimant cannot apply for summary judgment until the defendant has filed an **acknowledgment of service** or a defence, unless:

CPR 24.4(1)

- the court gives permission, or

- a practice direction provides otherwise.

Where a defendant has not filed an acknowledgement of service or a defence within the prescribed time periods, the claimant should apply for judgment in default (see page 60).

If a claimant applies for summary judgment before the defendant has filed a defence, the defendant need not, but may, file a defence before the hearing of that application.

CPR 24.4(2)

In contrast, there are no limitations on when the defendant can apply for summary judgment.

The application notice

In addition to the usual information required in the application notice, it must include a statement that it is an application for summary judgment under Part 24 CPR.

Furthermore, the application notice or the evidence contained (or referred to) in the notice must:[2]

- identify concisely any point of law or provision in a document on which the applicant relies

- state that the applicant believes, on the evidence, that the respondent has no real prospect of succeeding in her/his claim or defence

---

(or issue) and that s/he knows of no other reason why the matter should await trial

- identify the written evidence s/he relies on unless it is contained within the application notice

- inform the respondent of her/his right to file and serve written evidence in reply.

Listing the hearing

Where a summary judgment hearing is fixed, the respondent, or both parties if the hearing is fixed at the court's initiative, must be given at least 14 days' notice of:

CPR 24.4(3)-(4)

- the date of the hearing, and

- the issues which it is proposed the court will decide at the hearing.

Evidence

CPR 24.5(1)

The respondent to the application must file and serve any written evidence s/he wishes to rely on at least seven days before the hearing. If the respondent to the application has served a statement of case or other document such as a **witness statement**, verified by a **statement of truth**, s/he may rely on these as evidence for the summary judgment hearing.

CPR 24.5(2)

The applicant must file and serve any further written evidence in reply to the respondent's evidence at least three days before the hearing.

CPR 24.5(3)(a)
CPR 24.5(3)(b)

If the hearing has been fixed by the court of its own initiative, both parties must file and serve the written evidence that each wishes to rely on at least seven days before the hearing, unless the court orders otherwise. Where any party wishes to file and serve evidence in reply, they must do so at least three days before the hearing.

The hearing

In the county court, the hearing will normally take place before a **district judge** unless s/he directs that the hearing should be heard by a circuit judge.[3]

The court may make the following orders on hearing an application for summary judgment:[4]

- judgment on the claim

- striking out or dismissal of a claim

- dismissal of application

- a conditional order.

---

3 CPR PD 24 para 3   4 CPR PD 24 para 5.1

The court could make a conditional order where it appears that a claim or a defence may succeed, but that this is improbable. A conditional order requires a party to:[5]

• pay a sum of money into court, or

• take a specified step in relation to her/his claim or defence. The order will provide that the claim or statement of case will be struck out for non-compliance.

On reaching a decision on the summary judgment application, the court may also give directions for the future conduct of the case. This may include directions as to the filing and serving of a defence if one has not been filed.

CPR 24.6

Costs

The court may make any of the cost orders outlined in Chapter 13, but a successful applicant will normally be awarded fixed costs (see paragraph 13.9).[6]

Setting aside summary judgment

If summary judgment is given in the absence of the respondent, s/he may apply for the order to be set aside or varied. The court may make any order it thinks just on hearing the application.[7]

5.3   Judgment in default

A claimant may obtain judgment in default, frequently also referred to as "default judgment", where the defendant has failed to file an **acknowledgment of service** or a defence within the time specified by the CPR. In this way, the claimant may obtain judgment against the defendant at an early stage in the proceedings.

CPR 12.1 & 12.3

Default judgment is also available where a counterclaim has been brought and the claimant has failed to file a defence to the counterclaim within the specified time.

CPR 12.3(2)(b)

A claimant cannot obtain default judgment if the defendant has a pending application for:

CPR 12.3(3)

• the claimant's statement of case to be struck out under CPR 3.4, or

• summary judgment under Part 24.

Excluded claims

Default judgment cannot be obtained in respect of the following types of claim:[8]

---

5   CPR PD 24 para 5.2
6   CPR PD 24 paras 9.1-9.3 and see generally Part 44 CPR

7   CPR PD 24 paras 8.1-8.2
8   CPR 12.2 & 55.7(4)

- possession claims under Part 55 (see Chapter 14)

- Part 8 claims

- claims for delivery of goods subject to a Consumer Credit Act 1974 agreement

- any other case where a relevant practice direction provides that default judgment is not available, eg. arbitration proceedings, contentious probate proceedings and claims for provisional damages.

Procedure

The procedure to be used by the claimant differs depending on the nature of the claim against the defendant. In some circumstances, the claimant can obtain default judgment simply by filing a request at court in the prescribed form. In others, the claimant must make an application in accordance with Part 23 (see paragraph 9.1).

Default judgment by application

The claimant must make an application for default judgment where the claim:[9]

- consists of or includes a claim for a remedy other than a money claim (eg. includes a claim for an injunction)

- is a claim against a **child** or **patient**

- is a claim in **tort** by one spouse against the other

- is a claim against the Crown

- is a claim against a defendant where there are jurisdictional issues, for example against a defendant resident in Scotland or Northern Ireland.

Default judgment by filing request

CPR 12.4(1)

The claimant can obtain default judgment by filing a request in the relevant practice form at court, where the claim is not one which requires an application to be made (see previous section), and is a claim for:

- a specified amount of money, or

- an amount of money to be decided by the court, or

- delivery of goods as an alternative to payment, or

- any combination of these claims.

Evidence

Whether the claimant seeks default judgment by request or by application, the court must be satisfied that:[10]

- the defendant has been served with the particulars of claim, and

- the defendant has not filed an **acknowledgment of service** or filed a defence and, in either case, the relevant period has expired, and

- the defendant has not satisfied the claim, and

- the defendant has not returned or filed an admission accepting liability for the full amount of the claim.

Claims for specified amounts

CPR 12.5(1)-(2)

Where the claim is for a specified amount of money, the request for default judgment may indicate the date by which the claimant requires full payment of the debt, or the times and rates for payment by instalments. If the claimant does not give any indication then the court will normally give judgment requiring immediate payment. Fixed costs will be added to the debt (see paragraph 13.9).[11]

CPR 12.6 & 16.4

A default judgment for a claim for a specified amount may include interest claimed to the date of the judgment, but only where:

- the claimant included within the particulars of claim all the information required by CPR 16.4 (see page 26); and

- any claim for statutory interest under section 69 of the County Courts Act 1984 does not exceed the rate of interest payable on judgment debts at the time the claim form was issued. The rate payable on judgment debts is eight per cent; and

- the request for judgment includes a calculation of the interest from the date it was calculated on the claim form to the date of the request.

In all other cases judgment will be for an amount of interest to be decided by the court; this is usually done at a disposal hearing.

Claims for unspecified amounts

CPR 12.5(3)

CPR 12.7

Where the claim is for an unspecified amount, a default judgment obtained by request will be for an amount to be decided by the court, with costs added. The court will give directions and, where appropriate, will allocate the case to track (see page 79). It will not normally be appropriate for the court to allocate the case to track unless the amount payable is genuinely disputed on substantial grounds.[12]

In the majority of cases the court will list the matter for a disposal hearing and may give directions. The claimant should file and serve any documents, such as **witness statements** or reports, on which s/he

---

11 CPR 12.5(2) & 45.4   12 CPR PD 26 para 12.3

intends to rely on to prove the losses sustained. These documents should be served at least three days before the disposal hearing; this will enable the court to decide the amount payable at the hearing.[13]

Claim against co-defendants

A claimant may enter default judgment against one or more co-defendants, while proceeding with the action against the remaining defendants. However, this is possible only if the claim can be dealt with separately from that against the other defendants. If it cannot, then the court will not allow default judgment to be entered until the action against those other defendants is disposed of.

CPR 12.8

Setting aside or varying default judgment

The CPR provide that the defendant may apply to the court for the setting aside or varying of the default judgment. In some cases the court must set aside the judgment, while in others the court is given the discretion to set aside or vary. In addition, the claimant her/himself may have a duty to apply to set aside the default judgment order in her/his favour.

When the court must set aside

CPR 13.2

The court must set aside the default judgment if it was wrongly entered because:

- the defendant had filed a defence or **acknowledgment of service** within the prescribed time, or

- the defendant had applied for the claimant's statement of case to be struck out under CPR 3.4, or for summary judgment under Part 24 and the application has not been dealt with, or

- the whole of the claim was satisfied before judgment was entered.

When the court may set aside or vary

CPR 13.3(1)

The court has the discretion to set aside or vary the judgment if:

- the defendant has a real prospect of successfully defending the claim, or

- it appears that there is some other good reason why the judgment should be set aside or varied, or that the defendant should be permitted to defend the claim. For example, the defendant was abroad or in hospital and could not have filed an acknowledgment or defence.

CPR 13.3(2)

Applications to set aside or vary should be made without delay, as the court will have regard to any delay by the defendant in deciding whether to set aside the judgment.

13 CPR PD 26 para 12.8

CPR 13.4(3) An application for a set aside or variation where the court has a discretion must be supported by evidence, which may be provided in the application notice but only where it is verified by a **statement of truth**.

When the claimant must apply to set aside

CPR 13.5 Where the claimant has entered judgment against the defendant, and subsequently has "good reason to believe" that her/his particulars of claim had not reached the defendant at the time of judgment, s/he must either:

- file a request for judgment to be set aside, or

- apply to the court for directions.

Human Rights Act 1998

The default judgment procedure could be open to a challenge that it denies the defendant a "fair and public hearing" contrary to article 6(1) of the European Convention on Human Rights. The claimant can obtain judgment merely through the failure of the defendant to respond to the action, without presenting any evidence to the court to prove her/his claim. On the other hand, it may be argued that the opportunity for the defendant to have the judgment set aside, if her/his defence has a reasonable prospect of success, meets the requirements of article 6.[14]

5.4   Discontinuance

Discontinuance is the means by which a claimant can abandon all or part of a claim, thereby bringing the proceedings to an end. An important distinction should be made from the outset. If the claimant wishes to abandon her/his claim for one or more remedies, but wishes to proceed with the claim for other remedies, s/he should amend the statement of case rather than discontinue the claim.

Example 1

Marianne brings a claim for harassment and illegal eviction. In the statement of case she seeks relief by way of damages and an injunction allowing her back into the property. Marianne decides that s/he does not want to return to the property, but to continue with the claim for damages for harassment and illegal eviction. Marianne could apply to amend the statement of case to reflect this.

Alternatively, Marianne could simply inform the court at the directions hearing or trial that she does not wish to proceed with the claim for an injunction. If this approach is adopted, it is advisable at the earliest

---

14 Position taken by the Court of Appeal in the context of warrants for possession; see St Brice and Others v Southwark LBC, Housing Aid Update September 2001, CA

opportunity to inform the defendant of her intention. If this is not done then the defendant may incur further costs and could seek an order against Marianne in respect of these costs.

Example 2

If, however, Marianne wishes to abandon the claim altogether or to abandon the claim in respect of illegal eviction only, she should discontinue the claim in full or in part, as the case may be.

When the claimant can discontinue

CPR 38.2(1)

CPR 38.2(2)(a)

The fundamental principle is that a claimant has the right to discontinue the claim at any time. However, there are important exceptions to this general rule. A claimant must obtain the court's permission to discontinue where:

• the court has granted an **interim injunction**, or

• a party has given an **undertaking** to the court.

CPR 38.2(2)(c)

If there is more than one claimant, a claimant may not discontinue unless:

• every other claimant consents in writing, or

• the court gives permission.

CPR 38.2(3)

However, if there is more than one defendant, a claimant may discontinue against all or any of them.

Procedure

CPR 38.3(1)

In order to discontinue all or part of a claim, a claimant must:

• file a notice of discontinuance (Form N279), and

• serve a copy on every other party in the case.

CPR 38.3(2)-(3)

The notice should include a statement that every other party has been served with a copy of the notice. Where the consent of another party is required, a copy of this consent should be attached to the notice.

CPR 38.3(4)

Where there is more than one defendant, the notice must also state against which defendants the claim is discontinued.

Setting aside discontinuance

CPR 38.4

The defendant may apply to have the notice of discontinuance set aside within 28 days of receiving the notice. This would be appropriate where the permission of the court or consent from another party was not sought even though it was required.

Effect of discontinuance

CPR 38.5

The notice takes effect, and the proceedings are brought to an end against a defendant, on the date s/he receives the notice.

CPR 38.7

The claimant will need the permission of the court to make a subsequent claim against the defendant if:

• the claim is discontinued after the defendant has filed a defence, and

• the fresh claim arises from the same or similar facts as those of the discontinued action.

Costs

CPR 38.6(1)-(2)

Generally, a claimant who discontinues a claim will be liable for the defendant's costs, on the **standard basis**, up to the date of service of the notice. If part of a claim is discontinued, the claimant's liability for costs will be in respect of that part only, to be assessed at the end of the proceedings. The court retains the discretion in each case to make a different costs order from the "normal" order on discontinuance.

CPR 38.6(3)

These costs rules do not apply to claims allocated to the small claims track.

5.5   Offers to settle and payments into court – Part 36 CPR

The CPR encourage parties to settle cases as early as possible. Part 36 provides a framework to enable one party to apply pressure on another party to reach agreement.

There is nothing to prevent the parties reaching a settlement without reference to Part 36. However, for a party making an offer to settle, there are considerable advantages relating to costs in using the procedure. A settlement reached outside the scope of Part 36 will only have the costs implications outlined below where the court so orders.[15]

The Part 36 rules do not apply to claims allocated to the small claims track, unless the court orders otherwise.[16] This reflects the severe limitations on which costs can normally be recovered by a successful party to a small claim (see paragraph 13.8).

Disclosure of a Part 36 offer or payment

One of the fundamental principles of the Part 36 procedure is that any offers or payments, made in accordance with the rules, should not prejudice either party as far as liability in respect of the claim itself is concerned. Therefore, offers and payments made into court are treated

---

15 CPR 36.1 & PD 36 para 1.3   16 CPR 27.2 & 36.2(5)

as **without prejudice** except as to costs, and are not to be disclosed to the trial judge until such time as liability and the amount of any award have been resolved.

CPR 36.19

Part 36 offers/payments – general provisions

If the claim does not include a money claim, the claimant or defendant may make a Part 36 offer proposing settlement. This can take place either before the issue of proceedings or at any time thereafter.

However, in a money claim, the *defendant* may make a Part 36 offer (of money) before proceedings are issued, but once they are issued, must make a Part 36 payment, in order to take advantage of the costs implications of Part 36.[17] The *claimant* can make a Part 36 offer in respect of her/his money claim at any stage.

Form and content of a Part 36 offer

There is no prescribed form for a Part 36 offer. However, in order to be valid the Part 36 offer must:

CPR 36.5(1)-(3)

• be in writing

• state whether it relates to the whole or part of the claim and, if so, which part

• state whether it takes into account any counterclaim

• provide details of interest claimed.

CPR 36.5(6) If the offer is made not less than 21 days before the trial, the offer must:

• be expressed so as to remain open for acceptance for 21 days

• state that the offer can be accepted after 21 days, but only if the parties agree liability for costs or the court gives permission.

If the offer is made less than 21 days before the trial, then it must state that it may be accepted only if the parties agree liability for costs or the court gives permission.

CPR 36.5(7)

Part 36 payment notice

A defendant who makes a Part 36 payment must file a notice – Form N242A – at court stating:

CPR 36.6(1)-(2)

• the amount of the payment

• whether the payment relates to the whole or part of the claim and, if so, which part

---

17 CPR 36.3; see also Amber v Stacey [2000] 2 All ER 58, CA

- whether it takes account of any counterclaim

- details of interest.

The court will serve the notice on the claimant unless the defendant informs the court that s/he will serve the notice. In this case, the defendant must file a certificate of service once the notice has been served on the claimant.

CPR 36.6(3)-(4)

Once a Part 36 payment has been made, the defendant cannot withdraw or reduce it without the permission of the court.

CPR 36.6(5)

Clarifying a Part 36 offer or payment

The party receiving a Part 36 offer, or payment notice, has seven days to request clarification from the party making the offer or payment. S/he may apply to the court for an order requiring clarification if this is not forthcoming within seven days of the request.

CPR 36.9

Withdrawal of offer

It was confirmed in *Scammel v Dicker*[18] that offers to settle can be withdrawn at any time before acceptance, in accordance with general contractual law.

Response by claimant to defendant's offer or payment

When an offer or payment is made by the defendant then the claimant can decide to accept or reject. However, the consequences which may follow from rejecting the offer or payment place the claimant under considerable pressure to accept.

Acceptance of offer or payment

The claimant may accept the offer or payment, without the permission of the court, if s/he gives the defendant written notice of acceptance within 21 days of receiving the offer. If a payment into court has been made then the claimant obtains a payment out of court by filing a request at court (Form N243).[19]

CPR 36.11(1)

In this situation, the claimant would be entitled to her/his costs incurred in the proceedings on the **standard basis** up to the date of serving the notice of acceptance.

CPR 36.13(1)

If the defendant's offer or payment is made less than 21 days before the start of the trial or the claimant does not accept an offer within 21 days, the claimant can accept only:

CPR 36.11(2)

- if the parties agree on liability for costs, or

- if the parties do not agree on liability for costs with the permission of the court, in which case the court will make an order as to costs.

18 Scammel v Dicker [2000] 145 SJB 28   19 CPR 36.16 & PD 36 para 8.1

Non-acceptance of offer or payment

The consequences of not accepting the offer of payment depend on whether the claimant achieves a better result at trial. This may happen if the claimant either fails to better a Part 36 payment or fails to obtain a more favourable judgment than a Part 36 offer. In either of these situations, the court will order the claimant to pay any costs incurred by the defendant after the last day on which the claimant could have accepted the payment or offer without needing the permission of the court; ie. 21 days from receipt of the offer or payment notice.

CPR 36.20 & 44.3

However, the court may make a different costs order where it considers that this would be unjust having regard to all the circumstances. For example, the court may have regard to the defendant's failure to disclose material matters which may have influenced the claimant in deciding whether to accept an offer or payment.[20]

CPR 44.3(2)

On the other hand, if the claimant does better than the offer or payment, it is likely that the defendant will be ordered to pay the claimant's costs for the whole action in accordance with the general rule. Again, the court retains its discretion when awarding costs and may, among other things, have regard to any Part 36 offer or payment in the proceedings. It is possible, therefore, that the court will make no order as to costs or award costs to the defendant, even if the claimant

CPR 44.3(4)

does better than the offer or payment.

Response by defendant to claimant's offer

There is similar pressure on the defendant when faced with a Part 36 offer made by the claimant.

Acceptance of offer

The defendant may accept an offer made not less than 21 days before the start of the trial. S/he can do this without the permission of the court if s/he gives notice of acceptance in writing not later than 21

CPR 36.12(1)

days after receipt of the offer.

CPR 36.14

In this situation, the claimant is entitled to the costs of the proceedings up to the date when the defendant serves the notice of acceptance.

CPR 36.12(2)

If the claimant's offer is made less than 21 days before the start of the trial or the defendant does not accept an offer within 21 days, the defendant can accept only:

• if the parties agree on liability for costs

• with the permission of the court where the parties do not agree on liability for costs. In this situation the court will decide what order to make as to costs.

---

20 Ford v GKR Construction Ltd [2000] 1 All ER 802

Non-acceptance of offer

If the defendant does not accept the offer and at the trial the claimant does better than her/his offer, ie. the defendant is held liable to pay more or the judgment is more advantageous to the claimant, then:

CPR 36.21(1)-(3)

- The court may order the defendant to pay interest on the claimant's damages at a higher rate – up to 10 per cent above the base rate – for some or all of the period from the latest date the defendant could have accepted the offer without the permission of the court.

- The court may also order that the defendant pays the claimant's costs on an **indemnity basis** from the latest date for acceptance of the offer, and award interest on these costs up to 10 per cent above the base rate.

The court will not make either order where to do so would be unjust. It must take account of all the circumstances of the case, but in particular:

CPR 36.21(4)-(5)

- the terms of any Part 36 offer and the stage in the proceedings that the offer was made

- the information available to the parties

- the conduct of the parties with regard to information given or refused for the purposes of making or evaluating an offer.

Effect of acceptance of a Part 36 offer or payment

The effect of acceptance of an offer (by either party) or acceptance of a payment (by the claimant) is that the claim is **stayed**. If the offer or payment relates to only part of the claim then that part of the claim is stayed. In effect, the stay is conditional on the agreement between the parties. If one party is in breach, then the other may apply to lift the stay and continue with the proceedings.

CPR 36.15

Interest

An offer or payment into court is treated as being inclusive of interest (up to the last date on which it could have been accepted without the permission of the court) unless the contrary is indicated in the offer letter or payment notice.

CPR 36.22

Children and patients

A Part 36 offer or payment made in proceedings which involve a **child** or **patient** may be accepted only with the permission of the court. It follows that no payment out of court may be made without a court order.

CPR 36.18 & 21.10

Case management and allocation

Prior to the introduction of the CPR, critics of the civil court system complained about the length of time it took for a case to be resolved and the disproportionate cost often incurred. The court's duty to manage cases actively to further the overriding objective is facilitated by the court being given extensive powers to enable this. The guiding principles are to ensure that cases are dealt with justly, quickly and in a cost-effective manner.[1]

The court's core case management powers are contained in Part 3, The court's case management powers, and Part 26, Case management – preliminary stage. These are examined in detail below.

6.1 General case management powers

A full list of the court's general case management powers is set out in CPR 3.1(2). They are extensive and include the power to:

- extend or reduce time limits for compliance with any rule, practice direction or order

CPR 3.1(2)(b)
- **adjourn** or bring forward a hearing date

- **stay** the whole or part of any proceedings generally or until a specific date or event

- consolidate proceedings and try two or more claims together

- direct that there be a separate trial of a particular issue, decide the order in which issues are tried or exclude consideration of an issue

- **dismiss** or give judgment following a decision on a preliminary issue

- require a party or her/his legal representative to attend court

- hold a hearing and accept evidence by telephone.

To illustrate that these powers are non-exhaustive, the court also has a CPR 3.1(2)(m) general power to:

... take any other step or make any other order for the purpose of managing the case and furthering the overriding objective.

CPR 3.3(1)
The CPR allow the court to exercise its court management powers on its own initiative or following an application by one or more of the parties. If the court is minded to make an order on its own initiative, it may hold a hearing or give the parties the opportunity to make representations, but is not obliged to do so. If a hearing is to be held, the court should give CPR 3.3(2)-(4) each party affected at least three days' notice. The ability of the court to use its powers on its own initiative is a fundamentally important

---

1   CPR 1.4; see Chapter 1 The overriding objective

innovation of the CPR and promotes the duty of the court to manage cases actively. In practice, however, the exercise by the courts of its case management powers is curtailed by limitations on the number of judges and time.

6.2   Directions

The court will also give directions to the parties to ensure that the issues between them are identified and any evidence is prepared and disclosed in anticipation of the trial of the matter. The extent of these directions varies according to how the case is allocated. This is considered in more detail below. Again, the aim of directions is to ensure effective case management in accordance with the overriding objective.

6.3   Sanctions

In order to ensure the active management of cases, the court may use its case management powers to apply sanctions against a particular party. The most extreme sanction is striking out, but there are a number of other less drastic but effective sanctions which, in practice, the court will employ. The use of other sanctions will depend on the circumstances and this will be explored later in this chapter.

Striking out

CPR 3.4(2) gives the court the power to strike out a statement of case where it appears to the court:

(a) that the statement of case discloses no reasonable grounds for bringing or defending the claim;

(b) that the statement of case is an abuse of the court's process or is otherwise likely to obstruct the just disposal of the proceedings; or

(c) that there has been a failure to comply with a rule, practice direction or court order.

Statement of case discloses no reasonable grounds

The situations in which a statement of case discloses no reasonable grounds for bringing or defending a claim include those where:[2]

• there is no indication of what the claim is about

• no legally recognisable claim against the defendant is set out

• a defence simply denies the claim without any coherent set of facts

• a defence discloses no actual defence in law.

---

2   CPR PD 3A para 1.4 & 1.6

Statement of case is an abuse of the court's process

The situations in which a statement of case is an abuse of the court's process or otherwise is likely to obstruct the just disposal of the proceedings include:[3]

- a claim which is **vexatious** or ill-founded

- a claim which would result in a trial of matters already adjudicated on or settled between the parties

- a claim which should have been raised in an earlier action which has itself been concluded

- a claim which is founded upon **without prejudice** discussions or correspondence.

Striking out for non-compliance

The court can also strike out a statement of case where a party has failed to comply with any other rules or orders of the court, ie. a party fails to file evidence within the timetable set by directions (see page 82).

Effect of striking out

The effect of striking out a statement of case is that the document is effectively deleted and cannot be relied on.

Where the statement of case struck out is the claim form (including a counterclaim), then it follows that the case is brought to an end. If the defence is struck out then the claimant may obtain judgment in default (see paragraph 5.3).

Other sanctions

As mentioned above, striking out is an extreme sanction and often it will be appropriate to apply one or more of the other possible sanctions at the court's disposal.[4]

Indeed, the implementation of the Human Rights Act 1998 in October 2000 means that courts should recognise, at least the possibility, that striking out a case purely on the basis of a breach of the rules or an order of the court may infringe the party's right to a fair trial.[5] There would usually have to be a persistent or flagrant disregard for the rules or orders of the court before a case would be struck out for non-compliance.[6]

It is not possible to outline all the possible sanctions which the court may employ. This depends on the nature and circumstances of the case involved. Failure to file evidence in support of a claim or defence may result in the court preventing a party from relying on that evidence at

3 CPR PD 3 para 1.5; see eg., Wain v F Sherwood & Sons
  Transport Ltd [1998] 25 LS Gaz R 32, CA; Schellenberg
  v BBC [2000] EMLR 296
4 Biguzzi v Rank Leisure plc [1999] 1 WLR 1926
5 Arrow Nominees Inc. v Blackledge [2000] All ER (D) 854, CA   6 Habib Bank Ltd v Jaffer [2000], *noted* at *Times* 5 April

The Court of Appeal observed that striking out a claim, pursuant to CPR 3.4(2)(c), was not a disproportionate sanction where the breach of the rule or order itself suggested that it was no longer possible to have a fair trial

trial. A common sanction is an order that a party must pay certain costs of the other side, eg. those incurred as a result of delay.

CPR 3.5(1) Another common sanction is for the court to order that unless a specified act is taken, such as filing an amended claim form or defence, then it will strike out that statement of case. If the party fails to comply with the order, then the other party may obtain judgment by filing a request at the court if:

- the order specified that the whole of the statement of case would be struck out for non-compliance, and

- the party requesting judgment is the claimant and the claim is for:

  - a specified amount of money

  - an amount of money to be decided by the court

  - delivery of goods where the claim form gives the defendant the alternative of paying the value of the goods

  - any combination of the above remedies.

CPR 3.6(1)-(2) If judgment is entered in this way, then the party against whom judgment has been entered may apply to have the judgment set aside and the restoration of the statement of case. The application must be made within 14 days of notification of judgment being entered.

CPR 3.6(3)-(4) Where the right to judgment had not arisen at the time it was entered then the court must set aside judgment. If the application for a set aside is made for any other reason then the application is treated in the same way as other applications for relief from sanctions (see below).

Relief from sanctions

CPR 3.9 A party who has been penalised for breach of a rule or court order may apply for relief from the sanction imposed. The application should be made promptly and supported by evidence.

CPR 3.9(1)(a)-(i) The court has a discretion whether to grant relief. It will take into account a number of factors, including:

- the interests of justice

- whether the application has been made promptly and whether relief would delay the trial date

- the explanation for the default and whether it was intentional

- the conduct of the party in complying with other rules or orders of the court

• whether the default was by the party or her/his legal representative

• the effect of the default and the effect that relief would have on each party.

6.4 Allocation

CPR 1.1(2)

In the exercise of its case management powers and the furtherance of the overriding objective, the court aims to deal with cases expeditiously and fairly. One of the ways this is achieved is by allotting an appropriate share of the court's time and resources to each case.

Part 26 of the CPR provides a framework under which the court assigns all defended claims to a particular case management track. This is known as allocation to track. The particular track to which the claim is allocated will govern the way the case proceeds, in particular in relation to the directions given by the court (see page 81).

A case will be allocated to a track generally according to its value and complexity. In most cases, the court will ask each party to complete an allocation questionnaire to assist the court in making this assessment.

The court may, however, at any time, decide to hold an allocation hearing to resolve the issue. A hearing may be appropriate where there is uncertainty about which track the case should be allocated even after filing of the questionnaires. Alternatively, if an interim hearing is held in the case, the court may decide to deal with the matter of allocation and/or directions there and then, and dispense with the need for allocation questionnaires.

The allocation questionnaire

CPR 26.3

Once the defendant has filed a defence the court sends each party an allocation questionnaire (Form N150). Each party must complete and return the questionnaire by the date specified by the court, as indicated on the top right hand corner of the form. The date specified should be at least 14 days from the date on which the parties are deemed to have been served with the questionnaire.

The parties should consult with one another and co-operate in completing the questionnaires, and should at the same time try to agree directions which they may invite the court to make.[7]

A fee of £80 is payable unless the claim is for money of £1,000 or less, where no fee is payable. The claimant is responsible for the payment of the fee at the time the questionnaire is filed. However, where the case is proceeding on a counterclaim alone then it is paid by the defendant. This is because the defendant is the only party proceeding with a claim.

---

7 CPR PD 26 para 2.3

CPR 26.5(1) The court may decide that an allocation questionnaire is not required and dispense with the requirement. If so the fee must be paid by the claimant:

• within 28 days of the defence being filed, or

• on the filing of the last defence if there is more than one defendant or

• within 28 days of the expiry of the date for filing of all of the defences.

The questionnaire is Form N150 and contains notes to assist the parties in completing it. It is separated into the following sections.

A. Settlement

The parties are asked whether they require a one-month **stay** of proceedings so that they can attempt to settle the case. This reflects the principles behind the overriding objective by encouraging settlement of cases wherever possible.

Where all the parties request a stay, or the court on its own initiative considers it appropriate, then a stay of four weeks will be ordered. The court may extend this period on its own initiative or in response to a further request from the parties. If settlement is reached during the stay, the claimant must inform the court. Where settlement is not achieved, the court will allocate the case and give case management directions as set out below.[8]

B. Track

The parties are asked which track they consider is most suitable. Case management tracks are dealt with in detail further in this chapter and guidance on the tracks is contained in the notes to the questionnaire.

C. Pre-action protocols

The parties are asked, where appropriate, whether they have complied with any pre-action protocols and, if not, why not. Pre-action protocols are an innovation of the CPR, the purpose of which are to encourage more contact and exchange of information between the parties before court proceedings are commenced. It is hoped that the protocols will foster early settlement without the need for court action or, where litigation is inevitable, to ensure the parties are properly prepared so that the subsequent court proceedings will run efficiently.

To date, pre-action protocols have been introduced in only a few areas. This includes judicial review, personal injury and clinical negligence. It is anticipated that they will be introduced in other areas in due course, eg. cases, disrepair (for a summary of the draft disrepair pre-action protocol see Case Study 4, page 340).

8   CPR 26.4 & PD 26 paras 3.1-3.4

D. Applications

The parties must indicate whether they intend to apply for **summary judgment** or apply to join another party to the proceedings. Any such application should be made as soon as possible (see paragraph 5.2).

E. Witnesses of fact

The parties are asked to name any witnesses they intend to call and to specify the facts in the case which will be contained in the evidence to be given by the witnesses (see Chapter 8).

F. Experts' evidence

The parties are asked to identify any expert witnesses they propose to rely on, whether any expert has been jointly instructed and in what form the evidence is to be given (see paragraph 8.2).

G. Location of trial

The parties are asked whether there are any reasons why their case should be heard in a particular court (other than the court in which the case was issued).

H. Representation and estimate of hearing/trial time

The parties must state whether they intend to be represented at the trial, and if so, by whom and how long it will take to put their case to the court at the trial.

I. Costs

The parties are asked to indicate the costs incurred to date and the likely overall costs of their case. This section needs to be completed only in respect of costs incurred by legal representatives.

J. Other information

The final section asks the parties to provide any other documents or information they wish the court to take into account when allocating the case to a particular track.

The allocation questionnaire does not contain a **statement of truth** and can be signed by the party or by her/his solicitor (where appropriate).

The case management tracks

A claim will be allocated to one of the three tracks, which are:

- the small claims track (Part 27 of the CPR)
- the fast track (Part 28 of the CPR)
- the multi-track (Part 29 of the CPR).

An important factor for considering which track to allocate the case to is the financial value of the claim. CPR 26.6 provides the financial scope of each track and these are outlined in the following sections.

The financial value of the claim is only one of a number of factors which the court may have regard to in deciding whether a claim should be allocated to the normal track for that claim. They include:[9]

- financial value, if any (disregarding any amount not in dispute, claim for interest and any **contributory negligence**)

- type of remedy sought

- complexity of facts, law or evidence and amount of oral evidence required

- number of parties, their circumstances and views expressed by them

- value and complexity of any Part 20 claim

- importance of claim to any non-parties.

CPR 26.7(3)   In any event, the court will not allocate a claim to a particular track where the value of that claim exceeds the limit for that track unless all the parties consent. However, a claim may be allocated to a track where its value is less than the normal scope for that track. This may occur where, for example, a claim is particularly complex or there are wider public issues at stake. It follows that a claim that has no financial value is allocated according to the above factors alone.

The small claims track

The small claims track replaces the small claims court procedure that existed under the old County Court Rules. This track is designed to provide a relatively inexpensive means of resolving disputes that have a limited value. In general, any case with a value up to £5,000 will be dealt with in the small claims track. However, there are some important exceptions to this general rule and the following types of claim will not usually be allocated to the track:[10]

- disrepair claims brought by residential tenants which include a claim for work to be carried out where either the cost of the work, or the value of any damages, exceeds £1,000

- personal injury claims worth more than £1,000

- claims for injunctions and damages following illegal eviction or harassment

- claims for possession of land brought by a landlord, mortgagee or licensor

---

9 CPR 26.8(1)-(2), 26.7(2)   10 CPR 26.6, 26.7(4), 55.9(2) & PD 26 para 8.1(d)

- claims involving a disputed allegation of dishonesty.

It should be recalled that even if the claim is worth more than £5,000, or £1,000 as the case may be, the parties can consent to it being allocated downwards and may indicate their consent for other types of claim to be allocated to the small claims track, eg. possession claims. They can indicate such approval on the allocation questionnaire or at any allocation hearing. However, the final decision rests with the court, having regard to the factors described earlier.

CHARACTERISTICS OF THE SMALL CLAIMS TRACK

In accordance with the principle that claims should be dealt with proportionately to their value and importance, the small claims track is a streamlined procedure and has a number of characteristics distinct from the other two tracks. These include that:[11]

- the parties have only to comply with a limited set of directions (preparatory steps) before the hearing date (see below)

- the strict rules of evidence do not apply

- the hearing will take place in private in the judge's room, also known as in **chambers**, and will follow a more informal process (see page 150)

- the successful party can usually only recover a limited amount of legal costs; this is known as "fixed costs". Thus, the losing party does not run the risk of having to pay her/his opponent's full legal costs

- public funding will not normally be available unless there are exceptional circumstances.

STANDARD DIRECTIONS

Once allocated to the small claims track, the court gives limited directions to the parties and fixes a date for the hearing. The court gives 21 days' notice of the hearing unless the parties agree to accept less notice. The court usually gives directions without a hearing, though it retains the

CPR 27.6   power to hold a "preliminary hearing" in certain limited situations.

The CPR provide lists of standard directions which are tailored towards different types of claims.[12] One such standard list applies to claims by tenants for the return of a deposit and/or claims by the landlord for damage to the property.[13]

The general form of standard directions provides for:[14]

- the service by each party of copies of all the documents they intend to rely on at the hearing not less than 14 days before the hearing

---

11 For a full list of those parts of the CPR which do not
    apply to small claims, see CPR 27.2
12 Appendix to the Practice Direction to Rule 27 CPR 1998
13 ibid. Form D
14 ibid. Form A

- original documents to be brought to the hearing

- notice of when the hearing is to take place and the amount of time allowed for it

- an obligation on the parties to inform the court if they settle the case before the hearing.

The fast track

The fast track is an innovation of the CPR and was conceived as an attempt to reduce the cost and complexity of county court cases. The track is designed to ensure that relatively straightforward cases outside the jurisdiction of the small claims track proceed to trial quickly.

This aim is principally achieved at the directions stage by the court laying down a timetable for all the preparatory stages up to and including trial. The length of time from the making of directions to the trial is no more than 30 weeks.

CPR 28.2

Generally, claims are allocated to the fast track where they do not fall within the criteria for allocation to the small claims track and the financial value does not exceed £15,000.

CPR 26(4)

However, the court must also be satisfied that:

CPR 26(5)

- the trial is likely to last no longer than a day

- oral expert evidence will be limited to one expert per party in relation to no more than two expert fields, eg. surveyor, psychiatrist, engineer.

If the court is not satisfied of the above, or the value of the claim is more than £15,000, then the claim should be allocated to the multi-track. This is subject to a qualification that the parties may agree to allocation to another track where the value of the claim exceeds £15,000. This is subject to the court's approval.[15]

DIRECTIONS

Once allocated to the fast track then the court issues directions for the management of the case. It also provides a timetable within which the following steps should be taken:

CPR 28.2 & 28.3

- disclosure of documents (see Chapter 7)

- exchange of witness statements (see Chapter 8)

- obtaining and serving expert evidence (see paragraph 8.2)

- filing listing questionnaires (see below)

- filing trial bundles.

15 CPR 26.6(6) & 26.7(3)

Although the court may fix a trial date at the same time as it issues directions, it is more likely to fix a trial window. This is a specified period, such as three to four weeks, within the 30-week period when the trial may take place. Thus, all the parties know approximately when the trial will take place; ie. within the trial window period. It is not uncommon, however, for the trial window period to expire without the case being listed. Upon receipt of the listing questionnaires the court will then fix the precise trial date and inform the parties (see below).

CPR 28.6

THE LISTING QUESTIONNAIRES

CPR 28.5

CPR 28.5(1)-(2)

Prior to the trial the parties will usually be sent a listing questionnaire by the court. This is a document that both parties have to complete and return to the court. The parties should file the listing questionnaire by the date specified in the notice of allocation; this should not be more than eight weeks before the trial date or the trial window. The questionnaire contains questions about the number of witnesses and experts each party will be relying on at the trial. This will assist the court in fixing a trial date (or confirming the date if fixed earlier), and ensuring that sufficient time is allotted for the trial itself.

It is worth noting that courts often fail to send out the listing questionnaire when they should. If this happens the parties should obtain the forms from the court or the court service website.[16]

The claimant must pay a fee known as the trial fee when filing her/his listing questionnaire, except where the case is proceeding on a counterclaim alone. The fee is £200 for a fast track case.

CPR 28.5(1)

The court may consider that the claim can be listed without the need for listing questionnaires. If the court fixes the trial date or trial window without listing questionnaires the fee must be paid within 14 days of:

• the despatch of the notice of trial or trial window, or

• if no written notice is given, the date the claimant is told of the trial date or trial week.

Following this, the trial bundle will be prepared and lodged at court and the case will proceed to trial (see paragraph 10.2).

VARYING THE DIRECTIONS

CPR 1.3

CPR 2.11

The directions, once set by the court, should be complied with by the parties in accordance with their duty to further the overriding objective. However, minor variations (eg. extending the time for disclosure of documents by a few days) can be agreed between the parties without the need to obtain the court's permission.

---

16 The Court Service's website is www.courtservice.gov.uk

CPR 28.4(1)   However, the following cannot be varied without the court's permission:

- the date for filing the listing questionnaires

- the trial date or the trial window.

This is reflected also by the stipulation that any agreed variations should not have the knock-on effect of delaying the date for returning the listing questionnaire or the date of the trial.

CPR 28.4(1)-(2)

The court views the postponement or varying of a trial date as a last resort. The party seeking the variation, by an application, will need to convince the court that her/his circumstances are exceptional before the application will be allowed. The court has the power to make further directions to ensure that the trial date goes ahead, if appropriate.[17]

FAILING TO COMPLY WITH THE DIRECTIONS

The directions issued by the court constitute a court order. They can be enforced by the court if so required.[18]

For example, if one party fails to disclose her/his documents within the time given in the directions, the other party can apply to the court for an order that the defaulting party is forced to comply with or is made subject to a sanction by the court (see page 74). In this example, the court may decide to make one of the following orders:

- that the party discloses her/his documents within seven days

- that the party cannot rely on any documentary evidence at trial

- that unless the party discloses the documents then s/he cannot rely on any documentary evidence at trial; ie. a combination of the two orders above.

The offending party is normally also ordered to pay the costs incurred by her/his opponent in making the application.

However, the party making the application must warn the offending party of her/his intention to apply to the court in this manner before applying.[19] It is usual practice to give the offending party a final chance to comply with the direction (eg. seven days), after which time the application will be made. If a party does not warn the offending party of her/his intention to make an application, then the court may not award the costs of the application in her/his favour.

The making of applications before the trial are called interim or interlocutory applications, the rules for which are dealt with in more detail in Chapter 9.

---

17 CPR PD 28 para 5   19 CPR PD 28 para 5.2
18 CPR PD 28 para 5.1

The multi-track

The multi-track is intended for those cases with a value of over £15,000 or where the issues, evidence and estimated length of the trial are such CPR 26.7(6) that the small claims and fast tracks are inappropriate.

Unlike the small claims track and the fast track, the multi-track does not offer any standard procedure for how the claim should progress to trial. Instead, it allows the court to use a variety of case management tools, including standard directions, case management conferences and pre-CPR 29.2 trial reviews, depending on the individual claim. The court will adopt a flexible approach to ensure that each case is dealt with in an appropriate way. However, the principles of setting a trial date at the earliest possible time, as with the other tracks, applies equally to the management of CPR 29.2(2) multi-track claims.

DIRECTIONS

Upon the case being allocated to the multi-track, the court will either:

- give directions for the management of the case, including a timetable of when those steps must be taken (not unlike the standard directions used in the fast track), or

- fix a case management conference, a pre-trial review, or both, and give CPR 29.2 such directions as it thinks fit.

In addition, the court fix a trial date or trial window (see page 83) to ensure that the trial will take place as soon as practicable, and specify CPR 29.2(2) when the parties must file listing questionnaires. However, unlike the fast track, there is no requirement that the trial must take place within 30 weeks of allocation.

CASE MANAGEMENT CONFERENCE

A case management conference, if appropriate, usually takes place CPR PD 29 para 5 soon after allocation. The purpose is for the court to:

- determine how much preparation of their respective cases has already been carried out by the parties

- review any action already taken by the parties in compliance with any directions the court has already made

- give directions for the future conduct of the case

- encourage the parties to agree on as many matters as possible.

The conference is usually held in the judge's rooms and should be attended by the parties or their representatives. Any person who attends as a representative should be personally involved in the conduct of the

CPR 29.3(2)

case, and have the authority and the information to deal effectively with the issues which will be raised.

The Practice Direction to Part 29 of the CPR encourages the parties to prepare for the case management conference as follows:[20]

(1) *ensure that all documents that the court is likely to ask to see (including witness statements and experts' reports) are brought to the hearing,*

(2) *consider whether the parties should attend,*

(3) *consider whether a case summary will be useful, and*

(4) *consider what orders each wishes to be made and give notice to the other parties.*

THE LISTING QUESTIONNAIRE

CPR 29.6

As in fast track cases (see page 83), listing questionnaires are also required in multi-track cases unless the court dispenses with the need for them. Once completed, the questionnaire must be filed by a date set by the court, which will not be later than eight weeks before the trial date or start of the trial period.[21] The questionnaires should be served on the parties by the court for completion at least 14 days before that date.[22] The trial fee payable on filing of the listing questionnaire is £300 for a case in the multi-track.

If the court fails to send out a listing questionnaire when it should, then the parties should obtain a form from the court or the court service website.[23]

THE PRE-TRIAL REVIEW

CPR 29.3 & 29.7

Pre-trial reviews, in practice, differ from case management conferences in that they tend to be used to settle any outstanding matters and ensure the parties are ready for the trial itself. If the court feels that such a review is required, it will normally take place shortly before the trial and usually after receipt of the completed listing questionnaires.

VARYING DIRECTIONS IN THE MULTI-TRACK

CPR 29.5(1)-(2)

Minor variations can be made to the directions by agreement between the parties, without the need for an application to the court, provided such variation does not affect the dates fixed for the following:

• a case management conference

• a pre-trial review

• the date for returning the listing questionnaire

• the trial

• the trial period.

---

20 CPR PD 29 para. 5.6
21 CPR PD 29 para 8.1(3)
22 CPR PD 29 para 8.1(4)
23 The Court Service's website is www.courtservice.gov.uk

CPR 29.5(1) Any variation of the dates the court has fixed for these five steps must be by way of application to the court.

FAILING TO COMPLY WITH THE DIRECTIONS

As with the fast track, if a party fails to comply with a case management direction, the other party may apply to the court for an order compelling compliance, imposing a sanction or a combination of the two.[24] The application should be made without delay but the party making the application should warn the offending party of her/his intention.[25]

Similarly, the court will not allow a party's failure to comply with the directions to lead to a postponement of the trial date, except in very exceptional circumstances.[26] The CPR do not expand upon what would constitute exceptional circumstances, but paragraph 7.4(6) of the Practice Direction to Part 29 offers the following warning:

Litigants and lawyers must be in no doubt that the court will regard the postponement of the trial as an order of last resort. Where it appears inevitable the court may exercise its power to require a party as well as his legal representative to attend court at the hearing where such an order is to be sought.

LISTING THE TRIAL

CPR PD 29 para 9 Upon receipt of the completed listing questionnaires and after a pre-trial review (if appropriate), the court will:

• fix the trial date or the week within which the trial will take place

• give a time estimate for the trial

• make any other directions which the court feels appropriate. This will usually include the preparation of a trial bundle and may also include a detailed timetable for the conduct of the hearing.

Multi-track trials are generally heard only before a circuit judge, and not a **district judge**, because of their inherent value and/or complexity. District judges may hear trials in the multi-track only where the case is proceeding as a Part 8 claim or the parties give their consent.[27] The procedure at trial will be similar to that in the fast track (see Chapter 10).

---

24 CPR PD 29 para 7.1
25 CPR PD 29 para 7.2

26 CPR PD 29 para 7.4(1)
27 CPR PD 2 paras 1.1 & 4.1

7

Disclosure and inspection of documents

Disclosure is when a party lets the other parties in an action know that certain documents exist. The main purpose of disclosure is to allow the parties to evaluate the strength of their case before the trial. It is intended to encourage settlements between the parties, thereby saving costs.

When directions are given (see paragraph 6.2), one of the first directions the court tends to give is disclosure. As a result, disclosure usually takes place shortly after the defence is filed. However, with the increasing use of **pre-action protocols** (as illustrated in Case Study 4), there will be a growing number of cases where disclosure, of at least the most important documents relevant to a claim, has taken place before the claim is issued at court.

7.1 Documents which must be disclosed

CPR 31.5

An order to disclose documents is limited to standard disclosure unless the court orders otherwise. Under CPR 31.6, standard disclosure requires a party to disclose:[1]

a) the documents on which he relies, and

b) the documents which –

> *(i) adversely affect his own case;*

> *(ii) adversely affect another party's case; or*

> *(iii) support another party's case; and*

c) the documents which he is required to disclose by a relevant practice direction.

CPR 31.4

The word "document" has a wide meaning. As well as the usual meaning, it also includes photographs, computer hard and floppy disks, videotapes, audiotapes and emails.

In a possession case on the grounds of rent arrears, documents to be disclosed would include the tenancy agreement, the rent account, notices, correspondence, etc. For a homelessness appeal, this list would include interview notes, the housing file, etc. Case Study 4 contains a list of documents to be disclosed in a disrepair action.

Note that all relevant documents must be disclosed, unless they are privileged (see page 93), even if they are not helpful to the case of the party disclosing them.

---

1 At the time of writing, there is to be an annex to Practice Direction 31 which will list all the types of documents which must always be disclosed, but this has not yet been published.

Standard disclosure applies to fast track and multi-track cases. For the small claims track, a party need disclose only the documents s/he will be relying on.

7.2   Duty to search for documents

Under CPR 31.7, a party must make a reasonable search for documents to be disclosed. In determining what is reasonable, the following factors are taken into account:

• the number of documents involved

• the nature and complexity of the proceedings

• the ease and expense of retrieval of any particular document, and

• the significance of any document that is likely to be located during the search.

If a party considers it unreasonable to search for a document, then this must be stated in the disclosure statement (see below).

The overriding principle of proportionality (see Chapter 1) should be borne in mind when assessing whether or not to search for a document. For example, if the cost of finding a document would be far greater than the amount by which the claim would be increased/decreased were it located, then the principle of proportionality would suggest that the party need not search for that document.

7.3   How disclosure takes place

Generally, a list is compiled of all documents to be disclosed on Form N265 – List of Documents (for an example, see Case Study 4; page 364). The first page of Form N265 contains the disclosure statement. The party disclosing the documents must sign this. The statement sets out the extent of the search for documents and certifies that the party who signs the statement understands the duty to disclose documents, and has carried out this duty to the best of her/his knowledge. If the party is a company, firm, association or other organisation, the statement also has to identify the person making the statement and explain why s/he is the

CPR 31.10(6)-(7)   most suitable person to make the statement.

If the party has a **legal representative**, then this legal representative must endeavour to make certain that the party signing the disclosure statement understands the duty of disclosure. It is very important that this duty is carried out correctly because, if a false disclosure statement is made, this could constitute contempt of court (see page 24) on the implications of signing a **statement of truth**. In order to ensure the party understands the duty of disclosure, the legal representative should explain it in writing.

The second page of Form N265 sets out the list of documents to be disclosed. It is split into three parts.

Part one requires the disclosing party to list all the documents s/he has in her/his control which s/he does not object to the other parties inspecting. This includes all documents that are in her/his physical possession, as well as documents that s/he has or has had a right to possession of, and documents that s/he has or has had a right to inspect or take copies of.

CPR 31.8

These documents should be listed in a convenient order. This is usually by date order. The list should be numbered and a short description given of each document (eg. letter, defendant to claimant). If there are a large number of documents falling into the same category then these can be listed together as a category, (eg. [20] rent statements relating to [address] dated 22/10/2001 to 15/02/2002).

Part two lists the documents that a party has in her/his control but objects to the other party inspecting. The list is set out as above. The reason for the objection is most likely to be privilege regarding those documents. This is dealt with below.

Part three lists all the documents that were in the disclosing party's control but which s/he no longer has. The party must state when the document was last in her/his control and where it is now. This part covers, for example, documents that have been destroyed or lost.

7.4 The right of inspection

Once a list of documents is served, the disclosing party must let all the other parties inspect the documents mentioned in the first part of the list of documents in Form N265, ie. those that are within her/his control and s/he does not object to being inspected by the other parties.

CPR 31.3

A party must give written notice of her/his wish to inspect a document. This notice is given by letter, as there is no special form for it. The disclosing party must allow inspection within seven days of receiving the notice. Rather than going to inspect the documents, a party can request copies of the documents. S/he must agree to pay reasonable photocopying charges.

CPR 31.15

7.5 Withholding inspection – privilege

The most likely reason for not allowing a party to inspect a document is privilege. Privileged documents fall into three main groups:

1. documents protected by legal professional privilege

2. documents tending to incriminate the disclosing party

3. documents privileged on the grounds of public policy.

Legal professional privilege

Legal professional privilege has two heads: the privilege of advice (also known as advice privilege) and litigation privilege. These are explained below.

Advice privilege

Advice privilege relates to confidential communications between a party and her/his legal advisers. The communications must be written by or to the legal adviser in her/his professional capacity for the purpose of securing legal advice or assistance for the client.

This privilege would include communications between a party and her/his legal adviser's employee or agent. It also includes communications with a legal adviser in a party's employment. For example, a solicitor employed in a local authority housing department.

Instructions and briefs to counsel, counsel's opinions and counsel's drafts and notes are also privileged.

Litigation privilege

Litigation privilege applies to the same group of documents as above but where the main purpose of these documents is actual or pending litigation. This also includes:

• communications between a party's legal adviser and a third party, and

• communications between the party personally and a third party.

The documents will be privileged if they were created at the request or on behalf of the legal adviser or with the intention of getting her/his advice or to allow her/him to take legal proceedings.[2] This will include, for example, surveyors' reports in disrepair cases and witness statements.

If a party prepares a document with a third party, this document will be privileged only if the main reason for its creation was for it to be used in legal proceedings. Even if it is then not used in proceedings, it will still be privileged. It is the intention of the party at the time of creating the document that must be taken into account. For example, a report for a letting agency prepared by one of its employees would be privileged if the agency was considering possible legal proceedings. This report would still be privileged even if legal action was not commenced.

Parties cannot claim privilege against each other if they instruct the

---

2   Anderson v Bank of British Columbia (1876) 2 Ch D 644; Wheeler v Le Marchant (1881) 17 Ch D 675; Southwark Water Co v Quick (1878) 3 QBD 315

same legal adviser.[3] For example, if co-tenants have the same legal adviser, one tenant could not stop her/his adviser from showing the other tenants a document which would otherwise attract legal professional privilege. This situation will be rare. In cases such as these, the legal adviser should not act for both parties if there is, or is likely to be, any conflict of interest between the parties.

Legal professional privilege is a right that can be **waived**. However, it is the right of the party concerned and can only be waived by her/himself. The party's legal adviser could not make a decision to waive the right to legal professional privilege without the party's consent.

Documents tending to incriminate the disclosing party

A party can claim privilege for documents that would incriminate her/him if disclosed. This privilege might be relevant in a case involving unlawful eviction and harassment, but is generally rare in housing law cases.

Documents privileged on the grounds of public policy

This is also known as "public interest immunity" and is unlikely to affect a housing case. A document must be withheld from inspection if disclosing it would be harmful to the public interest. If a party has such a document, s/he will need to make an application to court (see Chapter 9) for an order permitting her/him to withhold disclosure of that document.

CPR 31.19(1)   The other party need not be put on notice of this application.

7.6   Withholding other documents from inspection

As well as the above, there are other types of documents that need not be disclosed. These include "without prejudice" documents.

"Without prejudice" communications are generally exchanges made to try to settle a case. Any record of such negotiations is privileged from disclosure. The reasoning behind this is that, during negotiations, a party might concede an issue in her/his claim solely in order to reach a settlement. If negotiations to settle were then not successful, the party making the concession would not wish to be bound by it and might be disadvantaged if it were known to the court and/or other parties who were not involved in the negotiations.

Any documents in such negotiations should be clearly marked "without prejudice". This will include written notes of telephone conversations and of meetings between the parties. However, a document might still be privileged from disclosure even if it was not clearly marked "without prejudice". The test is to assess whether the document in question was

3   Hellenic Mutual War Risks Association (Bermuda) Ltd v Harrison (1997) 1 Lloyd's Rep 160

created in a genuine attempt to settle the claim. Conversely, a document marked "without prejudice" might not necessarily be privileged if it was not created in a genuine attempt to settle the claim.

7.7   Disclosing privileged documents unintentionally

CPR 31.20

If a party unintentionally discloses privileged documents, then the other party can use these documents only if the court allows it.

7.8   Specific disclosure

CPR 31.12

If a party believes that the other party has not disclosed all the documents relevant to the case, s/he can force that party to produce the documents that appear to be missing. For example, if the local authority in a disrepair claim has not disclosed records from its maintenance department because they are not kept on the housing file, the tenant can make an application to the court (see Chapter 9) for an order to compel disclosure.

CPR 31.12(2)

In an application for specific disclosure, a court can order a party to do the following:

• disclose documents or classes of documents

• carry out a search for documents

• disclose any documents found as a result of the search.

7.9   The continuing duty of disclosure

CPR 31.11

The duty to disclose relevant documents continues throughout proceedings. Therefore, where a party obtains a relevant document while the case is ongoing (eg. housing benefit documents sent by the authority after Form N265 has been served), then this must be disclosed to the other parties. This can be done either on Form N265 or by letter. The same will apply where a party finds further documents in her/his possession after disclosure. S/he must disclose them immediately to the other parties on Form N265 or by letter.

Evidence

This chapter looks at the CPR as they relate to the presentation of evidence within proceedings. Although a detailed examination of the nature of evidence is outside the scope of this text, it is necessary to outline the interaction between evidence and its treatment under the rules. The rules on evidence are contained mainly in Parts 32 to 35 of the CPR, but the application of these rules to small claims is limited and an outline of the treatment of evidence in these claims is provided at the end of the chapter.

The court has a general power under CPR 32.1 to control the evidence in proceedings. This is exercised by giving directions on the issues it requires evidence to be brought, the nature of the evidence to be provided and the way in which that evidence is to be placed before the court.

The powers are extensive and complement the court's case management powers in Part 3 of the CPR. This is demonstrated by the ability of the court to exclude evidence which would otherwise be admissible under the rules of evidence, and limit cross-examination. In exercising these powers, the court has a duty to control the evidence to further the overriding objective (see Chapter 1). Thus, it may be appropriate to exclude evidence in the interests of limiting costs,[1] but not so as to exclude evidence potentially crucial to a party's case.[2]

8.1   Evidence given by non-expert witnesses

CPR 32.2

The way in which the evidence of witnesses is given depends on whether it is provided at the trial or at any other hearing (eg. interim hearings). Generally, a witness will be required to give oral evidence at the trial of a matter. However, this does not mean it is not necessary to provide written evidence in advance of the trial. As detailed below, the parties must serve witness statements in advance of the trial and this will normally stand as the witness's **evidence in chief.**

In any other hearing the evidence given should be written in the form of witness statements or affidavits. However, there is provision for one party to apply to the court for permission to cross-examine a witness at a hearing other than the trial. An application should be made prior to, rather than at, the hearing in question to ensure that the witness has adequate notice of the need for her/his attendance.

CPR 32.7

Although the use of affidavits has diminished greatly since the introduction of the CPR, there are certain types of cases where they must be used. They may also be used to provide evidence for hearings other than

---

1   See Grobbelaar v Sun Newspapers Ltd [1999], CA, noted at *Times* 12 August

2   See McPhilemy v Times Newspapers Ltd [1999] 3 All ER 775, CA

the trial. Therefore, although more attention will be given to the nature, form and content of witness statements, an outline of affidavits will also be given.

Witness statements

A witness statement is a person's signed written account relating to the particular case. There is no blueprint for the content of witness statements, as each case will be different depending on the nature and circumstances of the particular case.

It is possible, however, to provide some general guidance on contents and the form of statements from experience and from the requirements of the Practice Direction to Part 32.

CPR 32.8 The Practice Direction also provides for certain essential formalities for inclusion in every witness statement. These are examined after the general guidance. Examples of the form and content of witness statements in a number of different types of housing cases are included in Part II of this book (see pages 274, 300, 332, 334, 366, 387 and 404).

Contents of a witness statement – general guidance

As far as possible, a statement should be in the words of the witness, expressed in the first person and couched in plain, non-legalistic language. Moreover, it should not contain legal argument, which is more appropriate for inclusion in a statement of case.[3]

CPR 32.5(2)
CPR 32.4(1)
Where the witness is to give oral evidence, the statement will stand as **evidence in chief** unless the court orders otherwise. Witness statements should therefore be confined to evidence which that person would be permitted to give orally. It follows that hearsay evidence should be included only if it is admissible under the Civil Evidence Act 1995 (see page 107).

It is usually more convenient, and helpful to the court, to detail events or matters chronologically. Also, ideally, each paragraph should be confined to a particular subject or event. For example, a statement prepared for a possession claim for nuisance may separate out, by paragraphs and in date order, each alleged incident with appropriate details of what happened.

Opinion evidence

The witness statement must usually relate facts rather than the witness's opinions. However, it may be appropriate for a witness to express necessary comment on the facts that may be essential to the issue in question. For example, in a statement prepared for a statutory homelessness appeal, it will be legitimate for a person fleeing their

---

3   CPR PD 32 para 18.1 & Alex Lawrie Factors Ltd v Morgan [1999], CA, noted at *Times* 18 August

home because of domestic violence to say: 'the council are wrong in stating that it would be safe for me to return home'.

A witness will also be allowed to state an opinion if it relays relevant facts personally perceived by her/him.[4] This could include an opinion on matters such as:

• the identity and age of persons and articles

• the sobriety or otherwise of a person – though reasons for her/his perception should also be included. For example, if a witness refers to her/his opinion that a person was drunk, s/he should continue to explain reasons for this opinion, eg. the slurred speech and unsteadiness of the person concerned

• the condition of articles, eg. items in the person's home

• the state of the weather

• estimations of speed or distance.

A major exception to the rule on opinion evidence is statements given by experts. This is examined in more detail on page 113.

Contents of a witness statement – layout and required information

The Practice Direction to Part 32 prescribes the layout of the witness statement, and requires the statement to include certain details about the claim and the witness.

HEADING

Witness statements should be headed in the same way as statements of case. They should, therefore, provide the name and the number of the case, the court and details as to the parties to the case.

Additionally, in the top right hand corner, each of the following should be written clearly:[5]

• the party on whose behalf the statement is being made

• the witness's initials and surname

• the number of the statement in relation to that witness, eg. 1st statement of [name]

• the initials and number of the exhibits referred to in the statement

• the date of the statement.

BODY OF WITNESS STATEMENT

As far as practicable, the statement should be in the witness's own words. It must also be expressed in the first person and should state:[6]

---

4   section 3(2) of the Civil Evidence Act 1972   6   CPR PD 32 para 18.1
5   CPR PD 32 para 17.2

- the witness's full name

- the witness's place of residence or work address, the position the witness holds and the name of her/his firm or employer if the statement is being made in the witness's professional, business or other occupational capacity

- the witness's occupation or, if s/he has none, her/his description eg. 'I am an unemployed engineer'

- the fact that the witness is a party to the proceedings or is the employee of such a party, if this is the case.

EXHIBITS

Documents that are to be exhibited by the witness statement should be referred to in the body of the statement, with words like: 'I refer to the bank statements marked "JS5"'. "JS5" comes from the witness's initials followed by the number of the exhibit. The exhibited documents should be kept separate from the witness statement.

The cover sheet to the document should have the same heading as the statement. This should be followed by wording such as: 'This is the exhibit marked "JS5" referred to in the 2nd statement of John Smith made on the 22nd day of August 2000'.

Exhibits are numbered consecutively throughout all statements made by the same witness. For example the first exhibit referred to in the 2nd statement of John Smith may well be JS5 if there were four exhibits referred to in the 1st statement.[7]

FORMAT OF WITNESS STATEMENT

A witness statement should:[8]

- be on A4 paper with a 3.5 cm margin

- be typed on one side of paper only and be legible

- be bound securely or have the case number and witness's initials on each page

- have the pages numbered consecutively

- be divided into numbered paragraphs

- have all numbers written in figures, not words

- give the reference of any documents mentioned in the statement. This should be either in the margin or in bold text in the body of the statement.

7   CPR PD 32 para 18.6   8   CPR PD 32 para 19.1

STATEMENT OF TRUTH

As the witness statement will stand as evidence in interim hearings and as **evidence in chief** at the trial, the witness statement must be verified as being true. Thus a statement of truth must be included stating:[9]

'I believe that the facts stated in this witness statement are true'.

As for other documents, proceedings for contempt of court may be brought against a person who makes, or causes to be made, a false statement verified by a statement of truth without an honest belief CPR 32.14   in its truth.

Inability to read or sign the statement

Sometimes a witness may not be able to read or sign a statement prepared for her/him, eg. if the witness is illiterate. In this situation the statement must be certified by an authorised person stating that:[10]

• the content of the statement and the statement of truth has been read to the witness

• the witness appeared to understand and approve the contents of the statement, and understood the statement of truth and the consequences of making a false statement, and

• the witness signed or made her/his mark in the presence of the authorised person.

An authorised person is a person able to administer oaths and take affidavits (see page 106).

Non-English speakers

Many witnesses will not be fluent English speakers. In these situations it is crucial that the witness statement reflects the witness's version of events accurately. It will therefore be necessary to use an interpreter. The interpreter should certify that:

• the statement and statement of truth have been interpreted to the witness properly

• the witness appeared to understand:
  (a) the statement and approved its content
  (b) the statement of truth and the consequences of making a false witness statement

• the witness signed the document in her/his presence.

An example of the wording used is given in the witness statement in Case Study 1 on page 274.

9   CPR PD 32 paras 20.1 & 20.2

10   CPR PD 32 paras 21.1-21.4; see also annex 2 for the wording of the certificate

Alterations to witness statements

Any alterations must be initialled by the maker of the statement.
It is important to comply with this, as a witness statement that has
been altered, but not initialled, may be used in evidence only with the
court's permission.[11]

Defects in witness statements and exhibits

Where the form of witness statements and exhibits do not comply with
the requirements of Part 32 and the Practice Direction, the court may
refuse to admit them as evidence and may refuse to award costs to the
party who has prepared them.[12]

Exchange of witness statements

It is usually not necessary for a court to order the exchange of witness
statements in respect of Part 8 claims. This is because the parties are
required to file and serve all written evidence they wish to rely on at the
same time as the claim form and acknowledgment of service are filed
(see, respectively, pages 35 and 53). Similarly, appeals brought under
Part 52 – for example, a statutory homelessness appeal – have
different rules regarding the filing and service of evidence in support of
a claim or a defence (see paragraph 15.3).

For claims brought under Part 7, the court will usually order the parties
to exchange witness statements. Invariably, this will be at the same time
as the court allocates the case to the fast track or the multi-track, or at
a **case management conference**.

Generally, witness statements are not required for cases in the small
claims track. This reflects the emphasis on informality of such claims.
However, it may be very helpful to the court, and therefore advisable, to
prepare witness statements so as to ensure that all relevant evidence is
before the court. Indeed, for this reason, **district judges** will often direct
that witness statements should be prepared and exchanged in small
claims track cases.

Exchange of witness statements will normally be ordered to take place
a few weeks after disclosure and inspection, so that the witnesses may
refer to any of this documentation in their statements.

The exchange will generally take place simultaneously to ensure that a
party will not have the unfair advantage of taking into account the other
party's statements when preparing their own evidence. Simultaneous
exchange is commonly carried out by the parties agreeing to put the
statements in the post on the same day. Alternatively, if the parties
have reason not to trust one another sufficiently, eg. due to previous

non-compliance with directions, one of the parties could send her/his witness statements by courier to the other party with a specific instruction not to release the statements unless the courier is given the other party's statements.

Failure to exchange witness statements

CPR 32.10

If the statement of a witness is not served on the other party by the date given for exchange, the party will not be able to call that witness to give evidence at the trial without the court's permission. Although the defaulting party should as far as possible give good reasons for the delay, it would be extreme for the court to deny an extension for the exchange of witness statements. In *Mealey Horgan plc v Horgan,*[13] the judge stated that to deprive the party of the use of evidence would be appropriate only where s/he had deliberately flouted the court order, or there had been an inexcusable delay.

Use of witness statements at trial

CPR 32.5

Where a party has served a witness statement that s/he wishes to rely on at trial, s/he will normally be required to call that witness to give oral evidence. The only exceptions to this will be where the court orders otherwise, or the party has put in a statement as hearsay evidence (see page 107).

CPR 32.5(2)

A witness statement will stand as that witness's **evidence in chief** at trial unless the court orders otherwise. This means that when the witness is called to give oral evidence at the trial, s/he will generally be asked to confirm that the contents of the statement are true to the best of her/his knowledge.

CPR 32.5(3)

The witness may be permitted by the court to expand on her/his statement and/or give evidence on new matters that have arisen since the statements were exchanged. The court will allow this if there is good reason why the witness should not be confined to the evidence contained in the witness statement. For this reason it is advisable for witness statements to be comprehensive and deal with all the matters on which the party wishes to rely in the case.

Legal privilege

On occasions, at the trial, a party may decide not to call the witness to give oral evidence or seek to use the statement. As the statement would have been prepared for the purpose of contemplated or pending litigation, it would normally be **privileged**. It would not therefore need to be disclosed to the other party. However, if the witness statement has been exchanged, the document is no longer privileged and the other party may use it as hearsay evidence in support of her/his own case (see page 107).[14]

---

13 Mealey Horgan plc v Horgan [1999], noted at *Times* 6 July

14 CPR 32.5(5); Society of Lloyd's v Jaffray [2000], noted at *Times* 3 August

Affidavits and affirmations

An affidavit is a written, sworn statement of evidence. An affirmation is the same, except that the maker of the statement affirms rather than swears an oath that the contents of the statement are true. As with the CPR, any reference in this book to affidavits should be taken to include affirmations unless otherwise provided.

Affidavits were more widely used before the introduction of the CPR and were the usual form for giving evidence at hearings other than the trial. As outlined above, witness statements may be used for such hearings as well as for trials.

Affidavits are similar in content and form to witness statements, but they are more formal in that the maker of the affidavit must **swear** that its contents are true before one of the following:[15]

• a commissioner for oaths

• a practising solicitor

• an authorised court officer

• a district or circuit judge

• any justice of the peace or

• other persons specified in the CPR.

The person before whom the affidavit is sworn must be independent of the parties or their representatives.[16] There is usually a fee payable to the person. There is no fee if the affidavit is sworn before an authorised court officer of a county court.

Where a party has a choice, it is difficult to see any advantages in preparing affidavits rather than witness statements, in particular because if the affidavit was not required a party is unlikely to be able to recover the cost of any fee for swearing. However, an affidavit must be used for certain types of action. These include:

CPR 32.15(2)
CPR 32.15

• **contempt of court** proceedings

• an application for a **freezing injunction** or a **search order**

• where required by an enactment, statutory instrument, rule, order or practice direction.

Defects in affidavits

Where the form of affidavits do not comply with the requirements of Part 32 and the Practice Direction, the court may refuse to admit them as evidence and may refuse to award costs to the party who has prepared them.[17]

15 CPR PD 32 para 9.1
16 CPR PD 32 para 9.2
17 CPR PD 32 para 25.1-25.2

Hearsay

There are special rules governing the use of hearsay evidence for court proceedings. Although a detailed look at the nature and meaning of hearsay evidence is outside the ambit of this book, a basic outline is provided to enable advisers to recognise hearsay and understand how it should be submitted in evidence.

Hearsay is defined by section 1(2)(a) of the Civil Evidence Act 1995, and repeated in CPR 33.1 as:

... a statement made otherwise than by a person while giving oral evidence in the proceedings which is tendered as evidence of the matters stated.

Hearsay is evidence of an oral or written statement made outside the court, and which is repeated to the court, in order to establish the truth of the statement made outside court. It is crucial to distinguish between evidence which is provided as proof merely that a statement was made by someone, and evidence that is given to prove the contents of the statement are actually true.

Example

Harry is a housing officer for Anytown Housing Association. He is giving oral evidence in the trial of possession proceedings brought against Ryan on the grounds of nuisance and anti-social behaviour. He informs the court that one of Ryan's neighbours told him that he had seen Ryan spraying graffiti on the walls and of hearing Ryan play loud music on a number of occasions. The neighbour is unwilling to give evidence for fear of reprisals from Ryan. The evidence is clearly given by Harry in order to assert that the neighbour's statements are true and that Ryan committed the acts in question. It is hearsay evidence. It would not be hearsay evidence if the neighbour gave evidence that s/he had seen Ryan spraying graffiti on the walls and heard music emanating from Ryan's flat. This would be evidence of matters actually perceived by the neighbour with her/his own senses.

The Civil Evidence Act 1995 swept away the common law rule which largely prevented hearsay evidence from being submitted within proceedings. Section 1(1) of the Act provides:

In civil proceedings evidence shall not be excluded on the ground that it is hearsay.

All forms of hearsay are admissible in civil proceedings. On occasions this will include multiple hearsay, ie. where the statement has come to the witness third hand (or fourth hand and so on).

Using hearsay at trial

Commonly, there are two different situations when a party is likely to submit hearsay evidence to trial. These are where:

• a witness wishes to include hearsay evidence in her/his oral evidence. The hearsay evidence will have to be included in her/his witness statement too, or

• the witness will not be giving oral evidence at all, in which case the whole of the witness statement will be hearsay evidence.

When a party intends to rely on hearsay evidence at trial, s/he must notify any other party of this and, if requested, must provide details of the evidence involved.[18]

The requirement to notify another party that a witness wishes to include hearsay evidence in her/his oral evidence is in fact met by serving a copy of the witness statement on the other party. The other party has notice of the hearsay evidence as it should be included in the witness statement.

Where the maker of the statement will not be giving oral evidence at the trial, the requirements are met by:

• serving a copy of the statement on the other parties, and

• notifying them that the witness is not being called to give oral evidence, and the reasons for this.

CPR 33.2(3)

In all other cases where the party intends to rely on hearsay evidence, a notice must be served on the other party no later than the latest date on which witness statements must be served. There is no prescribed form of notice; it may be by letter, fax or email. It must:

• be in writing

• identify the hearsay evidence

• state that the party serving the notice wishes to rely on the hearsay evidence at trial

• give the reason why the witness will not be called.

If the hearsay is contained in any document then a copy should be provided to any party on request.

Failure to serve the notice does not make the hearsay evidence inadmissible, but it may be taken into account by the court in assessing the weight of hearsay evidence together with the other considerations which the court will have regard to and which are outlined below.

18 section 2 of the Civil Evidence Act 1995

Some of the possible reasons why a witness is not going to be called to trial include:

• s/he is dead

• s/he is abroad

• s/he is unfit by reason of her/his physical or mental condition to attend.

This list is not exhaustive and there may be other reasons why s/he will not be called.

Weight given to hearsay evidence

The weight given to hearsay evidence will vary depending on the nature of the evidence and a range of other considerations. It is clearly advisable, wherever possible, to provide first-hand evidence of any matter as more weight will be given to evidence within the knowledge of the person giving the evidence. In the example provided above, this would involve Ryan's neighbour giving evidence of the things s/he saw and heard. However, as in the example, often this will not be possible.

In assessing the weight to be given to hearsay evidence, the court may draw reasonable inferences on the reliability or otherwise of the evidence based on all the circumstances. The following are some of the considerations that the court will have regard to:[19]

• would it have been reasonable or practicable for the maker of the statement to have attended court as a witness?

• was the statement made soon after the event(s) it describes?

• does the evidence involve multiple hearsay?

• does anyone involved have a motive to misrepresent or conceal matters?

• was the original statement an edited version of events?

• was the original statement made in collaboration with another or made for a particular purpose?

Credibility of witness not called

CPR 33.5 Where a party is not proposing to call a witness to give oral evidence but is relying on hearsay evidence, the other party may call evidence to attack the credibility of that witness. The other party must give notice of her/his intention to do so not more than 14 days after the day on which the witness statement, or the hearsay notice, was served on her/him.

Power to call witness for cross-examination

The other party may also apply to the court for permission to call the

---

19 section 4 of the Civil Evidence Act 1995

witness to court for the purpose of cross-examination. Having regard to the overriding objective, the party seeking the attendance at court of a witness may wish to seek the other party's agreement to this witness's attendance, thus saving court time and expense.

CPR 33.4

Witness summaries

It may prove difficult for a party to file witness statements by persons s/he intends to call in order to give oral evidence. There are two main situations where this may occur:

- the witness is reluctant for some reason to give evidence on behalf of the party

- the witness is not able to provide and/or sign a statement before the time for exchange of witness statements, perhaps because the person is out of the country.

CPR 32.9(1)

If this occurs, then a party may apply to the court, without notice, for permission to serve a witness summary instead of a witness statement.

CPR 32.9(2)-(3)

If permission is granted, then the party may prepare a witness summary. This should include:

- the name and address of the intended witness, and
  either

- if known, the evidence which would have been included in a witness statement
  or

- if not known, the areas on which the party plans to question the intended witness.

In the situation where the witness is reluctant to give evidence, it may also be necessary to serve a witness summons on her/him (see below).

Witness summonses

Witness summonses are frequently issued within possession proceedings based on rent arrears so as to require housing benefit officers to attend court to explain why a defendant's claim has not been processed. Often the issue or threat of issue of a summons can galvanise the housing benefit department into processing a claim. They may be

CPR 34.2(1)

issued in any type of housing case where a party requires a witness to:

- produce documents to the court, or

- attend court to give evidence.

Before considering the procedure involved in issuing and serving a witness summons, it is worth noting that many judges will make an order requiring an officer of the housing benefit department to attend court to give evidence relating to a claim. Advisers should therefore consider making such a request where the judge indicates that a possession action will be adjourned and there are delays in processing a claim. This will avoid the need to issue a witness summons.

Procedure

The prescribed form for a witness summons is Form N20. This should be completed by the party seeking the witness summons. It should then be taken or sent (in duplicate) to the court, with the appropriate fee, to be issued. Witness summonses should be issued in the court where the case is proceeding or where the hearing is to be held.

A party will not need permission to issue a witness summons unless s/he wants a summons issued:

- less than seven days before the date of the trial, or

- for a witness to attend court to give evidence or to produce documents at a hearing other than the trial date, or on any other date other than the trial date.

Once the summons is issued, it must be served on the witness. This is done by the court unless the party issuing indicates in writing that s/he wishes to serve it. The court will usually send the summons by first class post; deemed service is the second day after the date it is posted. For this reason, if the date for service is close, a party should consider serving the summons by a method which ensures that service is deemed to have taken place earlier, such as personal service. (See page 31 for details of how time is calculated with examples.)

Where the witness to be summoned is a housing benefit officer, it is important to find out the identity of the relevant officer. This will be the person who is able to provide the necessary information on the housing benefit claim; it is not sufficient to simply name the head of the department. In this situation, it is extremely advisable for the party issuing the witness summons to arrange personal service on the relevant officer. There is a clear danger that if it is posted to the department, the witness summons will be "lost" in the system. The court may be able to provide a party with a list of process servers.

A witness summons is binding on the witness if it is served at least seven days before the hearing that the witness is required to attend. If it is served less than seven days before the hearing, it will not be binding unless the court directs otherwise. A party who is seeking permission

CPR 34.3(3)

CPR 34.3(2)

CPR 34.6

from the court to serve a witness summons less than seven days before a hearing should therefore also ask the court to include a direction that the summons is binding. The court may do this retrospectively by virtue of its **case management** powers in CPR 3.1. The summons remains binding on the witness until the conclusion of the hearing.

CPR 34.5

Witness expenses

CPR 34.7

The witness is entitled to a sum of money "reasonably sufficient" to meet her/his travelling expenses and compensation for loss of time. In the case of a housing benefit officer giving evidence on someone's claim, this is likely to need a simple estimation to be made of that person's bus or train fares. They are extremely unlikely to lose any income for attending. Other witnesses may, however, face losing income from work.

The amounts payable are based on the allowances for witnesses attending the crown court in criminal cases. These are updated from time to time but at the time of writing are:[20]

EXPENSES FOR LOSS OF TIME

Where the witness attends court up to 4 hours	£29.75
Where the witness attends for more than 4 hours	£59.50

TRAVELLING EXPENSES

Where the witness travels by public transport	25p (per mile)
Where the witness travels by car or motorcycle	45p (per mile)

The expenses should be offered or paid to the witness at the time of service. If the court is to serve the witness summons, the issuing party should deposit the money at court.[21]

Notice to admit facts

CPR 32.18(1)

As highlighted throughout this book, the CPR aim to confine and define issues of contention between parties; thus saving court time and costs. Another way this is promoted is to allow a party to serve a notice on another party requiring the latter to admit certain facts or part of a case. If a fact or a part of a case is admitted, then the party who has served the notice will not have to prove that matter in court.

CPR 32.18(2)

The notice can be in letter form providing it is clear about what exactly is being asked of the other party, though it is advisable to use Form N266. The form should be completed and served on the other party no later than 21 days before the trial. The other party may respond on the section of the form headed Admission of facts, or by letter.

20 Costs in Criminal Cases (General) Regulations 1986   21 CPR 34.7 & 34.6(2)

Any admissions made by the responding party may be used against her/him only in the proceedings within which the notice was served, CPR 32.18(3) and only by the party who has served the notice. A party may amend or withdraw an admission if the court gives permission. This will be given CPR 32.18(4) if it is just; it may be appropriate where an admission is made under a mistaken belief of certain facts.

Although CPR 32.18 does not specify any consequences with regard to costs for the failure of a party to admit certain facts which are later proved at trial, the court will clearly take this failure into account in accordance with its discretion in Part 44 (see paragraph 13.1).

Notice to admit or prove documents

If a document has been disclosed to a party, s/he is deemed to accept that the document is genuine unless s/he serves a notice requiring the disclosing party to prove the authenticity of the document at trial. Any CPR 32.19 notice must be served by the later of the following:

• the latest date for service of witness statements, or

• within seven days of disclosure of the document.

Use of plans, photographs and models

Usually plans, photographs and models will be capable of being exhibited to a witness's statement. For example, a tenant may have taken photographs of his accommodation for the purpose of a disrepair claim. These should be exhibited to the statement. Where this is not possible, a party intending to use such evidence must disclose her/his intention CPR 33.6 to do so at least 21 days before the hearing.

8.2   Evidence given by experts

Experts are instructed in many cases to give evidence on matters within their expertise. Expert evidence is one major exception to the general rule against the use of opinion evidence, in so far as the expert may express opinions on matters within her/his expertise.[22]

In the housing field, common examples of cases where a party may wish to use the evidence of an expert are:

• Disrepair cases, where an expert is instructed to survey accommodation and prepare a report on any disrepair. A medical practitioner or psychiatrist may be instructed to report on a person's health or any injuries arising from disrepair.

22 section 3(1) of the Civil Evidence Act 1995

- Possession cases, where a medical practitioner or psychiatrist may provide evidence on the health of the defendant, which could be relevant to the question of reasonableness.

- Statutory homelessness appeals, where the evidence of a medical practitioner or psychiatrist may be crucial to the question of a person's vulnerability or someone's capacity to commit a "deliberate act".

The court's power to restrict expert evidence

It is important to note from the outset that the parties do not have carte blanche to use expert evidence. This is because the court has a duty to limit the use of expert evidence to what is reasonably required to resolve the issues in the case, so as to restrict unnecessary costs.

CPR 35.1

A party has to obtain the court's permission if s/he wishes to call an expert to give evidence or use an expert's report within the proceedings. If the court is so minded, permission will usually be given at a **directions hearing**.

CPR 35.4(1)

It is frequently commented that some courts appear to unofficially exclude certain types of expert evidence. Practitioners have reported courts consistently refusing to entertain expert evidence from psychiatrists, employment consultants, accountants and care professionals.[23] On occasions this may lead to greater costs being incurred. For example, in the context of a disrepair claim, a solicitor may have to make a complex loss of earnings calculation following personal injury. In complex cases the services of an accountant could be more cost effective. Advisers should be alert to the possibility that denying a party the use of expert evidence amounts to an unfair trial, which could be challenged under article 6 of the Human Rights Act 1998.

CPR 35.4(2)

CPR 35.4(3)

The party making an application for permission to instruct an expert should specify the expert's field and, where practicable, her/his name. These details will normally be given in the allocation questionnaire. If permission is given it will relate only to the named expert or the expert's field.

CPR 35.4(4)

CPR 1.1(2)

The court has a power to limit the expert's fees and expenses that may be recoverable from any other party. In doing so, the court will take account of the complexity of the case, the amount of damages or other remedy sought, and the respective financial position of the parties.

Instructing an expert at an early stage

A party will often consider it necessary to instruct an expert at an early stage; in certain cases this will be appropriate prior to the commencement of proceedings. There is a clear risk that the court will subsequently

---

23 see *Legal Action* April 2000, p26

refuse to allow the evidence to be used in evidence within the proceedings. The court may also restrict the amount that can be recovered from the other side incurred in preparing the expert evidence.

A party may also struggle to recoup the costs incurred from **public funding** and, in any event, should have regard to Legal Services funding guidance and any pre-action protocol in place for the particular type of claim involved (see below). Although a party may not be allowed to use the evidence of experts at trial, and may not recover the costs of instructing the expert at the trial of the matter, adherence to the guidance and protocol should normally mean that the costs are recoverable under the Legal Help or Legal Representation schemes.

In any type of case, practitioners should consider whether instructing an expert is necessary and proportionate to the case in terms of both the complexity of the case and the remedies sought.

Pre-action protocols

The CPR must be read alongside any **pre-action protocol** in place with regard to a particular type of claim. The protocols promote the exchange of information between parties at an early stage and economy in the use and selection of experts.

There are three protocols in operation which are relevant to housing cases. These relate to: judicial review, personal injury and medical clinical disputes. Also in draft form is the disrepair pre-action protocol. The use of experts in disrepair cases and the relevant parts of the protocol on their use are considered later in this chapter. In addition, a general overview of the draft disrepair pre-action protocol is given in Case Study 4.

Providing a party observes a pre-action protocol, where one is in force for the type of claim involved, and acts reasonably in instructing experts, it is probable that in any subsequent proceedings the court will allow the use of this evidence and the cost in doing so.

Instructing an expert at an early stage in disrepair cases

One of the most common situations in which a party will wish to instruct an expert before commencing proceedings involves disrepair to residential accommodation. Certain types of disrepair will be prejudicial to the health of the occupier: it may be necessary to issue proceedings and seek an urgent injunction to force the landlord to carry out necessary repairs. Alternatively, it may be vital to obtain an expert's report to establish whether the disrepair involved is of a type within the landlord's repairing obligations, and therefore whether there is a case at all.

Moreover, the landlord may have given an indication that certain works are about to be undertaken; this could result in important evidence about the disrepair being lost.

Legal Help and Legal Representation

It is common to instruct an expert under the Legal Help scheme to ascertain whether a claim may be brought or to preserve evidence. A detailed discussion of the Legal Help and Legal Representation schemes is outside the scope of this book. Advisers who are contemplating instructing an expert should consult the most recent guidance available.

The guidance given to solicitors and agencies for the **General Civil Contract** states that, except in a case of urgency, an expert should not be instructed to prepare a report unless:[24]

• the disrepair appears serious enough to justify a surveyor's report, and

• the landlord has been served with notice of the disrepair and a request for remedial repairs and/or compensation within a reasonable period of time, but has failed within that time to make arrangements for, or take, appropriate action.

It will not normally be appropriate to obtain a surveyor's report if the only remedy to be sought is damages that are likely to be less than £1,000.[25]

The disrepair pre-action protocol

An overview of the draft **pre-action protocol** for housing disrepair cases is given in Case Study 4 (see page 340).

It is should be emphasised that the need to instruct an expert at an early stage is specifically recognised within the disrepair pre-action protocol. The draft protocol gives a non-exhaustive list of cases where this would be appropriate. They are:[26]

• Where the tenant considers there is a significant risk to health and safety – the risk may be to any of the occupants of the house including children and also visitors to the property.

• Where the tenant is seeking an interim injunction, ie. to require the landlord to carry out the works urgently.

• Where it is necessary to preserve evidence, ie. the landlord intends to carry out remedial works in the property.

However, the draft protocol also warns that it is not always necessary to instruct an expert where, for example, video evidence or photographs would suffice.

24 Community Legal Service – General Civil Contract (solicitors), Legal Aid Board, October 1999; General Civil Contract (not for profit), October 1999

25 ibid.
26 Pre-action protocol for disrepair cases, para (j)

Single joint experts

The role of experts in court proceedings caused particular concern to some members of the judiciary, Lord Woolf included. These concerns centred on the expense and delay caused by the use of experts, who were perceived to be partisan in favour of the instructing party.

One way the CPR tackle this issue is to attempt to make the use of single joint experts the norm in respect of relatively straightforward and lower-value claims. Anecdotal evidence suggests that the appointment of single joint experts has increased considerably. This is not only as the result of court order but by agreement between parties, who are no doubt wary of the possible costs implications where separate experts are instructed.[27]

CPR 35.7

Where proceedings have begun, the court may order that evidence on an issue be given by a single expert. The parties may agree an expert, but if they fail to reach agreement, the court will choose a single expert from a list prepared or identified by the parties.

CPR 35.8

If a single joint expert is used, each party may give instructions to the expert and must serve the other parties with a copy of these. The court will usually state who is to pay for the expert's fees and expenses, failing which, the instructing parties are **jointly and severally** liable for the payment.

The disrepair protocol

As mentioned above, pre-action protocols promote the use of single joint experts prior to any claim being brought. The protocol for disrepair claims provides specific guidance for the conduct of parties in relation to the use, or otherwise, of single joint experts. This is outlined within the overview of the disrepair protocol in Case Study 4 (on page 340) and is not repeated in detail here.

In practice, some courts do not insist on the use of single joint experts. It is often difficult to get the agreement of both parties as to which expert should be used. Many local authorities prefer to use their own surveyors. There may be variation between courts on this and advisers should take soundings from their local area.

This is recognised within the protocol which provides that, where it is not possible to reach agreement to instruct a single joint expert, the parties should arrange a joint inspection of the property by both instructed experts.[28]

In *Field v Leeds City Council*,[29] a local authority disrepair case, Lord Woolf stated that the use of a single joint expert was to be preferred to an in-house local authority surveyor. However, he added that, if the latter could demonstrate a proper understanding of the overriding duty of the expert to the court, the use of this expert should not be ruled out.

27 see *Legal Action* April 2000, p26
28 Pre-action protocol for disrepair cases, para (e)
29 Field v Leeds City Council [1999], noted at *Times* 18 January

Instructing an expert

There is no prescribed form for instructing an expert. The party simply writes a letter to the expert outlining details of the case, and the matters on which the expert's opinion is sought. For disrepair cases the protocol provides a specimen form of a letter of instruction, which may be adapted as necessary.[30] In any case, it is advisable for an agency or firm to have a standard letter of instruction to ensure that proper and full instructions are given and that the report is prepared in the correct form.

Advisers should be aware that, although letters to experts will not normally be disclosed to other parties, the court may order disclosure where there are reasonable grounds to do so and the instructions are not **privileged**.

CPR 35.10(4)

An expert's duty to the court

Although it is the parties to an action who instruct an expert to give evidence, the expert has an overriding duty to the court to assist on matters within her/his expertise. Any obligations owed to the party who gave the instructions and paid the expert are secondary to this duty. This means that experts must be objective in presenting their evidence to the court.[31]

CPR 35.3

Form and content of an expert's reports

An expert's report should be addressed to the court. This re-emphasises the fact that the expert's overriding duty is to the court, and not the party who instructed her/him. The evidence should be in the form of a written report unless the court orders otherwise. In fast track cases the expert will be required to attend a hearing only if the court considers that this is in the interests of justice.[32] The court will have regard to the overriding objective and will, in particular, balance the interests of justice against the proportionality of the cost of requiring the expert to attend court.[33] For these reasons an expert is likely to be required to give oral evidence in multi-track cases.

The expert's report must contain the following:[34]

- a summary of the substance of all oral and written instructions. This should include a summary of the facts and instructions relevant to the opinions expressed in the report or those which have influenced the expert's opinions

- details of the expert's qualifications

- details of literature or other material the expert has relied on in making the report

30 Pre-action protocol for disrepair cases, Annex C
31 Stevens v Gullis [1999], noted at *Times* 6 October; Whitehouse v Jordan [1981] 1 WLR 246
32 CPR 35.5; PD 28 para 7.2(4)
33 see CPR 1.1 & Chapter 1
34 CPR 35.10 & PD 35 paras 1.1-1.4

- details of what tests or experiments, if any, were used in the report, who they were carried out by and whether this was under the expert's supervision

- the qualifications of the person who carried out the tests or experiments

- a summary of the range of opinion, if applicable, and the reasons for the expert's opinion

- a summary of the conclusions reached

- a statement that the expert has understood and complied with her/his duty to the court

- a **statement of truth**.

Written questions to experts

On receiving an expert's report, a party has 28 days within which to put one set of written questions to the expert in order to clarify the report. The parties may agree an extension of the time with which to submit questions and may allow questions to be sent on more than one occasion. If agreement cannot be reached on these matters, a party may apply to the court for permission for what s/he is seeking. A copy of any questions should be sent to the other party's solicitors.

The answers form part of the expert's report and should therefore follow the requirements set out above.[35]

If the expert does not answer the questions, the court may order that the party who instructed the expert may not rely on the expert's evidence, and/or may not recover the fees and expenses of that expert from any other party.[36]

Useful guidance on some of the difficulties which may occur when parties instruct single joint experts was given in *Daniels v Walker*.[37] The Court of Appeal provided that:

- It is appropriate for parties, in the absence of agreement, to give separate or supplementary instructions to the expert.

- If a party is unhappy with the report, s/he should first ask the expert questions (see below).

- If the responses to the questions put to the expert are unsatisfactory then the court, having regard to the overriding objective, may give permission for that party to instruct another expert.

- It would be unjust, particularly in a substantial case and having regard to the overriding objective, to prevent a party relying on a further

35 CPR 35.6(3); see also Mutch v Allen [2001] All ER D 121, CA

36 CPR 35.6 & CPR PD 35 paras 4.1-4.3

37 Daniels v Walker (2000) 1 WLR 1382, CA; per Lord Woolf

report where the party objected to the report of the single joint expert and the objections are not "fanciful".

• The court would decide whether the evidence of a further expert was to be used at the trial only after the experts had met to resolve the differences between them.

Discussions between the experts

The court may, at any time within proceedings, order that experts hold discussions in order to identify issues and, where possible, reach agreement on any of these issues.

CPR 35.12

Expert evidence at trial

A party must disclose an expert's report if s/he wishes to rely on it in evidence. Indeed, any of the parties may use a disclosed expert's report in evidence.

CPR 35.11

8.3 Evidence in small claims

The strict rules of evidence are not applied in cases allocated to the small claims track. The general power of the court to control the evidence by directions in CPR 32.1 does apply and generally will be applied by the judge so as to ensure that the matter is dealt with informally, quickly and cheaply. Except for this general power and certain rules relating to the use of experts, the rules outlined above do not apply.

CPR 27.2

Generally, the use of expert evidence will not be permitted. If a party does wish to submit any expert evidence, either written or oral, then s/he should ideally ask the court to list a preliminary hearing. Although inadvisable, it is possible to ask for permission at the outset of the final hearing. The court is unlikely to entertain such a late application and, if it does, will almost certainly adjourn the case and impose a costs order against the applicant. This may be mitigated by giving the other party as much notice as possible of the intended application.

If permission to submit expert evidence is given, then certain provisions of Part 35 apply; namely:

CPR 27.2

• the expert's overriding duty to the court

• the power of the court to direct the use of a single joint expert

• the manner in which experts are instructed by the parties

• the court's powers to limit the amount payable to the expert and to give directions on payment of the fees.

Applications

Part 23 of the CPR provides the general rules for making applications at different stages of proceedings. For this reason they are known as interim applications.

Throughout this book, references are made to various occasions when a party may wish to apply to the court to deal with issues relating to such matters as case management, or to request a particular remedy such as an injunction or a suspension of a warrant. This chapter outlines the general procedure for making applications, and also the specific rules that modify the general procedure for certain interim remedies such as **declarations**. In addition, a separate section is devoted to applications for injunctions – another example of an interim remedy – to which particular rules apply. Finally, the procedure for enforcement of injunctions by committal proceedings is outlined.

9.1 General applications

Part 23 establishes a framework within which such applications are made, and which may be supplemented by rules specific to any particular type of application. Thus, applications for **summary judgment** should be made in accordance with the specific requirements imposed by Part 24, in addition to the general provisions in Part 23.

Applications to the court are generally made by an application notice using Form N244. The party making the application is called the applicant. The other party is known as the respondent. (For an example of Form N244 see Case Study 3, page 329.)

In making an application to the court, the applicant must bear in mind the overriding objective at all times (see Chapter 1). The applicant should be able to show, for example, all of the following:

• that s/he has done her/his best to co-operate with the opponent on the issue

• that the costs of making the application are justified by the benefit, and

• that s/he is dealing with as many aspects of the case as s/he can at the one hearing.

When to make an application

Applications should be made as soon as it becomes apparent that one is needed or desirable.[1] In addition, certain types of applications should

---

be made within a specified time or by reference to another event. For example, an application for an **interim payment** cannot be made before the expiry of the period for filing an acknowledgement of service, and, further, must be made at least 14 days before the date of the trial.

CPR 25.6

The parties should also, as far as possible, seek to make applications so that they can be heard at a hearing already fixed or about to be fixed (eg. a **directions hearing** or **case management conference**).

How to make an application

The general rule is that an application must be made by filing an application notice at the court. However, the applicant may make an application without filing a notice, where:

CPR 23.3(2)

• a rule or practice direction allows, or

• the court dispenses with the requirement for a notice.

A party may therefore ask the court to dispense with the requirement for a notice and make an oral application to the judge. This may occur where, for example, an application is particularly urgent or the need for the order on which the application is based only becomes apparent at the hearing, eg. the need to amend a statement of case. If this happens prior to the hearing, then normally the applicant should inform the other party and the court, in writing and as soon as possible, of the nature of the application and the reasons for it.[2] This may be contrasted with a situation in which an application is made without notice for a specific reason, for example, where an injunction is needed to protect the applicant from violence and giving notice to the respondent could place the applicant at risk.

If an application is made by filing an application notice, it is deemed to have been made at the time that the court receives a request for it to be issued; usually by lodging the application at the court. This is of particular relevance where a rule, court order or practice direction specifies that an application should be made within a specified time, eg. appealing against a court order. In *LB Islington v Harridge*,[3] a case concerning an application to suspend a warrant for possession, the Court of Appeal held that the application was made when the applicant's solicitor attended court although he had been wrongly turned away and told to return on the following day.

CPR 23.5

Where to make an application

Generally, an application should be made to the court where the claim was started. However, if an application is made in another court, the

CPR 23.2(1)

---

2   CPR PD 23 para 2.10

3   LB Islington v Harridge (1999), CA, noted at *Times* 30 June

court has no jurisdiction to refuse to accept it on the basis that it should be filed in the court where the claim began.[4]

CPR 23.2(2)-(3)

If the case has been moved or the trial is to be in a different court, the application should be made to that court.

CPR 23.2(4)

If the claim has not yet been issued, the application should be made to the court where it is likely to be started. For example, this would apply where a potential claimant for an illegal eviction case needs to make an immediate application to the court to order that s/he be reinstated in her/his home (see Case Study 5).

The application notice

The applicant should normally complete Form N244 (for an example of Form N244 see Case Study 3, page 329). However, an application may be made by another document as long as it is signed and contains the following information:[5]

- the order being sought (see below)

- brief reasons for seeking the order (see page 126)

- the title and reference number of the claim

- the applicant's full name and, if s/he is not yet a party to the proceedings, an address for service

- either a request for a hearing or a request that the application be dealt with without a hearing (see page 126)

- the applicant's **statement of truth** if s/he wishes to rely on the contents of the application notice as evidence.

The court has a general power in CPR 3.10 to rectify matters where there has been an error of procedure which may include the form and content of an application notice.

A fee is payable. The fee for general applications is £50 for those made on notice, and £25 for those made without notice or applications made by consent. Other fees are prescribed for certain kinds of application. However, if an application is made orally at a hearing the court may not require the payment of a fee. Anecdotal evidence suggests that practice in this regard varies widely between the courts.

Order being sought

The wording of the order sought should be included in this section. Also, if the application is dealt with at a hearing, the applicant should take a draft of the order to the hearing except in the simplest of applications.[6]

---

4   Gwynedd County Council v Grunshaw (1999)
    149 NLJ 1286

5   CPR 23.6 & CPR PD 23 para 2.1
6   CPR PD 23 para 12.1

Brief reasons for seeking the order

This section should be kept as brief and concise as possible. For example, where the applicant is applying to set aside a possession order, under CPR 39.3(3), because s/he was not present at the hearing, the reasons could be set out as follows:

(1) I was an inpatient in hospital prior to, and on the date of, the possession hearing.

(2) I made this application as soon as I found out about the judgment after being discharged from hospital.

(3) I believe I have a good chance of defending the claim successfully because the rent arrears, which existed at the time of the possession hearing, have now been reduced considerably by payment of housing benefit. It is not reasonable in the circumstances for the court to make a possession order.

Further details showing the reasons for the application, and the relevant factual background, should be provided as evidence (see page 127).

Hearing or no hearing

Applications can be dealt without a hearing if:[7]

• the parties consent to the terms of the order (see paragraph 11.3), and the parties agree that the court should deal with the application without a hearing, or

• the court does not consider that a hearing is necessary.

CPR 1.4(2)(j)

As seen in Chapter 1, the court has a duty to manage cases without the parties needing to attend court whenever possible. Therefore, applications should be dealt without a hearing whenever possible. In practice, this is largely confined to situations where the parties have reached agreement on the terms of an order. Ideally, each party should forward to the court a signed consent order (for an example see Case Study 4, page 374) and a covering letter indicating that agreement has been reached, and asking for the court to deal with the matter without the need for attendance by the parties or their representatives.[8] Often agreements are not reached until shortly before the hearing. In this situation the parties should immediately fax the court a consent order or letters indicating the terms of the agreement.

If a hearing is necessary, then, if feasible, it should be dealt with by written submission or by telephone. There is a detailed procedure for telephone hearings outlined in the Practice Direction to Part 23.[9] Telephone hearings are possible only where arrangements are made in

---

7   CPR 23.8; PD 23 paras 10.1-10.5; see also CPR 40.6
    for general rules relating to consent orders

8   CPR PD 23 paras 10.1-10.5

9   CPR PD 23 paras 6.1-6.5

advance with the court. However, few parties or courts seem to be proactive in arranging hearings in this manner.

Evidence

A detailed outline of what written evidence should be included is contained in chapter 8. Broadly, the evidence should provide sufficient detail of the circumstances of the case to enable the court to consider, with any evidence from the respondent, whether or not to make the order sought.

The evidence necessary for certain types of application may be set out in the rules or a practice direction, but for other types there may be no specific requirement for evidence. However, the applicant and respondent should bear in mind that the court will need to be satisfied of facts being relied on to support or oppose the application.[10] Therefore, invariably, evidence of these facts will be necessary.

The applicant should indicate the form of any evidence s/he will be relying on in Part B of the N244 form. This evidence may be set out in one or more of the following:

• a **witness statement** or an **affidavit**

• Part C of the N244 form

• a statement of case, eg. a claim form or defence filed in the proceedings.

For most applications, one of the first two options will be used for giving evidence in support of an application. If the applicant wishes to rely on evidence contained in Part C of the N244 form then the application notice must be verified by a **statement of truth**. If a witness statement or affidavit has been filed recently in the substantive proceedings and it contains all the necessary and up to date information to support the interim application, it will not usually be necessary to file a further witness statement or affidavit.

It is important to note the general rule that written evidence should be in the form of a witness statement rather than an affidavit.[11] If an affidavit is filed then a party may not recover any additional costs incurred in its preparation, such as the fee for administering the oath. However, evidence must be given by affidavit where this is required by the court, a rule, practice direction, or other enactment. An example of this is found in the rules relating to committal proceedings where the application must be supported by evidence contained in an affidavit.

CPR 32.15(2)

CPR 32.15(1)

CCR Ord. 29r1(4A)

The evidence should be served with the application unless it has already been served.[12] The respondent should serve her/his evidence

10 CPR PD 23 para 9.1
11 CPR 32.6. see also Chapter 8
12 CPR PD 23 para 9.3

as soon as possible or in accordance with any directions the court may have given.[13]

If written evidence has already been filed and served, eg. as part of the statement of case, it need not be filed and served again as part of an application notice and can be relied upon as evidence.

CPR 23.7(5)

Service of the application notice

Once the application notice has been filed, a copy should be served on all the respondents as soon as possible, and usually at least three days before the court is to deal with the application. This means three clear days excluding weekends and Bank Holidays and also excluding the date of service and the date of the hearing. The court may allow a shorter period than three days. A more detailed consideration of the calculation of time is contained on page 30.

CPR 23.7(1)

CPR 23.7(4)
CPR 2.8

The application notice can be served by the applicant or the court. If the court is to serve the notice, the applicant must file a copy of any written evidence in support when s/he files the notice. Details of how to serve documents together with the deemed dates of service for each method are also contained on page 31.

CPR 23.7(2)

Applications without notice

An application notice need not be served on all the respondents in certain circumstances:[14]

• cases of exceptional urgency

• where the overriding objective is best furthered by not serving

• with the consent of all the parties

• with the permission of the court

• where a date for a hearing has already been fixed but there is not enough time to file and serve a notice. The applicant should then give informal notice, if possible in writing, to the other parties and to the court and make her/his application orally

• where a court order, rule or practice direction allows.

These include the situations in which the court may dispense with the need for the filing of a notice (see above), and those in which the court recognises that the other party should not have notice of the application. These used to be known as "ex parte" applications.

A human rights issue arises in applications without notice because the respondent will not have had the chance to prepare and present

---

13 CPR PD 23 para 9.4   14 CPR PD 23 paras 2.10 & 3

her/his case. This is potentially an infringement of article 6 of the European Convention on Human Rights, which provides for 'fair and impartial' hearings. However, it is likely that an application made without notice would withstand a human rights challenge. This is because there is a procedure for the respondent to be heard at a later date on whether the order should be set aside (see page 130), and the court needs to act quickly where a party's rights are in danger.

Alternatively, the court may make an interim order to last only until a further hearing and list the matter for a return date. At this further hearing the court can consider evidence from the respondent as well as the applicant, and decide the matter accordingly. This is likely to meet the requirements of article 6.

The hearing

Interim applications are usually dealt with in private, ie. in **chambers**, before a **district judge** and decided largely on the basis of written evidence. The judge may ask the parties, or their advocates if they are represented, to clarify, or elaborate on, certain matters within the written evidence. The judge will then decide whether to make the order sought or any other order as appropriate. As mentioned above, the applicant should attend the hearing with a draft of the order sought.

A more detailed discussion of hearings is contained in Chapter 10 while evidence is considered in Chapter 8.

If the court makes an order following an application without notice then the respondent must be served with:

CPR 23.9

• the order

• a copy of the application notice

• a copy of any evidence in support.

The order must inform the respondent of the right to set aside or vary the order.

Costs

Once the court has decided the outcome of the interim application, the issue of which party will bear the costs of the application will be discussed. Advocates should be prepared to argue their point on this issue at the hearing.

For the same reason, each party should prepare a statement of costs, as the court may make an order for summary assessment.[15] The court will not make an order for summary assessment where the receiving

---

15 Under its powers in CPR 44.7

party is either **publicly funded**, or a **child** or **patient**. However, there is nothing to prevent the courts making a summary assessment of costs if any of these is the paying party.[16]

Setting aside or varying an order

If a person was not served with a copy of the application notice before the order was made, s/he will have seven days from the date s/he is served with the order to seek to have it set aside or varied.

CPR 23.10

9.2 Interim remedies

An interim remedy is a remedy which is granted by the court at any time other than at the trial of the claim.

The court has wide powers to grant interim remedies such as:[17]

• interim injunctions (see page 131)

• **interim declarations**

• **interim payments**

• orders for disclosure and inspection of information or property before a claim has been commenced

• orders for the sale of relevant property

• an order under section 4 of the Torts (Interference with Goods) Act 1977 to deliver up goods.

It is worth noting that in many cases the court will need to consider many of the substantive issues of the proceedings before granting an interim remedy. An example of this would be an application by a tenant, who has been illegally evicted, for an injunction requiring the landlord to reinstate the tenant in the property. The court will need to be satisfied of the tenant's status and that the eviction had not been lawfully effected before granting the injunction.

When an order for an interim remedy can be made

An order for an interim remedy can be made at any time, including before proceedings are started and after judgment has been given.

CPR 25.2(1)

For an interim remedy to be granted before proceedings have started, the court has to be satisfied that:

CPR 25.2(2)(b)

• the matter is urgent, or

• it is otherwise desirable to grant the remedy in the interests of justice.

---

16 CPR PD 44 paras 13.10 & 13.11(2)   17 CPR 25.1 for a more comprehensive, although not exhaustive, list

CPR 25.2(3)

Generally, if an interim remedy is granted before proceedings have started, the court will direct that a claim should be brought as soon as possible. The court is unlikely to direct this where the interim remedy sought is for the disclosure and inspection of information or property, which the applicant requires to assess the merits of commencing proceedings.

CPR 25.2(2)(c)

A defendant will usually need to file either an **acknowledgement of service** or a defence before s/he can apply for an interim remedy.

How to apply for an interim remedy

An application for an interim remedy is made in accordance with the general rules for applications contained in Part 23, as outlined in paragraph 9.1 above.

CPR 25.3(2)

The application must be supported by evidence. An application may be made without notice to the other party where there are "good reasons" for not giving notice. The evidence in support of the application must include the reasons why no notice was given to the other party. These matters are considered in detail in the section dealing with applications for interim injunctions below.

Certain interim remedies have additional rules contained in Part 25, which supplement and modify the general rules in Part 23. One of the interim remedies to which this is particularly applicable is the interim injunction. These are frequently encountered within the housing field and are therefore discussed in detail below.

9.3 Interim injunctions

As mentioned earlier, injunctions are frequently sought in the context of landlord and tenant law; for example to reinstate tenants who have been illegally evicted (see Case Study 5). The specific rules relating to interim injunctions are contained in Part 25 and the accompanying Practice Direction. These rules should be read alongside the general rules for applications in Part 23, as outlined in paragraph 9.1 above. The general rules apply unless modified by a particular provision in Part 25.

The remit of this book does not permit an extensive examination of the substantive law relating to injunctions and advisers should, therefore, refer to a specialist text on the subject.

Jurisdiction of the courts

The county court has jurisdiction to grant interim injunctions by virtue of section 38 of the County Courts Act 1984, which provides that a county court may make any order that may be made by the High Court.

The power of the High Court to grant injunctions derives from section 37 of the Supreme Court Act 1981, which states:

(1) *The High Court may by order (whether interlocutory or final) grant an injunction or appoint a receiver in all cases in which it appears to the court to be just and convenient to do so.*

(2) *Any such order may be made either unconditionally or on such terms and conditions as the court thinks just.*

The substantive claim

It is important to appreciate that applications for injunctions should normally be made only where there is a related substantive claim. The application is not a substantive claim in itself but is a remedy sought within the proceedings. The remedy sought within the actual claim may be confined to an injunction, but, invariably, will also include a claim for damages (see Case Study 4, page 345).

Therefore, where there is no pre-existing related claim, the claimant should issue a claim form in the usual form (see page 22) together with the application for an injunction. This will often arise where the need for an injunction arises at the same time as the need for the claim itself; for example, a claim for damages for unlawful eviction or disrepair where an injunction is also appropriate.

However, the urgent nature of some cases, such as unlawful eviction, means that it is not always possible to prepare a claim before applying for an injunction. CPR 25.2(2) allows the court to grant an interim injunction where:

• the matter is urgent, or

• this is otherwise desirable in the interests of justice.

In these circumstances, the court will usually ask for an **undertaking** from the applicant to issue a claim and pay the prescribed fee on the same day or on the next working day.[18]

The circumstances in which the court will exercise its discretion to grant an injunction, before a claim has been brought, are similar to those in which it is appropriate to apply for an injunction without giving notice to the other party. This is considered below.

Types of injunction

Injunctions can be restraining (forbidding an act) or mandatory (compelling an act). The courts are generally more reluctant, at an interim stage, to grant a mandatory injunction than a restraining

---

18 CPR PD 25 para. 5.1(4)

injunction.[19] For the court the emphasis is more on preserving the existing state of affairs between the parties. However, the court will grant a mandatory injunction where a compelling case for doing so is made out, having regard to the test the court applies to granting all injunctions (see below).[20]

When the courts grant injunctions

Before granting an injunction the court will need to be satisfied that:[21]

• the applicant has made out a serious issue

• damages are not an adequate remedy. This does not mean that damages will not be awarded when the claim itself is decided. It refers to situations where damages alone are not sufficient

• the balance of convenience lies in favour of granting an injunction. In other words, granting the relief to the applicant will do more good than harm. However, there are a number of circumstances where the balance of convenience is not strictly applied (see below)

• the applicant is able to compensate the respondent for any loss which may be caused to the respondent in the event that the substantive claim fails, and it is adjudged that the injunction should not have been granted. However, an injunction may still be made if the applicant is of limited financial means (see below).

The court has a very wide discretion when considering whether to grant an injunction order. One matter the court will have particular regard to is whether the applicant comes to court with "clean hands". This refers to the conduct of the applicant in the matter. For example, the court may not be sympathetic to a tenant who applies for an injunction to restrain harassment from her/his landlord where there is evidence that the applicant has been guilty of similar acts of harassment or violence against the landlord. The principle does not extend as far as to prevent the court granting an injunction because the tenant is in rent arrears; though all the circumstances of the case will be considered.

Another consideration for the court is whether the applicant has acted promptly in bringing the application.

Exceptional cases

There are a number of circumstances when the courts will not apply a strict balance of convenience test. These include:

• The interim injunction will dispose of the case. This applies where the granting of an injunction will effectively give the applicant all s/he wants and effectively disposes of the action. For example, an

19 Shepherd Homes Ltd v Sandham [1970] All ER 402
20 Redland Bricks Ltd v Morris [1969] 2 All ER 576
21 American Cyanamid Co v Ethicon Ltd (1975)
   1 All ER 504, HL

application for an injunction within judicial review proceedings requiring the local authority to provide accommodation to a homeless person, pending the outcome of a review by the local authority of a homelessness decision. If an injunction is granted, it is quite possible that the local authority will have completed the review and issued a decision before the trial of the judicial review claim itself is heard. It would not normally be appropriate to pursue the judicial review claim further as there would be no outstanding remedy sought. In these cases the court will look beyond the normal test of weighing up the balance of convenience, and will form a view of the likelihood of success of the parties if the matter were to proceed to court.[22]

- The defendant has no arguable defence. For example, the applicant has established a clear right to property and the defence lacks any real substance.[23]

- The interim injunction is sought to restrain the defendant from breaching a negative covenant. For example, an injunction that a tenant does not cause a nuisance to her/his neighbours in breach of an express term of her/his tenancy.[24]

How to apply for an interim injunction

An application for an interim injunction is made by filing an application notice at court. Form N16A is the general form used to apply for an injunction in the county court. There is no prescribed form for applications to the High Court. The application should be completed and signed by the applicant and must include the following information:

- the wording of the injunction order sought

- whether or not the case raises issues under the Human Rights Act 1998

- a reference to the evidence filed in support of the application (see page 135)

- the title and reference number of the substantive claim (if already issued)

- the applicant's full name and address for service

- the name and address of the respondent.

A completed N16A form is contained in Case Study 5, on page 386.

A fee is payable as for other applications (see above).

In addition to providing the terms of the injunction order sought, the applicant, wherever possible, should also file a draft of the order sought

---

22 NWL Ltd v Woods (1979) 3 All ER 614, HL
23 Official Custodian for Charities v Mackey (1984)
3 All ER 689
24 A-G Barker (1990) 3 All ER 257, CA

and a computer disc containing the draft. This will enable the court to speedily amend the draft order to match the actual order made by the court. The word processing system which is used by the court is WordPerfect 5.1.[25]

Written evidence

CPR 25.3(2)

An application for an interim injunction must be supported by evidence unless the court orders otherwise. Unlike the N244 form, the N16A form does not provide space for the written evidence relied on by the applicant to be included on the form. For this reason it does not include a **statement of truth**.

The evidence will invariably be given by a **witness statement** which must be verified by a statement of truth. An applicant may rely on evidence filed in connection with the substantive claim (if filed) which could be included in a statement of case or a witness statement.

The evidence required to support the application will vary according to the type of claim and circumstances of the case. Generally, the evidence should set out all the material facts relied on by the applicant for the claim.

The evidence should also set out, if applicable, the reasons why no notice of the application has been given to the respondent (see page 136). Furthermore, where the application is made without notice the applicant is under a duty to put all relevant facts before the court, even where these may be adverse to the application. A failure to disclose facts in this way may result in an injunction order being set aside.[26]

An example of a witness statement in support of an application for an injunction in an unlawful eviction case is given in Case Study 5, page 387. A detailed examination of the rules relating to evidence is contained in Chapter 8.

Service

Unless the application is made without notice, the application notice and evidence in support should be served on the respondent in accordance with the general rules in Part 23 outlined earlier, ie. as soon as practicable and at least three **clear days** before the hearing listed for consideration of the application.[27]

Where it is not possible to effect service at least three clear days before the hearing, the applicant should ask the court to allow a shorter period.[28] This request may be made at the outset at the hearing. The court will consider the reasons for the short notice in much the same way as it would consider whether to allow an application without notice.

25 CPR PD 25 para 2.4
26 Chanoch v Hertz (1888) 4 TLR 331
27 CPR PD 25 para 2.2; CPR 23.7(1)
28 under the court's powers in CPR 23.7(4)

Service may be effected by the court. The applicant should provide a copy of the application notice and evidence for the court and each of the respondents.[29] However, the urgent nature of injunctions and strict time limits for service means that it will almost always be advisable to personally serve the respondent (see page 31 for the rules relating to service).

Applications made without notice

CPR 25.3(1)

The court may grant an interim injunction on an application made without notice if there are good reasons for not giving notice.

A distinction should be made between the two most common situations where it is appropriate not to give notice of the application:

(1) It is not appropriate because giving notice is likely to lead to the respondent taking the very action which the injunction seeks to prevent and the application is extremely urgent. This is commonly the situation in domestic violence cases where there is an urgent need for an injunction, and a risk of further violence to the applicant if notice is given. It may equally apply to a tenant who is suffering severe harassment from her/his landlord.

(2) It is not appropriate because the matter is so urgent that there is no time to issue and serve an application. An example of this could be an application for an injunction requiring a local authority to provide interim accommodation, under section 188 of the Housing Act 1996, where the applicant is street homeless. In such cases, the respondent should, at the very least, be given informal notice of the intention to make the application and details of the time and place of the hearing, eg. by telephone.

Notwithstanding the informal notice given, the application will be viewed as one made without notice.

Where an urgent application is made without notice the applicant should, wherever possible, file the application notice, evidence in support and a draft order two hours before the hearing.

CPR 23.3(2)

It was noted above that urgent applications for injunctions may be considered by the court where no substantive claim has been brought. The court has a similar discretion to hear an urgent application for an injunction without an application notice having being filed. In these cases, the applicant should still provide a draft order and must file the application notice and evidence in support on the same or the next working day, or when the court may otherwise specify.[30]

---

29 CPR PD 25 para 2.3   30 CPR PD 25 para 4.3(2)

Injunction hearings

The general rule is that applications for injunctions will be dealt with at a court hearing.[31]

Where the application is one made on notice, or informal notice has been given, the respondent may be present and the hearing will be conducted in much the same way as a trial. The court will consider any written evidence filed in relation to the case and may invite the parties, or their advocates, to clarify or elaborate on the evidence. Where the respondent has had insufficient time to file any evidence because s/he was informed of the hearing at a late stage, the court will ask for their response to the facts contained in the applicant's evidence.

Where the application is made without any notice then the respondent will not be present. The court will consider the written evidence of the applicant and may ask the applicant or her/his advocate for clarification.

Telephone hearings

As an exception to the general rule that an application should be considered at a hearing, cases of extreme urgency may be dealt with by telephone.[32] Such applications may be made only where the applicant is acting by a solicitor or by counsel. The most common situation where this may be necessary is if the injunction is sought when the court offices are closed, ie. after 5pm and before 10am. If an application is made outside office hours, the applicant's solicitor or counsel should ring the appropriate court and ask to speak to the clerk to the duty judge. A draft order will normally be required where it is possible to fax it to the judge.

If the telephone procedure is used, the application notice and evidence in support must be filed with the court on the same or on the next working day, together with two copies of any order granted by telephone.[33]

The order

The order should set out clearly what it is that the respondent must do or not do. It may state that it is effective until trial or further order of the court.[34]

Unless the court orders otherwise, an injunction order must always contain the following:[35]

- An **undertaking** from the applicant to pay any damages which the respondent sustains as a result of the injunction, and which the court considers the applicant should pay. This is likely to be relevant where the claim proceeds, it transpires that the applicant was not entitled to an injunction and the substantive claim fails. However, an

---

31 CPR PD 25 para 4.2
32 procedure contained in CPR PD 25 para 4.5
33 CPR PD 25 para 4.5(4)

34 CPR PD 25 para 5.2-5.3
35 CPR PD 25 para 5.1(1)-(5)

injunction may still be made if the applicant is of limited financial means – most commonly someone who is publicly funded – thereby rendering any undertaking worthless to the respondent.[36]

• If the order was made without notice, an undertaking by the applicant to serve the respondent with the application notice, evidence in support and the order as soon as is practicable, and a **return date** for a further hearing to enable the respondent to be present.

• If the order was made before the filing of an application notice, an undertaking to file it and pay the fee on the same or the next working day.

• If the order was made before issue of a claim form, an undertaking to issue and pay the fee on the same or the next working day, or directions for the commencement of the claim.

Injunction applications made on notice and with the respondent present are, instead of an injunction order, sometimes dealt with by the respondent giving an **undertaking** to do or not to do the act requested.

Costs

Once the court has decided the outcome of the interim application, the issue of which party will bear the costs of the application will be discussed. Advocates should be prepared to argue their point on this issue at the hearing. The most common order following the hearing of an interim application will be costs in the case. For further information on the types of costs orders likely to be made, see Chapter 13.

Service of the order

It is crucial that the applicant serves a copy of the order on the respondent by personal service. The respondent is not bound by the order, and enforcement by committal proceedings cannot usually be brought until service has been effected (see page 140).

Injunctions under Housing Act 1996

Applications by local authorities for injunctions under section 152 of the Housing Act 1996, restraining anti-social behaviour, follow a different procedure; advisers should consult Order 49 Rule 6B of the CCR.

Breach of order and undertakings

If the respondent breaches the injunction order or any party breaches an **undertaking** given to the court, that person may face **committal**

36 Allen v Jambo Holdings Ltd [1980] 1 WLR 1252, CA

proceedings. The purpose of committal proceedings is to enforce the order or undertaking so as to ensure compliance, and to punish the party for **contempt of court** for the breach.[37] The court has power to commit a party to a maximum of two years' imprisonment.[38]

In order that committal proceedings may be brought, the injunction or undertaking should include a **penal notice** warning the party of the consequences of breaching the injunction or undertaking.[39] The only exception to this is where the party in breach was well aware of the consequences of disobedience of the order.[40] This may be difficult to prove; consideration should be given instead to making a request to the court for the order to be redrawn to include a penal notice.[41] In any case the advocate for the applicant should ensure that a penal notice is attached to the injunction when it is drawn up.

A power of arrest may be attached to certain injunctions. The power of arrest enables a police officer to arrest, without a warrant, a person suspected of breaching an injunction; the person may be held in custody and taken before a judge for committal proceedings. In the housing field this is likely only to include injunctions restraining anti-social behaviour under sections 152 and 153 of the Housing Act 1996. A power of arrest may not be attached to an undertaking.

Application for committal

Where there is no power of arrest on an order, or the police will not arrest a party under a power of arrest, the party in whose favour the order was made may apply to the court. The party may issue a claim form or application notice asking for the offending party to be committed for **contempt of court**.

An application should be made with evidence in support in accordance with Part 23 of the CPR and Order 29 Rule 1 of the County Court Rules 1981. The claim form or the application notice should provide the following information:[42]

• details of the provisions of the injunction

• details of breaches by listing the incidents

• other relevant information in support to be provided by **affidavit**.

It is important to note that the information contained in the claim form or application notice must set out the acts alleged to constitute the contempt; it is not sufficient for this information to be contained in the affidavit alone.[43] The evidence as a whole should enable the party against whom the application has been brought to know the nature of the allegations against her/him.[44]

37 James v Cliffe (1987), CA, noted at *Times* 16 June
38 section 38 of the County Courts Act 1984
39 CCR O29 r1(3); Hampden v Wallis (1884) 26 Ch D 746
40 Sofroniou v Szgetti (1991) FCR 332n, CA
41 CCR O29 r1(3)
42 CCR O29 r1(4A)
43 Dorrell v Dorrell (1985) FLR 1089, CA
44 Chakravorty v Braganza (1983), noted at *Times* 12 October

The applicant must personally serve the claim form or application notice on the respondent unless the court dispenses with the need for service.[45] The court will dispense with service only in exceptional circumstances.[46]

The hearing

CCR O29 r1(2)

The court will only entertain enforcing an injunction by committal where it is satisfied that:

- a copy of the order has been served personally on the person required to do or not do the specified act, and

- in the case of an injunction requiring a person to do an act (ie. a mandatory injunction), the order was served before the expiration of the time within which the act was required to be done.

The **standard of proof** which applies to committal proceedings incorporates the criminal test; the applicant must therefore show that the breaches are proved "beyond reasonable doubt". The person alleged to be in breach will be invited to bring evidence in her/his defence, and should be informed of the right to legal representation.

The order

If the court is satisfied that the breaches have taken place, it does not have to order a term of imprisonment. The court may make a committal order but suspend it for a period of time, indefinitely or until further order. Alternatively, the court may fine or just reprimand the person in breach. What order the court makes will depend on the nature and seriousness of the breaches.

If the court makes an order for committal, a warrant for that person's arrest will be issued and, unless the court orders otherwise:

- a copy of the order will be served on the person to be committed either before or at the time the warrant is executed, ie. the person is arrested; or

- where the warrant is signed by the judge, the order may be served on the person to be committed at any time within 36 hours of the execution of the warrant.

CCR O29 r3

The person who is in custody may apply to discharge the committal order. An application may be made in writing attested by the governor of the prison showing that s/he has **purged,** or desires to purge, her/his contempt. The application should be served on any party at whose instance the committal order was made.

---

45 CCR O29 r1 (4)&(7)   46 Lamb v Lamb (1984) FLR 278, CA

Hearings

This chapter looks at what happens at hearings and the preparation required for them. In particular, the final hearing – ie. the trial – is examined. Although there are generally hearings for interim applications throughout proceedings, these are not looked at specifically as they tend to follow the same basic outline as trials.

The majority of cases started in court are resolved before they get to trial. The main reason for this is that the parties reach a settlement rather than go to court. Other reasons include judgment being entered in default (see paragraph 5.3) and striking out a claim (see page 74).

CPR 28.2(4)

The final direction given by the court in both fast track and multi-track cases (see pages 82 and 85 respectively) tends to be about setting down for trial. This is when all the parties let the court know they are ready for trial and that a date can be set for the hearing. The direction will specify when a case should be ready for trial. In the fast track, a case should be ready for trial within 30 weeks of allocation. There is no similar time limit for a case in the multi-track.

10.1 Preparation for trial

After all the directions have been complied with, a number of things need to be done in preparation for the final hearing in a case. These include:

• completing a listing questionnaire

• compiling a trial bundle.

The court can hold a hearing prior to the trial. This will be either a listing hearing or a pre-trial review. The hearing might be to encourage a settlement or to ensure that all the parties are ready for trial. The court may order that further directions are complied with, such as a deadline for filing the trial bundle (see page 145).

Listing questionnaire

The listing questionnaire is Form N170. (For an example of a listing questionnaire see Case Study 4, page 370.) The court will send this form out to all the parties in the case. There is usually a deadline for completing the form and sending it to the court. The parties cannot agree to extend this deadline without the permission of the court.[1] The claimant must pay a fee when returning her/his listing questionnaire.

It often happens that the court, in error, does not send out the listing questionnaire; but the parties are still under an obligation to file it.

---

1 CPR 28.4(1)(a) & 29.5(1)(c)

Most of the court forms, including the listing questionnaire, are available on the internet and can be completed online.

Listing questionnaires are generally only completed for **fast track** and **multi-track** cases. **Small claims track** cases are intended to be more informal, and so listing questionnaires are not required.

In completing the listing questionnaire, the parties are requested to state:

• which directions have been complied with and what further directions are needed

• details of any expert witnesses being used (see paragraph 8.2)

• details of other witnesses who are giving evidence (see paragraph 8.1)

• who is representing the case for the party completing the questionnaire

• a time estimate of the trial and an estimate of how many pages the trial bundle is likely to have

• in a fast track case, whether the parties could go to trial with less than three weeks' notice.

It is important at this stage to state on the form any dates when the witnesses or the advocate presenting the case will not be available. The court will take these dates into account when fixing a date for the trial.

In fast track cases, the parties are generally given at least three weeks' notice of when the trial will be. This can be shortened if the parties so agree or if the court decides shorter notice is sufficient.[2] Fast track trials should last no longer than one day (see page 82 on allocation to CPR 28.6(1) the fast track).

As discussed in Chapter 1, one of the underlying principles of the CPR is co-operation between the parties. The CPR encourage all parties to exchange copies of the listing questionnaires with each other before they are sent to the court. They can then come to an agreement on any major differences, eg. how long the trial will last, and amend the questionnaires so that the information contained in all the questionnaires is similar. This will then allow the court to deal with setting down a case for trial more efficiently.

Once the court receives the listing questionnaires, it will decide whether or not to have a listing hearing or a **pre-trial review**. After this, CPR 28.6(1) & 29.8 the court will:

• set a trial timetable if appropriate

• fix the date for the trial or, for multi-track cases, the week within which the trial is to begin

2 CPR 28.6(2) & CPR PD 28 para 7.1(2)

• specify any other steps to be taken before trial.

A trial timetable deals with what is expected to happen at the trial. For example, the court may outline how long a party should spend in presenting her/his case, or at what times certain experts are to give their evidence. The court might also decide that an opening speech by the claimant (ie. the speech that is made at the start of the hearing outlining her/his case) is not needed (see page 148).

Trial bundles

A trial bundle consists of all the documents relevant to the case including pleadings, **disclosed** documents and **witness statements**. It has to be filed with the court between three and seven days before the trial.

CPR 39.5(2)

CPR Practice Direction 39 para 3 deals with how a trial bundle should be put together and what it should contain. Particular points to note are:

• the bundle is compiled by the claimant or her/his legal adviser and should be filed by her/him at court

• it should normally be contained in a ring binder or lever arch file

• it should be numbered continuously throughout

• there should be an index with a description of each document and the page number

• a copy of the bundle should be supplied to all the parties and for the use of the witnesses at the trial

• a bundle containing original copies of documents should be available at the trial.

It is usual for the claimant to agree the contents of the trial bundle with the other party. A copy of the index to the bundle should be sent to the other party before the bundle is compiled. This allows the other party to add any documents that have been missed out. An example of an index is found in Case Study 1, page 266.

10.2 The trial

This section also applies to the hearings of interim applications.

Representation

Solicitors, barristers and parties conducting their own cases have **rights of audience** in the county court and are therefore able to represent parties at hearings.[3] Legal executives also have rights of audience at

---

3   section 60(1) of the County Courts Act 1984

hearings that are in private; this is usually in the judge's room. Interim applications are generally heard in private.

Where a local authority has given permission for its employee to act on its behalf, that employee has full rights of audience in the county court in possession cases and/or any other claim in respect of the occupation by any person in its accommodation, eg. the recovery of rent, mesne profits, damages.[4]

Lay advocates (ie. those without a professional qualification) have rights of audience in small claims hearings, but the party s/he is representing must be present.[5] For all other hearings, the lay advocate must ask for the court's permission to speak. This permission should be sought by application (see paragraph 9.1) before the hearing, where possible, or at the hearing just before the case is heard. If permission is sought at the hearing, it need not be in writing and can be made orally to the judge.

Public or private hearings?

CPR 39.2(1)

The general rule, reinforced by article 6(1) of the Human Rights Act 1998, is that a hearing is to be in public. However, CPR 39.2(3) states that a hearing may be in private in certain circumstances. These include situations where:

- publicity would defeat the object of the hearing
- the hearing involves confidential information and publicity would damage that confidentiality. This includes information relating to personal financial matters, eg. in possession proceedings on the grounds of rent arrears
- it is a hearing of an application made without notice where the respondent is not present, and it would not be fair to the respondent for there to be a public hearing
- the court considers a private hearing to be necessary in the interests of justice.

In addition to this rule, the Practice Direction to CPR Part 39 lists certain proceedings that should be held in private because they involve confidential information. These include:

- a claim by a mortgagee against one or more individuals for an order for possession of land
- a claim by a landlord against one or more tenants or former tenants for the repossession of a dwelling house based on non-payment of rent

---

4 section 60(2) of the County Courts Act 1984   5 CPR PD 27 paras 3.2(1) & (2)(a)

- an application to suspend a warrant of execution or a warrant of possession, or to stay execution where the court is being invited to consider the ability of a party to make payments to another party (see page 222)

- an attachment of earnings order (see page 166), a third party debt order (see page 167) or a charging order (see page 173)

- an order to obtain information from judgment debtors (see page 177).

District judges tend to hold *all* hearings in possession cases in private.

What happens at the hearing

On arrival at court, all parties and the advocates for the hearing should report to the usher. The usher will take down the advocates' names to inform the judge. S/he will also be able to inform an advocate if the other party has arrived and when the case is likely to be heard. This could be very important if last minute negotiations are needed.

If an application for permission to speak at the hearing has not already been made, if the advocate is a lay advocate then it would be a good idea at this point to inform the usher that permission is going to be sought at the hearing. The usher will tell the judge and might be able to give an indication to the advocate as to whether s/he will be allowed to speak at the hearing.

Trials in the small claims track are generally heard by a district judge in private. Fast track cases are heard by a district judge or a circuit judge. A multi-track trial is normally heard by a circuit judge.

A circuit judge should be called "Your Honour" in open court, ie. in public, and "Judge" in private. A district judge should be addressed as "Madam" or "Sir". If the hearing is in open court, then the advocate must stand up when addressing the court and when the court addresses her/him. The advocate remains seated when the hearing is in private.

The hearing will generally take place as follows:

- the claimant (or her/his advocate) makes a short opening speech outlining her/his case

- the claimant presents her/his evidence, which includes any documentary evidence s/he is relying on. Witnesses are called and:

  - examined in chief by the claimant

  - cross-examined by the defendant

        – re-examined by the claimant, and

        – might be asked questions by the judge

- the defendant (or her/his advocate) gives her/his opening speech

- the defendant presents her/his evidence as above

- the defendant gives her/his closing speech

- the claimant gives her/his closing speech

- the defendant responds

- judgment is given

- costs are considered (see Chapter 13).

Opening speech

The opening speech is when the claimant outlines her/his case. The judge may decide that an opening speech is not necessary. This is likely to happen where the claimant has provided a case summary; this will contain much of the same information that would have been included in the opening speech.

Drafting a case summary is becoming usual as one of the further directions that a court orders prior to trial. It is a summary of the case outlining the matters still in issue. There will generally be a limit on the number of words to be used. The summary will be drafted by the claimant but should be agreed by all parties. The aim of the summary is to help the court in reading the papers before the trial. Therefore, it should refer to documents included in the trial bundle where appropriate.

Examination in chief

Examination in chief is the initial questioning of a witness by the advocate of the party calling her/him. There is a tendency for **witness statements** to stand as **evidence in chief**, thus disposing of the need for examination in chief. Where this happens, a witness will be called to the witness stand and, after being sworn, be asked simply to confirm the contents of her/his statement as correct.

CPR 32.5(3)   S/he will be allowed to expand on or add to the contents of the statement only with the court's permission. As a result, it is extremely important that witness statements are complete in dealing with all the matters that the party wishes to rely on in the case.

Where the witness statement is not to stand as evidence in chief, the advocate of the party calling her/him will ask the witness questions. The advocate cannot ask the witness leading questions. These are questions that suggest the answer that is expected. For example, in a disrepair case where the advocate is trying to establish the effect of the disrepair, a leading question might be: 'Did the damp in the house cause your daughter to develop asthma?' The other party's advocate would be entitled to object to such a question. The question should be asked in more general terms, eg. 'Describe how the disrepair has affected you and your family'.

Cross-examination

After the witness has given her/his evidence in chief, the other party's advocate will cross-examine her/him. Leading questions are allowed in cross-examination. The purpose of cross-examination is to discredit the witness in order to weaken the impact of her/his evidence, or to bring new evidence to light that contradicts the **evidence in chief**. This does not necessarily mean that the advocate should be aggressive as, very often, the best results are achieved by a more gentle approach.

The rules of cross-examination are as follows:

- If evidence is not challenged in cross-examination, it is taken to be accepted. Consequently, it is necessary to challenge a witness on all material facts that are disputed.

- The cross-examining advocate must put her/his own party's case to the witness. For example, where the claimant has given evidence that the defendant knew of the disrepair in her/his house from a particular date and the defendant denies this in her/his witness statement/examination in chief, it must be put to the defendant in cross-examination that s/he knew of the disrepair from the date given.

- The questions asked must either be relevant to the issues in the case or aim to discredit the witness.

Re-examination

Re-examination follows cross-examination. The advocate is given the opportunity to ask further questions of her/his own witness. The questions that can be asked in re-examination are firmly restricted to points arising out of cross-examination. The advocate cannot ask questions of the witness that s/he forgot to ask her/him in examination in chief.

Closing speeches

This is an opportunity for the advocate to round up all the points in her/his case in order to persuade the court to make a judgment favourable to the party s/he is representing. Any new matters arising from evidence given should be incorporated into the closing speech. A closing speech should be concise.

Small claims cases

The trial in small claims cases will usually be dealt with by a **district judge**, conducted in the judge's room, ie. in private, rather than in a court room. The hearing is comparatively informal, with the parties often representing themselves. The strict rules of evidence (see paragraph 8.3) do not apply.

The parties and their witnesses will all be seated around the district judge's table. A small claims track hearing may proceed as above but with less formality. However, the judge usually tends to control the hearing more in a small claim case and can conduct the case as s/he wishes. S/he will often indicate at the start what will happen. Commonly, the judge will ask the witnesses questions first, and the parties can ask questions only when the judge has finished.

Possession cases

The importance of being prepared for defending possession cases cannot be stressed enough. Very often, the first hearing of the possession case can result in a final order being made. The advocate should come to court prepared to argue that making a possession order would be unreasonable.

Requesting an adjournment

A party defending a possession claim may be able to get an adjournment of the first hearing for a number of reasons. These are frequently brought to light once the party secures **legal representation**. This often happens at the last moment before the trial (eg. at a court duty advice scheme). Reasons for the adjournment in a case concerning rent arrears could include:

• A delay in the payment of housing benefit has caused the rent arrears, and an adjournment is necessary in order to try to resolve the housing benefit issues.

• The party has brought to light that there could be a potential counterclaim for disrepair, and this needs to be examined in greater detail.

In cases such as these, the courts tend to allow an adjournment for a limited amount of time, and will usually inform the parties when they are next to come to court; this is known as the "return date". The courts tend to grant adjournments more frequently on the first hearing of the possession claim. They are less likely to grant an adjournment if one has already been given; especially if the need for the adjournment has been caused by delay by the party requesting the adjournment.

The party requesting the adjournment should inform the other party of her/his intention to do so as soon as possible. S/he should also try to get the other party to agree to an adjournment. This will have costs implications as the party will be able to show that s/he has tried to co-operate with the other party.

Possession on the basis of rent arrears under Ground 8

It is important to request the adjournment *before* the landlord's evidence of rent arrears has been given. This is because, once the landlord has proved the mandatory ground of rent arrears, the court has no option but to grant a possession order.

For a more detailed look into possession claims, see Chapter 14.

10.3 Settlement or discontinuance after the trial date is fixed

The court officer responsible for listing the trial for hearing (the listing officer) must be notified immediately if there is no longer a need for the trial to go ahead. This would be due to:

CPR PD 39 para 4.1

• an offer to settle a claim being accepted

• a settlement being reached

• a claim being discontinued.

Offers to settle

Part 36 of the CPR deals with offers to settle and payments into court. The purpose of these is to put pressure on the other party to bring the proceedings to an end. There will be costs implications if the offer to settle, or the payment into court, is not accepted and the court then gives a final judgment that awards a party less than the amount offered by the other party (see paragraph 5.5).

Discontinuance

CPR 38.2(1)

A claimant may discontinue her/his claim at any time. This is not always straightforward as, in certain circumstances, the consent of the other parties or the court's permission is needed. For example, if there is more than one claimant, all the claimants must agree in writing to discontinue the action or the court must give permission.

CPR 38.2(2)

CPR 38.3

Form N279 (notice of discontinuance) needs to be completed and served on all the other parties. This form is also filed at court.

See paragraph 5.4 for more details on discontinuance.

Judgments and orders

A judgment is a final decision of the court on an issue before it ends the claim. An order is an interim decision but may, in some circumstances, also end the claim, eg. a consent order.

11.1 Drawing up and filing judgments and orders

CPR 40.3(1)

Generally, the court will draw up the judgment or order, ie. it will write the terms of the judgment or order. However, there are some situations when this does not happen:

- The court orders a party to draw it up.
- A party agrees to draw it up with the court's permission.
- The court states there is no need to draw it up.
- It is a consent order (see below).

CPR 40.2

The judgment or order must state the name and the judicial title of the person who made it and the date on which it is given or made. The court must also **seal** it.

CPR 40.3(3)

A party drawing up a judgment or order has up to seven days to file it at court. If this is not done, any other party can draw it up and file it.

11.2 Service of judgments and orders

CPR 40.4(1)

If a party has drawn up a judgment or an order, s/he must file enough copies at the court with copies for service on her/him and on the other parties. On receipt of these copies, the court will seal them, retain one copy and serve the others on each of the parties.

CPR 40.4(2)

Orders made as a result of an **interim application** must be served on the applicant, the respondent and any other person the court orders.

11.3 Consent judgments and orders

CPR 40.6(1)-(2)
CPR 40.6(3)

Certain judgments or orders may be entered without the court's approval provided they are agreed and none of the parties is a **litigant in person**. The court will then seal and serve the judgment or order as above. The types of judgments or orders include:

- a judgment or order for the payment of money
- an order for the dismissal of the whole or part of proceedings
- an order for the stay of proceedings on agreed terms that disposes of the proceedings

- an order staying the enforcement of a judgment
- an order setting aside a default judgment (see page 157)
- an order paying out money from payments into court
- an order for the assessment, waiver or payment of costs.

Where the above circumstances do not apply, but the parties have reached an agreement, any party (including a litigant in person) may apply for a consent order. This will require the court's approval, but the court may deal with the application without a hearing.

CPR 40.6(5)-(6)

A consent judgment or order must:[1]

- be drawn up in the agreed terms
- have the words "By Consent" on it
- be signed by each of the parties' **legal representatives** or the litigant where the party is a litigant in person.

An example of a consent order can be found in Case Study 4.

11.4 Complying with a judgment or order

CPR 40.7(1)

CPR 40.11(a)

A judgment or order will usually take effect from the day when it is given or made. A party has 14 days to comply with a judgment or an order for the payment of money. However, the court may specify a different date for compliance, including specifying payments by instalments.

11.5 Interest on judgments

Interest is payable on all county court money judgments of £5,000 and more under section 17 of the Judgments Act 1838 and the County Court Act 1984.[2] Interest is also payable on county court judgments for any amount of money where the debt is a qualifying debt under the Late Payment of Commercial Debts (Interest) Act 1998. A qualifying debt would be one which was created by virtue of a requirement under a contract to which the Act applies.[3]

CPR 40.8

The interest on the debt will start running from the day the judgment is made, but the court may order that it runs from an earlier date.

11.6 Correction of errors in judgments and orders

A party can apply for a judgment or order to be corrected where it contains an accidental mistake or omission. The application need not be formal or on notice. It simply requires a letter to be written. The court can deal with the error without a hearing.[4]

---

1   CPR 40.6(7) & CPR PD 40B para 3.4
2   this is charged at a rate of 8% per annum

3   section 3(1) of the Late Payment of Commercial Debts (Interest) Act 1998
4   CPR 40.12 & CPR PD 40B paras 4.1-4.3

11.7 Setting aside or varying a judgment or order

Three instances of where a court might set aside or vary a judgment or order are dealt with below.

Non-appearance at a hearing

A party can make an application (see Chapter 9) to set aside a judgment or order if s/he did not attend the hearing and the court then gave
CPR 39.3(3)
CPR 39.3(4)-(5)
judgment or made an order against her/him. The court will grant the application only if it is supported by evidence showing that the party:

• acted promptly when s/he found out the court had entered judgment or made an order against her/him

• had good reason for not attending the trial, eg. s/he was in hospital, s/he did not receive the application notice. However, in practice, less good reasons may be accepted. These reasons include attending the wrong court, or making a mistake about the date/time of the hearing or a possession claim where the tenant has been told not to attend the hearing by her/his housing officer. A party should not be discouraged from making an application because the non-attendance is due to mistake or carelessness

• has a reasonable prospect of success at the trial.

The party will need to show evidence supporting *all three* of the above points.

Default judgment

A default judgment is a judgment given without trial where a defendant
CPR 12.1 did not file an acknowledgment of service or a defence. It is explained in more detail in paragraph 5.3.

The court must set aside the judgment if it was wrongly entered because
CPR 13.2 one of the conditions of obtaining a default judgment was not satisfied. Additionally, the court has the power to set aside or vary a default
CPR 13.3(1) judgment if:

• the defendant has a real chance of successfully defending the claim, or

• the court can see a good reason why the judgment should be set aside or varied, or the defendant should be allowed to defend the claim.

The court will set aside or vary the default judgment only if the defendant can show that s/he acted promptly in making the application to set
CPR 13.3(2) aside or vary the judgment.

Fresh evidence

A new trial may be allowed because fresh evidence has been discovered. This will only be in special and exceptional cases. The party asking for the new trial will have to show that:[5]

- s/he could not have obtained the evidence with reasonable diligence for use at the original trial, and

- the evidence would probably have an important influence on the outcome of the case, and

- the evidence must appear credible.

CPR 40.9
A person who is directly affected by the judgment or order but is not a party, can apply to have it set aside or varied.

11.8 Appealing a judgment or an order

Other than dealing with statutory homelessness appeals, this book does not explain the procedure for appealing a decision of a court. However, it is important to point out the initial steps that need to be taken in order to make an appeal and the time limits for appealing.

CPR 52.11(1)

CPR 52.11(2)

CPR 52.11(3)
Appeals are limited to a review of the lower court's decision unless otherwise suggested by a practice direction, or the court considers that a re-hearing is in the interests of justice. An appeal court does not generally consider oral evidence or evidence that was not before the lower court. Therefore, an appeal hearing usually consists entirely of legal argument. The appeal will be allowed if the decision of the lower court was wrong or unjust due to a serious procedural or other irregularity in the proceedings in the lower court. The three main types of appeal are:

- appeals on points of law

- appeals on findings of fact

- appeals against a judge's exercise of discretion.

Appeals on points of law

An appeal will succeed if a judge is wrong on a matter of law central to her/his decision. An example of this would be where a judge decides incorrectly that s/he has no choice but to make an outright possession order where a protected tenant has two months' rent arrears. This would be wrong as the judge has a discretion not to order possession for protected tenants. However, permission to appeal will be granted only if the appeal court considers that there is a realistic chance of success in the appeal.

---

5 Ladd v Marshall (1954) 3 All ER 745 CA, & CCR Ord 37 r1

Appeals on findings of fact

Appeals against the lower court's findings of fact are very rare. The appeal court will generally attach great weight to any finding of fact made by the judge in the lower court. This is because the appeal court will not usually have before it the evidence that the lower court would have had, eg. oral evidence from a witness.

Appeals against a judge's exercise of discretion

In order for an appeal to succeed on this ground, it must be shown that the judge had done one of the following:[6]

• misunderstood the facts

• taken into account irrelevant matters

• failed to exercise her/his discretion

• came to a conclusion that no other reasonable judge could have come to, or made a decision that could not be justified by any material before her/him.

Once again, it is usually very difficult to succeed on this ground of appeal.

Initial steps

CPR 52.3(1)
CPR 52.3(2)

The permission of the court is needed to appeal a judgment or an order in most cases. Permission is requested in one of two ways:

• by the advocate simply asking the court that made the decision for permission at the hearing when the decision was made

• if after the hearing, to the appeal court in an appeal notice, ie. Form N161. (For an example of a completed Form N161, see Case Study 2; page 286.)

In the county court, a **district judge** or a circuit judge will have made the decision being appealed. In these cases, the appeal will be made to a circuit judge and a High Court judge respectively unless otherwise specified by a practice direction.[7] An appeal of the final judgment in a multi-track case will be made to the Court of Appeal.

Time limits

A party wishing to make an appeal must file her/his appeal notice in the appeal court either:

• within 14 days after the date of the decision being appealed, or

• within such a period that the court specifies.

Most decisions of the county court in housing cases have a deadline of 14 days within which to appeal them.

6   G v G (1985) 2 All ER 225   7   CPR PD 52 paras 2A.1-2A.2

Enforcing judgments

This chapter looks at the position after the making of a court order or judgment where a party fails to comply with its terms. The mere fact that an order has been made by the court does not mean that the party ordered to do something or not do something will abide by that order. If it is not complied with, the party in whose favour it was made will need to enforce the judgment or order.

Example

Mrs Smith brought a claim against her landlord, Mr Jones, for the return of her deposit when she moved out of her flat. The court ordered Mr Jones to pay Mrs Smith £750 within 28 days. After the 28 days have elapsed, Mrs Smith is still waiting for her money. How can she get her money from Mr Jones?

For the purposes of this chapter, the person who has obtained judgment and wishes to enforce it (in this instance, Mrs Smith) is referred to as the 'judgment creditor' and the person against whom the judgment is to be enforced (Mr Jones) is referred to as the 'judgment debtor'. These are also the terms used within the Civil Procedure Rules.[1]

The right to enforce a judgment or order does not arise until any time limits for complying with the terms of the judgment or order have elapsed. The actual judgment or order itself will usually contain details of any such time limits. In the absence of a specified period, a judgment or order for the payment of money (including costs) is payable within
CPR 40.11   14 days.

12.1 Review of enforcement of civil court judgments

In March 1998 the Lord Chancellor announced a comprehensive review of the methods of enforcement of civil court judgments. The report of the first phase of the enforcement review was published in July 2000. The general conclusion of the report was that the enforcement procedures should be reformed to enable them to operate more effectively and a series of proposals were made to achieve this aim. A number of these have been implemented by a statutory instrument, which introduced Parts 70 to 73 of the CPR.[2] These replace those parts of the old County Court Rules preserved in Schedule 2 of the CPR that relate to:

• garnishee proceedings – now called 'third party debt orders'

• charging orders, stop orders and stop notices

• oral examinations – now called 'orders to obtain information from judgment debtors'.

1   CPR 70.1(2)(a)-(b)   2   The Civil Procedure (Amendment No 4) Rules 2001, SI 2001/2792

The rules, in these areas of enforcement, apply to all proceedings issued after 25 March 2002. Proceedings issued before 25 March 2002 are dealt with according to the procedure contained in the old County Court Rules.

Advisers should be aware that this chapter incorporates only those changes implemented at the time of writing. Further changes will follow in relation to other methods for enforcement, such as warrants and attachment of earnings orders. It is important, therefore, to check the up to date position before advising.

12.2 Methods of enforcement

There are a number of ways a judgment or order can be enforced and it is for the judgment creditor – rather than the court – to decide on the best option for her/him. The various methods of enforcement allow for flexibility and reflect the different circumstances that may face the judgment creditor when s/he is considering enforcement. The different methods include warrants, attachment of earnings, third party debt orders, charging orders and insolvency. Each of these methods is examined in outline below. In addition, an outline is given of the ways in which a judgment creditor can obtain information about the judgment debtor.

Warrants

A warrant is an order issued by the court giving court officers – in the form of bailiffs – the authority to put the terms of the judgment into effect. This will usually involve seizing goods belonging to the judgment debtor or recovering goods or property belonging to the judgment creditor. The warrant gives the bailiff, on behalf of the court, the authority in law to take such action. Carrying out the terms of the warrant is known as executing the warrant.[3]

A warrant is applied for by the judgment creditor completing the necessary form (see page 165) and paying a prescribed fee. The court will keep the judgment creditor informed of progress in executing the terms of the warrant.

There are three types of warrants, depending upon what the judgment creditor is seeking to recover:

- warrant of execution
- warrant of delivery
- warrant of possession.

Warrant of execution

Where the judgment is for a sum of money (including court costs), a warrant of execution entitles the bailiff to seize goods owned by the judgment debtor and sell them so as to settle the judgment debt and court costs from the proceeds of sale.[4] Any money left over is returned to the judgment debtor. Where the judgment is for payment of a sum of money by instalments, then if the judgment debtor fails to pay an instalment, a warrant of execution can be issued for either the whole of the remaining sum or just the missed instalment payment. If the amount to be recovered exceeds £5,000, only the High Court can execute the warrant.[5] In these circumstances, it would be necessary to transfer the claim from the county to the High Court (for the procedure, see CCR Ord 25 r13, Schedule 2 of the CPR).

Warrant of delivery

Where judgment is for the return or delivery of any goods by the judgment debtor to the judgment creditor, a warrant of delivery entitles the bailiff to seize those goods. Where judgment is for the return or delivery of certain goods or payment of their monetary value, a warrant of delivery can be used to either seize the goods themselves or recover their monetary value. If judgment is for both delivery of goods and payment of money (including costs), a warrant of delivery can be used in the same manner as a warrant of execution (see above) to seize and sell goods. As with warrants of execution, if the money judgment exceeds £5,000, it can only be enforced by the High Court.[6]

Warrant of possession

This particular method used to enforce a possession order is examined in detail in Chapter 14 (see page 219).

Applying for a warrant of execution or delivery

To apply for a warrant, the judgment creditor needs to confirm that the terms of the outstanding judgment or order have not been complied with by the judgment debtor. This is done by completing one of the following forms:

• Form N323 for a warrant of execution

• Form N324 for a warrant of goods.

There is a fee, which can be added to the judgment debt and recovered by the bailiff. Upon receipt of the completed form and fee, the court will issue the warrant.

However, in certain circumstances the court's prior permission will be

---

4 Note that the bailiff cannot force her/his way into the debtor's house to gain entry, Vaughan v McKenzie [1969] 1 QB 557

5 High Court and County Courts Jurisdiction Order 1991, art 8
6 High Court and County Courts Jurisdiction Order 1991, art 8

required before the warrant is issued, including where six years or more have elapsed since the judgment or order was made.[7]

Warrants of execution or delivery are valid for 12 months from the date of issue and, if they are not executed within this period, the judgment creditor must apply to the court to have the warrant renewed before it can be enforced.[8]

Once issued, the court sends a warning notice to the judgment debtor informing her/him that a warrant has been issued and when it is to be executed. The warrant will not be executed until seven days after the notice was sent.[9]

Preventing execution

Upon receiving notice that a warrant has been issued, the judgment debtor has three options to prevent the warrant being executed:

- Comply in full with the terms of the judgment or order, including paying any costs incurred by the judgment creditor in issuing the warrant.

- Apply to the court to have the warrant set aside. This action should be taken where the judgment debtor disputes that s/he has not complied with the terms of the judgment or order.[10]

- Apply to the court to have the warrant suspended. This should be used where there is no dispute that the judgment debtor has failed to comply with the terms of the judgment or order but s/he wishes to propose an alternative way of settling the judgment.[11]

Applications are made using Form N244 and are considered in more detail in Chapter 9.

Committal for breach of an order or undertaking

This is used as a method of enforcement and/or punishment against persons who have breached an injunction or an undertaking to court. The procedure involved is outlined in Chapter 9 (see page 138).

Attachment of earnings

Where a money judgment has not been complied with by the judgment debtor, the judgment creditor can apply to the court for an attachment of earnings order (AEO).[12] The AEO directs the judgment debtor's employer to deduct specified amounts from her/his earnings and pay them directly to the court.

Obviously, this method of enforcement is only appropriate where the judgment debtor is in employment. AEOs will usually result in the

---

7 CCR Ord 26 r5, CPR Schedule 2. Other circumstances requiring permission are: (1) where there has been any change, whether by death or otherwise, in the identity of the original judgment creditor and debtor; (2) the judgment or order is against the assets of a deceased person, which are now in the hands of the deceased's executors or administrators; (3) the goods to be seized are in the hands of a receiver appointed by the court
8 CCR Ord 26 r6, CPR Schedule 2
9 CCR Ord 26 r1, CPR Schedule 2

judgment debt being settled in instalments rather than a lump sum payment. Both these factors should be borne in mind by the judgment creditor before applying for the order.

Applying for an AEO

The judgment creditor applies to the court on Form N337, certifying the amount of money remaining due under the judgment and, where applicable, any instalments that remain unpaid. There is a court fee, which can be added to the judgment debt. Notice of the application is served by the court on the judgment debtor who must file a reply on Form N56 within eight days.[13] Contained within the form of reply will be details of the judgment debtor's employer. The court can, at any time, request further details of the judgment debtor's earnings from her/his employer.[14] The judgment debtor does not have to file a reply if s/he pays the money outstanding to the judgment creditor within the eight days referred to above.[15]

If the court believes it has sufficient information, it will make an AEO. However, if there is insufficient information for the court to be satisfied about making the order, a hearing will take place to consider the judgment creditor's application for an AEO in more detail. Where an AEO is made without a hearing, the judgment creditor or debtor may within 14 days of service of the order apply to have the terms of the AEO reconsidered. Upon receipt of such an application, the court fixes a hearing date.[16]

Once the AEO is made, it is sent to the judgment debtor and her/his employer. Deductions are made at source by the employer from the judgment debtor's earnings and sent to the court. The court then passes the payments to the judgment creditor.

The court can vary the terms of the AEO, which will itself lapse if the judgment debtor leaves the employment of the employer named in the order. The AEO will be of no effect until the court again directs it to a person who appears to be the judgment debtor's employer.[17] There is a duty on the judgment debtor to inform the court when s/he changes or leaves employment.[18]

Third party debt orders

Third party debt orders are the means by which the court can require third parties to pay money that they owe or hold on behalf of the judgment debtor directly to the judgment creditor. This may be the whole amount held by the third party, or such part of it as would be sufficient to satisfy the money outstanding under the judgment, together with the costs incurred by the judgment creditor in making the application.

10 CCR Ord 25 r8. Set aside by court under Ord 25 r8 (6)
11 CCR Ord 25 r8. Set aside by court under Ord 25 r8 (6)
12 CCR Ord 27, CPR Schedule 2
13 CCR Ord 27 r5, CPR Schedule 2
14 CCR Ord 27 r6, CPR Schedule 2
15 CCR Ord 27 r5 (2A), CPR Schedule 2
16 CCR Ord 27 r7, CPR Schedule 2
17 CCR Ord 27 r1(9), CPR Schedule 2
18 CCR Ord 27 r1(15), CPR Schedule 2

Commonly, the third party will be a bank or a building society that holds money in an account in the name of the judgment debtor.

Third party debt orders were previously called garnishee orders. The garnishee was the third party owing or holding money on behalf of the debtor. Applications for third party debt orders are brought under Part 72 of the CPR, which came into effect on 25 March 2002. However, any garnishee proceedings brought before that date will continue to be dealt with under the previous rules.

CCR Ord 30

The reforms to the procedure followed on from the review of enforcement proceedings carried out by the Lord Chancellor's Department (see paragraph 12.1 above). The central aims were to make the procedure less complicated and easier for creditors to use, while placing a greater emphasis on the individual circumstances of the debtor.[19]

Application for third party debt order

The judgment creditor applies to the court for a third party debt order by filing an application notice in Form N349.[20] The application must be made in the court that made the judgment or order that the judgment creditor is seeking to enforce. The only exception to this is where the proceedings have been transferred to a different court, in which case the application should be issued at that court.

CPR 72.3(1)(b)

Applications may, and generally will be, made without notice to either the third party or the judgment debtor.

CPR 72.3(1)(a)

The application notice must be verified by a statement of truth and include the following information:[21]

• the name and address of the judgment debtor

• details of the judgment or order which the judgment creditor seeks to enforce. This should include the date of the judgment and name of the court

• the amount under the judgment which remains unpaid including any instalments which have fallen due and remain unpaid

• the name and address of the third party

• confirmation that the judgment creditor believes, to the best of her/his knowledge, that the third party owes money to or holds money on behalf of the judgment debtor

• details of any other person who has a claim to the money owed by the third party and details of that claim

• details of any other applications for third party debt orders made by the judgment creditor in relation to the same judgment debt.

19 para 201, *Report of the First Phase of the Enforcement Review*, LCD, July 2000. Available from www.lcd.gov.uk
20 CPR 72.3(2) & PD 72 para 1.1
21 CPR 72.3 (2) & PD 72 para 1.2

If the third party is a bank or a building society then the application notice should include the address of its head office in England and Wales. It should also include the name and address of the branch at which the account is believed to be held and the account number. However, if any or all of this information is not known the judgment creditor should indicate this fact on the application notice.[22] The need for the details of the branch and account number to be provided has been lessened due to the requirement on the bank or building society to carry out a search of all accounts held by the debtor (see the next page). However, the judgment creditor should include sufficient information to justify her/his belief that the judgment debtor has an account with the bank or building society in question. The court will not entertain 'speculative applications for third party orders'.[23]

A fee of £50 is payable.

Interim third party debt order

CPR 72.4

The application is considered by a **district judge** without a hearing. If the judge makes an interim third party debt order, s/he will:

• fix a hearing to consider making a final third party debt order. The date of the hearing must be not less than 28 days from the date on which the interim order is made, and

• direct that, until that hearing, the third party must not make any payment that reduces the amount s/he owes to the judgment debtor to a level below that specified in the interim order.

CPR 72.4(4)

It is important to note that until the interim order has been served on the third party it will not be binding on them.

Service of the interim third party debt order

CPR 6.3

Generally service will be effected by the court. However, the judgment creditor may notify the court that s/he wishes to serve the order. This is advisable where s/he believes that the judgment debtor intends to move funds from accounts at short notice. In this situation personal service on the third party should be considered (see general rules on service on page 31).

CPR 72.5(1)

In any event, the interim third party debt order, the application notice and any documents in support must be served:

• on the third party, not less than 21 days before the hearing date, and

• on the judgment debtor, not less than seven days after the service of the order on the third party and not less than seven days before the hearing date.

---

22 CPR 72.3 (2) & PD 72 para 1.2   23 CPR PD 72 para 1.3

CPR 72.5(2)

If the judgment creditor serves the order then s/he must either file at court a certificate of service not less than two days before the hearing, or failing that, produce a certificate of service at the hearing.

Effect of interim third party debt order

Once the interim order is served, the effect is that the debt or money held in an account is "frozen" and cannot be settled or paid out in any way. Where the interim order is made in respect of a bank or building society account, that institution must not allow the judgment debtor to withdraw funds so as to reduce the amount held in the account to below the amount referred to in the order.

CPR 72.4(3)

The amount of money to be retained by the third party as specified in the order will be the total of:

• the amount which remains unpaid under the judgment or order, and

• the judgment creditor's fixed costs of the application.

The Practice Direction to Part 72 makes it clear that a bank or building society served with an interim order is only required to retain money in accounts that are held solely in the name of the judgment debtor. Therefore the order would not be effective to freeze a joint account in the name of the judgment debtor and another person. The order would, however, be effective to freeze a joint account where the account holders are also joint judgment debtors.[24]

CPR 72.6(1)

Another effect of the interim debt order is that once a bank or building society has been served with the order, they are required to carry out a search to reveal all accounts held by it in the name of the judgment debtor. This was not a requirement of the former rules relating to garnishee orders.

CPR 72.6(2)

Within seven days of service of the order the bank or building society must disclose, to the court and the judgment creditor, the following information in relation to each account held by the judgment debtor:

• the account number

• whether the account is in credit

• if the account is in credit:

– whether the amount in the account covers the amount specified in the order

– the amount in the account at the time that the order is served where this is less than the amount specified in the order

– whether the bank or building society wishes to assert any right to the money in that account, eg. by way of a set-off.

---

24 CPR PD 72 para 3.1 (1)

CPR 72.6(3)

If the judgment debtor does not have an account with the bank or building society, or the bank or building society is unable to comply with the order for any other reason, it should inform the court and the judgment creditor within seven days of service of the order. This may arise where the bank identifies more than one account holder whose details match those in the order.

CPR 72.6(4)

Where the third party is an individual or institution other than a bank or a building society, s/he must inform the court and the judgment creditor in writing within seven days of service of the order if s/he claims:

- not to owe any money to the judgment debtor, or

- to owe less than the amount specified in the order.

Application for a hardship payment order

In carrying out its review of the enforcement procedures the LCD highlighted the possible hardship caused to a judgment debtor where an interim third party debt order has been made.[25]

CPR 72.7(1)

Consequently, the Part 72 rules introduced in March 2002 allow the judgment debtor to apply to the court for a hardship payment order. The court may make an order permitting the bank or building society to make a payment out of the account concerned, on application by the judgment debtor, but only where:

- the judgment debtor is an individual who is prevented from withdrawing money from a bank or building society account due to the making of an interim third party debt order, and

- as a result, the judgment debtor or her/his family is suffering hardship in meeting ordinary living expenses.

CPR 72.7(2)

CPR 72.7(4)(a)

CPR 72.7(4)(b)

An application for a hardship payment order should be made on the general N244 application form (see page 125). The judgment debtor may apply to any county court (or District Registry if proceedings are in the High Court); not just the court that made the original judgment or order being enforced. The Form N244 should contain sufficiently detailed evidence to explain why the judgment debtor needs the payment requested. This should include any documents that prove her/his financial situation such as payslips, bank and mortgage statements.[26] The application must be verified by a **statement of truth**. A fee of £50 is payable. However, given the fact that most applicants applying for a hardship payment will implicitly have financial difficulties, a request for remission of the fees should be made to the court concerned.

Normally, the judgment debtor must serve the application notice and

---

25 para 210 of the *Report of the First Phase of the Enforcement Review*, LCD, July 2000, available at www.lcd.gov.uk   26 CPR PD 72 para 5.6

CPR 72.7(5)

supporting evidence on the judgment creditor at least two days prior to the hearing of the application. It need not be served on the third party.

However, the court does have the discretion to allow an application without notice to the judgment creditor in cases of exceptional urgency.[27] At the very least, the court is likely to direct that the judgment creditor be informed that the application has been made and is given the opportunity to make representations. This may be achieved by telephone, fax or other form of communication.[28]

Objecting to making of final third party debt order

The judgment debtor and the third party may object to the court making a final third party debt order. The reasons for any objections should be contained in written evidence and filed at court. This should be filed and served on all the other parties as soon as possible, and in any event not less than three days before the hearing.

CPR 72.8(1)&(4)

If the judgment debtor or the third party knows or believes that a person other than the judgment debtor has a claim to the money referred to in the interim order, s/he must file and serve written evidence detailing this information. The evidence must be filed and served on each other party as soon as possible and not less than three days before the hearing. If the court receives such notification then it will serve the other person with a notice of the application and date of hearing.

CPR 72.8 (2)&(4)

CPR 72.8(5)

If a third party has informed the judgment creditor and the court that s/he does not owe money to the judgment debtor or that the amount s/he owes is less than that specified in the interim debt order, the judgment creditor may dispute this. If so, s/he must file and serve written evidence on all the parties as soon as possible, and not later than three days before the hearing.

CPR 72.8(3)

The hearing

CPR 72.8(6)

At the hearing the court may:

- make a final third party debt order (see below)

- discharge the interim third party debt order and dismiss the application

- decide any issues in dispute between the parties, or between the parties and any other person with a claim to the money specified in the interim order. Alternatively, the court may give directions and direct that a trial take place to resolve these issues.

If the court makes a final third party debt order, this is an order to pay money, which may be enforced against the third party by the judgment creditor.

CPR 72.9

---

27 CPR PD 72 para 5.4   28 CPR PD 72 para 5.5

Charging orders

A judgment creditor may apply to the court to enforce a judgment by imposing a charge, by way of a charging order, on any property held by the judgment debtor.[29] In practice, a judgment creditor will seek to charge the judgment debtor's land with the amount due under the judgment. Upon the sale of the judgment debtor's interest – for example, the sale of land – the judgment creditor's charge is paid.

This method of enforcement can provide good security for the judgment creditor and is only suitable for a money judgment. However, it may not be suitable where the judgment creditor requires urgent settlement of the judgment – although there are provisions for enforcing the sale of land (see page 176) – and consideration should always be given to other charges, particularly over land, which may have priority. For example, upon the sale of land, an existing mortgage will be settled first out of the proceeds of the sale.

Applications for charging orders made after 25 March 2002 are dealt with in accordance with Part 73 of the CPR. The rules, which to a large extent mirror the former rules, were introduced following the review of enforcement proceedings undertaken by the Lord Chancellor's Department (see paragraph 12.1). Any applications made before 25 March 2002 will continue to be dealt with under the previous rules.

CCR Ord 31

Application for charging orders

An application for a charging order is made by filing an application notice in Form N379, if the application relates to land, or Form N380, if it relates to certain types of securities.[30] Applications may be made without notice.

CPR 73.3(1)

Generally, the application must be issued in the court that made the order which the judgment creditor is seeking to enforce. Exceptions to this include where:

CPR 73.3(2)

• the proceedings have since been transferred to another court

• the application is made under regulations for the enforcement of council tax liability.

A judgment debtor may, however, apply to the court asking for the proceedings to be transferred to her/his local court.

CPR PD 73 para 3

The application notice must be verified by a statement of truth and contain the following information:[31]

• the judgment debtor's name and address

• details of the order that the judgment creditor seeks to enforce

---

29 Applications under section 1 of the Charging Orders Act 1979 or Regulation 50 of the Council Tax (Administration & Enforcement) Regulations 1992

30 CPR PD 73 para 1.1
31 CPR PD 73 para 1.2

- the amount of money remaining unpaid under the judgment, including any instalments which have fallen due and remain unpaid

- if known, details of any other creditors of the judgment debtor

- identification of the asset(s) intended to be charged and details of the judgment debtor's interest in the asset

- names and addresses of persons who must be served with the interim charging order (if made).

Interim charging order

CPR 73.4

An application for an interim charging order will be dealt with by a judge without a hearing. The judge may make an order which:

- imposes a charge over the interest held by the judgment debtor in the asset concerned

- fixes a date for a hearing to consider whether a final charging order may be made.

If the charge relates to land, the judgment creditor should then register the interim charging order at HM Registry or the land charges department at the local council. This serves to warn anyone proposing to acquire an interest in the property that an interim charging order has been made.

Service of the interim charging order

CPR 6.3

Generally, service will be effected by the court, but the judgment creditor may notify the court that s/he wishes to serve the order.

CPR 73.5

In any event, the interim charging order, the application notice and any documents in support must be served not less than 21 days before the final hearing on the following persons:

- the judgment debtor

- other creditors specified by the court

- where the interest charged is held under a trust, on trustees specified by the court.

CPR 73.5(1)(d)-(e)

The rules specify other persons to be served where the interest charged relates to securities or funds in court.

CPR 73.5(2)

If the judgment creditor serves the order, then s/he must file at court a certificate of service not less than two days before the hearing, or failing that, produce a certificate of service at the hearing.

Objecting to the making of a final charging order

The judgment debtor or other person may object to the court making a final charging order by filing and serving written evidence that details the grounds for those objections. This should be filed and served not less than seven days before the hearing.

CPR 73.8(1)

The hearing

CPR 73.8(2)

At the hearing, the court may:

- make a final charging order

- discharge the interim charging order and dismiss the application

- decide any issues in dispute between the parties, or between any of the parties and other person who objects to the making of a final order. Alternatively, the court may give directions and direct that a trial takes place to resolve these issues.

If a final charging order is made then this will act as a charge on the property that may be enforced by an order for sale (see below). The order must be served on all those who were required to be served with the interim charging order.

CPR 73.8(4)

Discharge or variation of order

Any application to discharge or vary a charging order must be made to the court that made the charging order. If an application is successful, the order must be served on all those persons on whom the charging order was required to be served on.

CPR 73.9

Enforcement of charging order by sale

CPR 73.10

The judgment creditor may wait until the house is disposed of by the judgment debtor voluntarily or may seek to realise the interest they have in the property by forcing its sale. To do this, the judgment creditor must make a fresh claim under the Part 8 procedure. S/he must complete and file Form N208, together with a copy of the charging order and written evidence in support containing the information prescribed in the **practice direction**.[32] The claim proceeds under the Part 8 procedure (see paragraphs 3.3 and 4.2 respectively).

At the final hearing, the court will balance the interests of the judgment creditor with those of the judgment debtor's family (where appropriate).[33]

Insolvency

The type of insolvency proceedings available to the judgment creditor will depend on the nature of the judgment debtor (considered below).

---

32 CPR 73.10 & PD 73 paras 4.1–4.4

33 see for example, Jones v Challenger [1961] 1QB 176; Lloyds Bank plc v Byrne [1993] 23 HLR 472, CA

Insolvency proceedings are only available where the judgment debt is for £750 or over and are not suitable for non-money judgments.

Bankruptcy

Where the judgment debtor is an individual, the judgment creditor may choose to pursue bankruptcy proceedings. This is done by serving a demand for payment in the prescribed form on the judgment debtor; this is known as a statutory demand. Three weeks after service, the judgment creditor can file a bankruptcy petition with the court, supported by an **affidavit** confirming that the judgment debtor owes the amount claimed, that a statutory demand has been served and the amount owed remains outstanding. A hearing will take place and, if the judgment creditor can prove that the judgment debt remains outstanding, a bankruptcy order may be made.

If a bankruptcy order is made, control over all the judgment debtor's property and assets is placed in the hands of a trustee in bankruptcy. The trustee (who is usually a qualified insolvency practitioner) is responsible for settling all of the judgment debtor's liabilities out of her/his assets. This process is subject to complex regulations which are beyond the scope of this book. Advice should be sought from an insolvency specialist.

Winding up

If the judgment debtor is a company, the judgment creditor can apply to wind up the company. The procedure is very similar to the bankruptcy procedure and specialist advice should be sought.

Insolvency proceedings can be lengthy and expensive. In addition, if the judgment debtor has a number of other debts, these may take priority over the judgment debt. It is often the case that creditors in insolvency proceedings only ever recover part of what is owed to them. The rules relating to insolvency are laid down by the Insolvency Act 1986.

Which method of enforcement to adopt

The following factors should be borne in mind when deciding which method of enforcement to adopt:

• what is the judgment for (eg. money, property)?

• what assets, if any, does the judgment debtor have?

• what is the "value" of the judgment to the judgment creditor, both in monetary and non-monetary terms?

• are the whereabouts of the judgment debtor known?

Type and value of the judgment

The type of judgment to be enforced will determine the options available to the judgment creditor. For example, a judgment for money can be enforced in a number of ways; whereas a judgment for the return of land is usually only enforced in one way (see warrant of possession on page 219).

It is also important to bear in mind the value of the judgment or order. Some methods of enforcement aim to recover all the judgment debt at once, whereas other methods produce the debt in instalments over time or upon the sale of a property.

Information about the judgment debtor

The financial means of the judgment debtor will have an influence on which method of enforcement is chosen. There is little point in trying to enforce a money judgment against a judgment debtor who has little or no assets or income. The judgment creditor should also be aware that further court fees are incurred when enforcing judgments.[34] These can be added to the judgment itself and recovered from the judgment debtor. However, if the judgment debtor has limited means, difficulties may also arise in recovering these extra costs.

If the judgment debtor cannot be traced, difficulties can arise in enforcing the judgment. It may prove impossible to establish the means of the debtor or to use any of the enforcement methods.

If the judgment debtor is a firm rather than an individual, the judgment or order can be enforced against any property owned by the firm or any partner of the firm.[35]

Establishing the debtor's means

The type of judgment to be enforced will be clear from the judgment or order itself. Establishing the judgment debtor's means may not be so straightforward. Unless the judgment debtor has volunteered information about her/himself in the course of the court proceedings – for example, when completing the form of admission if the claim is not being defended (see page 46) – it will be for the judgment creditor to satisfy her/himself of the judgment debtor's ability to meet the outstanding judgment.

Orders to obtain information from judgment debtors

The CPR allow the court, upon application by the judgment creditor, to order the judgment debtor to be questioned by a court officer, or in certain circumstances by a judge, to establish her/his means. The

34 County Court Fees Order 1999 (SI 1999/689) for enforcement in the county court; Supreme Court Fees Order
1999 (SI 1999/687) for enforcement in the High Court.
35 CCR Ord 25 r9, CPR Schedule 2

CPR 71.2 court can also order the judgment debtor to produce any books or documents in her/his possession that may be relevant to her/his means (eg. accounts or bank statements). The information obtained is then passed to the judgment creditor.

This process was previously known as an oral examination, applications for which were made under the old County Court Rules. The reforms arose from the review of enforcement procedures by the Lord Chancellor's Department and apply to all applications made after 25 March 2002 (see paragraph 12.1). Applications made prior to that date continue under the old rules.[36]

APPLICATION

CPR 71.2(2)(a) Where the information is sought from an individual judgment debtor, the judgment creditor must file at court an application notice in Form N316. An alternative form, N316A is used if the information is sought from an officer of a company or corporation.[37] Applications may be made without notice.

CPR 71.2(2)(b) Unless the proceedings have since been transferred to another court, the application must be issued in the court that made the order that the judgment creditor seeks to enforce. A fee of £40 is payable.

The application notice must contain certain information prescribed by the **practice direction**, comprising details of the judgment debtor, the judgment or order that the judgment creditor seeks to enforce, and details of any specific documents that s/he wants the judgment debtor to provide.[38]

In addition, if applicable, the judgment creditor is required to provide reasons for wanting the questioning undertaken by a judge rather than a court officer. If s/he makes such a request, the application will be referred to a judge. Alternatively, the court officer may consider it appropriate to refer the application to a judge even if no request has been made.[39]

Once referred, the judge may make an order that the questioning itself takes place before a judge, but will only do so where there are "compelling reasons".[40]

If the judgment creditor has not asked for the questioning to be undertaken by a judge, a court officer will consider the application.

THE ORDER

CPR 71.2(5)-(6) If the application notice is in the appropriate form and contains the prescribed information, then an order will be made. The order will require the person concerned to:

---

36 CCR Ord 25 r3, CPR Schedule 2
37 CPR 71.2(3)(a) & PD 71 para 1.1
38 CPR 71.2(3)(b) & PD 71 para 1.2
39 CPR PD 71 para 1.3 & CPR 3.2
40 CPR PD 71 para 2.2

- attend court at the time and place specified

- when s/he attends court, produce the documents described in the order, where this is possible, and

- answer on oath, any questions asked by the court.

Generally, the judgment debtor will be required to attend the county court for the district in which s/he resides or carries on business.[41]

CPR 71.2(7) The order will also contain a notice warning the person required to attend court that:

'you must obey this order. If you do not, you may be sent to prison for contempt of court'.

SERVICE OF THE ORDER

CPR PD 71 para 3 Generally, the rules require service of the order to be undertaken by the judgment creditor. However, an important exception applies where the judgment creditor is an individual **litigant in person**, when the order will be served by the court bailiff. Unless the court orders otherwise, the order must be served on the person who is required to attend court, not less than 14 days before the hearing.

CPR 71.3(1)

CPR 71.3(2) If the judgment creditor attempts service, but is unsuccessful, s/he must inform the court of that fact not less than seven days before the hearing date.

TRAVELLING EXPENSES

CPR 71.4 The person served with an order may, within seven days of service, ask the judgment creditor to pay money to cover her/his reasonable travelling expenses to and from court. If such a request is made, the judgment creditor must pay a reasonable sum of money.

JUDGMENT CREDITOR'S AFFIDAVIT

CPR 71.5(1) The judgment creditor must file an **affidavit**:

- stating how much of the judgment debt is still unpaid

- confirming either that the judgment creditor has paid a sum to cover the travelling expenses of the person ordered to attend court, or that no request has been made by that person

- if service was not undertaken by the court, by the person who served the order, stating how and when the order was served.

CPR 71.5(2) The affidavit should be filed at court not less than two days before the hearing, or failing that, must be produced at the hearing.

---

41 CPR PD 71 para 2.1

HEARING BEFORE COURT OFFICER

At the hearing, the person ordered to attend court is questioned on oath by a court officer who asks a standard list of questions. The questions are contained in Form EX140 or Form EX141. The former is used where the person questioned is the judgment debtor, whilst the latter should be used where that person is an officer of a company or corporation.[42]

The judgment creditor or her/his representative may attend and ask additional questions at the hearing. Alternatively, s/he may provide additional questions for the court officer to ask in advance by attaching a list to the application notice when it is filed at court.[43]

The court officer will make a written record of the evidence given, read it to the person questioned and ask her/him to sign it at the end of the hearing. A refusal to sign the record will be noted.[44]

HEARING BEFORE JUDGE

If the hearing is before a judge, the judgment creditor or her/his representative must attend and undertake the questioning. The standard forms referred to above are not used and the proceedings are tape recorded.[45]

FAILURE TO COMPLY WITH ORDER

CPR 71.8(1)

The court will refer the matter to a circuit judge where the person ordered to attend the court:

• fails to attend court

• refuses to take the oath or answer any question at the hearing, or

• otherwise fails to comply with the order.

CPR 71.8(2)-(4)

The judge to whom the case has been referred may make a **committal** order against the person who has failed to comply with the order. However, the committal order will automatically be suspended as long as that person:

• attends court at a time and place specified in the order and

• complies with the terms of the order and those of the original order requiring her/him to attend court, eg. the production of documents at the hearing.

If the person fails again to attend court or fails to comply with a term of the order, then a warrant may be issued for that person to be arrested and brought before a judge who will decide whether the debtor should be committed to prison for failure to comply with the order.[46]

---

42 CPR 71.6(1)-(2) & PD 71 para 4.1
43 CPR 71.6 (3)(a) & PD 71 para 4.2
44 CPR PD 71 para 4.3

45 CPR 71.6(3)(b) & PD 71 para 5.1-5.2
46 CPR PD 71 paras 8.1-8.6

Credit search

The judgment creditor may prefer to establish the judgment debtor's means without recourse to the court. This can be done by using one of the many private investigative agencies which can carry out a credit search on the judgment debtor and any potential third party and undertake any other enquiries (see page 177). These can sometimes be expensive and there are limits as to what information such organisations are lawfully allowed to access.[47]

---

47 Statutory controls exists over the access to some personal information eg. Data Protection Act 1998

Costs

This chapter examines how the court decides which party, if any, should pay the costs of a case, how much those costs should be and ways of financing litigation. Costs are incurred throughout the life of a case and can include:

• the costs of a solicitor

• the cost of disbursements, eg. barrister's fees, court fees.

The overriding objective (see Chapter 1) is just as applicable to the issue of costs, with courts attempting to deal with cases as cost-effectively as possible. One of the major criticisms of the pre-CPR civil justice system was the prohibitive expense of seeking justice. The CPR have attempted to address this issue in a number of ways.

CPR 44.3(1) Who should pay the costs and how much they should pay is at the discretion of the court. The court exercises this discretion in the form of costs orders. These are made at the conclusion of a case – known as "final costs orders" – and also during the case, where interim applications have been made – known as "interim costs orders". The types of costs orders that the court can make are considered later in this chapter.

13.1 The court's discretion

CPR 44.3(2) The general rule is that the unsuccessful party will be ordered to pay the successful party's costs. However, this general rule is always subject to the factors set out below.

In exercising its discretion about who should pay the costs of a case and how much those costs should be, the court is required to have regard to all the circumstances of the claim, and in particular:[1]

• the extent to which the parties have followed any pre-action protocol (see paragraph 2.1; for an example see Case Study 4, page 340)

• the extent to which it was reasonable for the parties to raise, pursue or contest each of the allegations or issues

• the manner in which the parties pursued or defended the action or particular allegations or issues

• whether the successful party exaggerated the value of their claim

• whether a party was only partly successful

• any payment into court or offer to settle (see paragraph 5.5).

The purpose of these considerations is to ensure that the overriding objective is adhered to – and to penalise a party which fails to adhere to it – and to take account of the extent to which the successful party was in fact successful on the various issues or parts of the claim being pursued.

13.2　Interim costs orders

Interim costs orders are made during the course of proceedings. Generally, they will be made after an interim application has been considered (see chapter 9).

Example

During the course of a possession claim, it is ordered that **disclosure** must take place by 1 May, with the landlord and the tenant sending each other their respective lists of documents. By 7 May, the tenant has still not sent his list of documents to the landlord. The landlord applies to the court for an order that the tenant must serve his list of documents by 28 May, failing which, his defence will be struck out. The court makes an order in those terms, which the tenant complies with by serving his list of documents before 28 May.

The court also makes an order in respect of the costs incurred by the parties relating to the application. This is known as an interim costs order and will be one of the types described below.

If the court makes no reference to costs when making the interim order, then each party will have to be responsible for paying her/his own costs.[2] Thus it is important to ensure that, if a party expects to be entitled to a costs order in her/his favour, this should be specifically raised with the judge during the course of the application. Generally, the issue of costs would be considered after the court has decided the main point of the application.

Types of interim costs orders

For each application, there will be just one interim costs order (if any at all) that the court will make in deciding which party, if any, is to pay costs. The types of interim costs orders that can be made are outlined below. These types of orders can also be final costs orders.

An order for costs

The court can order that one party pays the other party's costs. This is sometimes called "costs or costs in any event". The party in whose favour the interim order is made is entitled to the costs incurred in respect of that part of the proceedings to which the order relates.

2　CPR 44.13(1) & CPR PD 23 para 13.2

In the example above, the landlord would be entitled to recover the costs incurred in applying to court for the order, *even if* the tenant was ultimately successful in defending the claim and secured a final costs order against the landlord. The tenant would not, of course, be entitled to the costs of the application.

This order is commonly made in respect of adversarial applications where one party can be identified as the winner. This order would be most appropriate to the example given above and would ensure that the landlord could recover his costs from the tenant whatever the ultimate outcome of the case.

Costs in the case

The party in whose favour a costs order is made at the end of the proceedings – a final costs order – is entitled to the costs incurred in respect of the interim order. The final paragraph of the interim order will state that there are to be costs in the case. This is also sometimes called "costs in the claim" or "costs in the cause".

In the example above, if the tenant was successful in defending the claim for possession and the court ordered the landlord to pay the tenant's costs at the end of the case, those costs would include the costs incurred by the tenant in respect of the interim order.

This order is commonly made in respect of case management hearings where there is no "winner".

Costs reserved

The court will decide that costs are to be reserved if the decision about who should pay the costs is deferred to a later occasion. If no later order is made, the costs will be costs in the case.

This order is commonly made when an application is adjourned to a specific date in the future, eg. an adjourned possession hearing. It is also frequently made when some issue is raised as to why the successful party should not recover the costs of an application, but the court does not have time to hear an argument about costs.

Claimant's/defendant's costs in the case/application

If the party in whose favour the costs order is made is awarded costs at the end of the proceedings, that party is entitled to her/his costs of the part of the proceedings to which the order relates. If any other party is awarded costs at the end of the proceedings, each party bears her/his own costs in respect of the part of the proceedings to which the order relates.

Costs of and caused by

Where, for example, the court makes this order on an application to amend a statement of case, the party in whose favour the costs order is made is entitled to the costs of preparing for and attending the application and the costs of any consequential amendment to her/his own statement of case.

Costs here and below

This order is only relevant when there is an appeal from a decision of a lower court. The party in whose favour the costs order is made is entitled to her/his costs in respect of the proceedings in which the court makes the order, ie. "costs here", and to her/his costs of proceedings in any lower court, ie. "and below".

No order as to costs or each party to pay her/his own costs

Where the order states "no order as to costs", each party pays her/his own costs of the part of the proceedings to which the order relates regardless of the final costs order.

13.3 Basis of assessment

Once the court has decided which party is to pay costs (see the above orders), the next step is to assess how much the party will have to pay. There are two bases upon which costs can be assessed. These are the standard basis and the indemnity basis. In either case, costs that are

CPR 44.4(1)   unreasonable will not be allowed. If an order does not specify which basis the costs are to be assessed on, then the standard basis will apply. The standard basis also applies if the order states some other

CPR 44.4(4)   form of assessment, eg. a solicitor/client basis.

Standard basis

If costs are assessed on this basis, the court will only allow costs that are proportionate to the matter in issue. Additionally, any doubt as to reasonability and proportionality will be resolved in favour of the

CPR 44.4(2)   paying party, ie. the party who must pay the other party's costs.

The majority of costs orders are assessed on the standard basis.

Indemnity basis

The indemnity basis of assessment is generally used to penalise a party. Issues on proportionality are not considered. Any doubts as to whether costs were reasonably incurred or were reasonable in amount are resolved in favour of the receiving party, ie. the party that is getting

CPR 44.4(3)   her/his costs paid.

Factors in assessing the amount of costs

CPR 44.5(3) The court must have regard to the following matters when assessing costs:

• the conduct of all the parties both before and during the proceedings, and any efforts made in trying to resolve the dispute

• the amount of money or value of property involved

• the importance of the case to all the parties

• the complexity of the issues

• the skill, effort, specialised knowledge and responsibility involved

• the time spent on the case

• the place where and the circumstances in which work or any part of it was done.

This list is not exhaustive and is simply an indicator of the types of matters the court should consider.

Bearing in mind the conduct of the parties, it is very important that pre-action protocols (see paragraph 2.1) are followed, letters before action are written (see paragraph 2.3), and there is full co-operation between the parties. The party who has not done so could face a heavy costs bill even if s/he goes on to win the case. This is because the courts are likely to be hard on a party who has proceeded with litigation where this could have been avoided.

The place where the work is done is relevant to costs because, in some areas such as London, the fee earner (ie. the **legal representative** who is running the case) will have higher charges than in other areas. This is due to the greater overheads, eg. rent and salaries. Also, the rates permitted on inter partes assessments are based on the indemnity principle and reflect the private rates which would be charged by a legal representative. Guidance from the Supreme Court Costs Office has been published for the purposes of summary assessment (see below) as to appropriate rates for different levels of fee earner (based on experience) in different parts of the country.[3] There is some debate as to whether the area rate to be charged should be where the case is proceeding or where the fee earner is working. It seems that where the fee earner is based is a relevant factor, but the courts may not allow a higher rate if it would have been reasonable for the party to have instructed a legal representative in the area where the court is situated.

3   the guidance is available on www.courtservice.gov.uk

13.4 Assessment procedures

The two methods that the courts use for assessing costs are summary assessment and detailed assessment. These are explained below.

Summary assessment

When the court decides the sum of money to be paid under a costs order at the time the order is made, this is called summary assessment. For example, at the conclusion of an interim application, the court will assess the costs to be paid as soon as the order is made. Courts are generally being encouraged to use this procedure for assessment where they can.

The court will not make a summary assessment of costs where the receiving party is:[4]

• an assisted person or a **public-funded** person

• a **child** or a **patient** within the meaning of Part 21, unless her/his solicitor has waived the right to further costs.

However, there is nothing to prevent the courts making a summary assessment of costs if these people are the paying party.[5]

When it is likely that there will be summary assessment at a hearing, the parties and their legal representatives are under a duty to assist the court.[6] The advocate should come prepared to argue that the costs incurred are reasonable. A written statement should be prepared showing the costs to be claimed; this is known as a statement of costs. The following should be shown separately:[7]

• the number of hours to be claimed

• the hourly rate to be claimed

• the grade of the fee earner (the different levels of fee earner are suggested by the Supreme Court Costs Office[8])

• the amount and nature of any disbursement to be claimed except for counsel's fee for appearing at the hearing

• the solicitor's costs for attending or appearing at the hearing

• counsel's fees in respect of the hearing

• VAT on these amounts.

Form N260 contains all of the above and should be used where possible or, at the very least, be closely followed.[9] The statement of

4 CPR PD 44 paras 13.9 & 13.11(1)
5 CPR PD 44 paras 13.10 & 13.11(2)
6 CPR PD 44 para 13.5(1)
7 CPR PD 44 para 13.5(2)

8 guidance from the Supreme Court Costs Office is available on www.courtservice.gov.uk
9 CPR PD 44 para 13.5(3)

costs should be filed at court and served on the potential paying party as soon as possible and, at any rate, at least 24 hours before the date fixed for the hearing.[10]

Detailed assessment

A detailed assessment is carried out when a costs officer, who will be a **district judge** in the county court, assesses the costs to be paid at the conclusion of the proceedings. Part 47 of the CPR outlines the procedure for detailed assessment. A costs officer has all the powers of the court when making a detailed assessment (and therefore can decide if costs are unreasonable, etc.), but s/he cannot make:

CPR 47.3(1)

• a wasted costs order (see page 196)

• an order in relation to misconduct

• an order specifying a sanction for delay in commencing detailed assessment proceedings

• an order dealing with an objection to a detailed assessment by an authorised court officer.

However, both the court and the Legal Services Commission have the power to reduce costs where there has been a delay in commencing detailed assessment proceedings.[11]

Detailed assessment proceedings take place in the court that was dealing with the case when the judgment or order was made.[12] Proceedings are started by the receiving party serving on the paying party and all other relevant persons:[13]

• a notice of commencement on Form N252

• a copy of the bill of costs (this is a breakdown of all the legal costs incurred and is usually compiled by a costs draftsman)

• copies of any counsel's fee notes

• copies of any experts' bills to be claimed

• written evidence of any disbursement over £250 which is to be claimed

• a statement giving the names and addresses of other persons that are to be sent the notice of commencement.

This procedure also applies where a party receiving **public funding** is awarded costs. The other party will pay the assisted party's legal costs and the rates charged will be inter partes rates. The assisted party will go through detailed assessment as above. If the paying party fails to pay, the assisted party's legal representative can make a claim for

10 CPR PD 44 para 13.5(4)
11 under reg 10 of The Civil Legal Aid (General) (Amendment) Regulations 2000 and CPR 44.14 respectively
12 CPR PD 47 para 31.1(1)
13 CPR PD 47 para 32.3

payment from the LSC as below. The LSC will then pursue the paying party for the costs.

Where costs are to be paid out of **public funds,** the request for detailed assessment is made on Form N258A and sent to the court rather than the other party. The court will check the reasonableness of the claim before the LSC pays the money out of public funds. In addition to the above, the following must be provided:

• copies of all the orders made in relation to costs

• all civil legal aid and CLS certificates and amendments to them; notice of discharge or revocation and specific legal aid authorities.

CPR 47.8(4)

In public-funded cases, the costs rules apply as if the solicitor to whom the costs are payable is the receiving party and the LSC is the paying party.

The proceedings must be started within the following timescale as specified by CPR 47.7:

Source of right to detailed assessment	Time by which detailed assessment proceedings must be commenced
Judgment, direction, order, award or other determination	Three months after the date of the judgment, etc. Where detailed assessment is **stayed** pending an appeal, three months after the date of the order lifting the stay
Discontinuance under Part 38 (see paragraph 5.4)	Three months after the date of service of notice of discontinuance under CPR 38.3; or three months after the date of the dismissal of application to set the notice of discontinuance aside under CPR 38.4
Acceptance of an offer to settle or a payment into court under Part 36 (see paragraph 5.5)	Three months after the date when the right to costs arose

The rules are slightly different for public-funded cases and, in some cases, the costs will be assessed by the LSC. Regulation 105 of The

Civil Legal Aid (General) Regulations 1989, as amended by regulation 10 of The Civil Legal Aid (General) (Amendment) Regulations 2000, contains the rules for these cases. They are looked at below.

The LSC must assess costs where:

• proceedings have not been issued

• proceedings have been issued and the total amount of the claim, including all disbursements but excluding VAT, is £500 or less.

The LSC may assess costs where proceedings have been issued and the total amount of the claim is £1,000 or less. For claims over £1,000, the court must assess the costs. Proceedings for detailed assessment must be started within the timescales set by CPR 47.7 (see page 192).

Where the LSC is assessing costs, it must receive CLSCLAIM1 either within the timescales set by CPR 47.7 or within three months of the revocation or discharge of the funding certificate.

In cases where the court is assessing costs, if proceedings are not commenced within the above times, the paying party can apply for an order requiring the receiving party to commence proceedings. The court will specify the time by which they must be commenced. The court can also direct that part of all of the costs to which the receiving party would be entitled are disallowed unless the proceedings are commenced within the specified time.

If the receiving party starts proceedings after the period specified in CPR 47.7 and the paying party has not made an application above, then the court has the power to disallow all or part of the interest otherwise payable to the receiving party. No other sanctions can be imposed except those in relation to misconduct.

The paying party has 21 days to serve points of dispute on all parties to the detailed assessment proceedings. If this is not done, s/he will not be heard further in the proceedings unless the court gives permission. Additionally, the receiving party may file a request for a default costs certificate.

If the points of dispute are served, the paying party must file a request for a detailed assessment hearing within three months of the expiry of the period for starting detailed assessment proceedings as above. This means the request must be filed within six months after the order giving the right to detailed assessment.

Once a request for detailed assessment has been served, the court will set a date for a hearing to take place. Generally, the **legal representatives** will attend this hearing to make representations on what costs should

CPR 47.8(1)

CPR 47.8(2)

CPR 47.8(3)

CPR 47.9(1)-(2)

CPR 47.9(3)
CPR 47.9(4)

CPR 47.14(1)-(2)

be allowed. Parties are also entitled to attend the hearing and make representations where they have an interest in the costs to be paid. This will be relevant where the party will ultimately have to pay the costs.

It should also be noted that parties to the proceedings have a right to have her/his legal representative's bill assessed by the court, attend an assessment hearing and make representations. This will be relevant where the party has paid, or contributed towards, her/his legal representative's costs.

13.5 Third parties and costs orders

The court has a discretion to order a person who is not a party to the proceedings to pay costs.[14] This is particularly helpful, for example, in possession cases where the whole of the arrears are due to delays in the payment of housing benefit. To make a costs order against such a party, s/he must be:

CPR 48.2(1)

• joined as a party to the proceedings for the purposes of costs only

• given a reasonable opportunity to attend a hearing at which the court will decide who is to pay costs.

13.6 Costs orders where there are multiple parties

This is where a claimant is suing two defendants. If s/he is successful against one but loses against the other, the first defendant would normally have to pay the claimant's costs and the claimant would pay the second defendant's costs. However, there are two special types of order that the court can make instead.

Bullock order

The court can order that the claimant pays the successful defendant's costs. Once paid, they can be claimed back as part of the claimant's costs from the unsuccessful defendant.

Sanderson order

The unsuccessful defendant is ordered to pay the successful defendant's costs and the claimant's costs insofar as they relate to the claim against the unsuccessful defendant.

13.7 Counterclaims and set offs

Where the claimant succeeds on her/his claim and the defendant succeeds on her/his counterclaim – or both parties fail on their

14 section 51 of the Supreme Court Act 1981

respective claim and counterclaim – the court may order that the two awards of costs are set off against each other. The party entitled to the higher award will receive the balance.

If a party is successful on both the claim and the counterclaim, general rules provide that the other party will pay her/his costs.

13.8 Small claims track

CPR 27.14(2)

Costs in the small claims track are usually limited to the costs of issuing the claim. This will be a fixed amount specified in CPR 45. However, if a party has behaved unreasonably, for example, in making unnecessary applications or refusing to co-operate, the court could order that party to pay the other party's costs.

CPR 27.14(3)

The court can also order a party to pay:

• court fees paid by another party

• travelling expenses and expenses arising out of staying away from home incurred by a party or witnesses required to attend a hearing

• loss of earnings by a party or witnesses due to attending a hearing; this is limited to £50 per day for each person[15]

• a maximum of £200 for the fees of each expert.[16]

13.9 Fixed costs

CPR 45.1

The fixed costs which are allowed are set out in CPR 45. In some circumstances, a party is entitled to fixed costs without any court order for costs being made. Fixed costs apply when the claim is for a specified sum of money that exceeds £25 and one of the following applies:

• **default judgment** is obtained under CPR 12.4(1)

• judgment on admission is obtained under CPR 14.4(3)

• judgment on admission on part of the claim is obtained under CPR 14.5(6)

• **summary judgment** is given under Part 24 of the CPR

• the court has made an order to **strike out** a defence under CPR 3.4(2)(a) as disclosing no reasonable grounds for defending the claim

• the full amount of the money claimed is paid within 14 days of service of the claim, or the claimant accepts an offer of payment that has been made within 14 days of service of the claim, under CPR 45.3

---

15 CPR PD 27 para 7.3(1)   16 CPR PD 27 para 7.3(2)

• the only claim is a claim where the court gave a fixed date for the hearing when it issued the claim and judgment is given for the delivery of goods.

13.10 Fast track trial costs

CPR 46.2(1)

There are set amounts that an advocate can claim as costs for preparing for and appearing at the trial of a fast track trial.

Value of the claim	Amount of fast track trial costs which the court may award
Up to £3,000	£350
Between £3,000 and £10,000	£500
More than £10,000	£750

CPR 46.2(2)(b)

CPR 46.3(2)

The court can award more or less than this amount if it decides not to award any fast track trial costs. The court can also award an additional £250 in respect of a party's **legal representative** attending the trial to assist the advocate if it considers that this attendance was necessary.

CPR 46.4(1)

see CPR 46.4(3)

Where there is more than one claimant or defendant, and the same advocate is acting for more than one party, the court will only make one award in respect of fast track trial costs payable to that advocate. The parties for whom the advocate is acting are jointly entitled to any fast track trial costs awarded by the court. However, if each claimant has a separate claim against the defendant, the claimants' advocate may be allowed an increased award.

13.11 Wasted costs orders

Costs are wasted if they were incurred:[17]

• as a result of any improper, unreasonable or negligent act or omission by a **legal representative**, or

• even if the costs were incurred before this act or omission, the court still considers it unreasonable to expect the party to pay them in light of the act or omission.

The court can order that these costs be disallowed or be paid by the legal representative.[18] In order to decide whether a wasted costs order should be made, the court must apply a three-stage test:[19]

1. Has the legal representative acted improperly, unreasonably or negligently?

17 section 51(7) of the Supreme Court Act 1981
18 CPR 48.7(1), section 51(6) of the Supreme Court 1981
19 Ridehalgh v Horsefield (1994) Ch 205 and confirmed in CPR PD 48 para 53.4

2. If so, did such conduct cause the applicant to incur unnecessary costs?

3. If so, is it just to order the legal representative to compensate the other party for the whole or part of the relevant costs?

"Improper" covers conduct that would lead to a serious professional penalty such as striking off or suspension from practice. It also includes conduct that would be considered improper by the consensus of professional opinion.

"Unreasonable" conduct is that which is vexatious or is designed to harass the other side rather than advance the case. This is regardless of whether the legal representative knowingly acted in this manner.

"Negligent" is not given a technical meaning and refers to failing to act with the competence reasonably expected of ordinary members of the legal profession.

Applying for wasted costs orders

An application is made in the usual way using Form N244 (see paragraph 9.1 for general information about applications). The court deals with the application in two stages:[20]

1. the applicant submits all the evidence which is likely to result in the making of a wasted costs order and shows that the wasted costs proceedings are justified in spite of the costs involved

2. the court gives the legal representative the opportunity of presenting her/his reasons why a wasted costs order should not be made.

In practice it is usually after some omission or negligence has come to light at an actual hearing that the possibility of a wasted costs order is raised. For example, a late application by one party to adjourn when the other party attends court and is prepared to go ahead. As the court can make an order of its own initiative, it is often enough to ask the court orally to issue a notice to show a reason, or reasons, why a party or legal representative should not bear the costs wasted by her/his negligence.

The issue of a wasted costs order would usually be raised at some abortive hearing, or could be applied for if a party is maintaining that the proceedings are an abuse of process or should be struck out for some reason. It would rarely arise that a party just decided to make an interim application for an order without it being connected to a particular hearing or application.

---

20 CPR PD 48 para 53.6

If a party is making an application for a wasted costs order on Form N244 it could be made in conjunction with an application for a claim/defence to be **struck out,** with a witness statement exhibiting all of the relevant evidence. It would be for the party against whom the wasted costs order is directed to show why s/he should not pay the costs.

13.12 Litigant in person

The court may order that any other person pay the **litigant in person's** costs. If the litigant in person can show s/he has suffered financial loss (effectively, loss of earnings) in preparing for and attending the hearing, the amount allowed must not exceed two-thirds of the amount
CPR 48.6(2)   that would have been allowed if s/he had been legally represented. The two-thirds limitation relates to two-thirds of the overall costs that a hypothetical competent solicitor would have been entitled to charge.

CPR 48.6(3)   Allowable costs to the litigant in person are:

• such costs that would have been allowed if the work had been done or the **disbursements** incurred by a legal representative on her/his behalf

• payments reasonably made by her/him for legal services relating to the conduct of the proceedings

• the cost of expert assistance (eg. from a barrister or a law costs draftsman) with the assessment of her/his claim for costs.

If the litigant in person cannot show financial loss, then s/he will be entitled to a standard hourly rate[21] in respect of the time spent reasonably doing the work.[22]

13.13 Costs orders where a party receives public funding

Where a party is unable to afford legal advice and representation, s/he may be entitled to **public funding**. Being eligible for funding will depend on the party's financial situation and the merits of her/his case. The party's **legal representative** will make an application for funding on the party's behalf to the LSC. If the application is accepted, the LSC will pay the legal representative's fees on behalf of the party. There are various considerations to take into account when one or more of the parties receives public funding to assist her/him with her/his legal costs.

Where a party is receiving public funding, s/he is liable to pay the legal costs incurred in her/his case under the CLS Public Funding Certificate.[23] This liability can be discharged in three ways:

21 this is £9.25 per hour
22 CPR 48.6(4) & CPR PD 48 para 52.4
23 section 10(7) of the Access to Justice Act 1999;
this is similar to section 16(6) of the Legal Aid Act 1988 which applied to cases funded by the Legal Aid Board (now the Legal Services Commission)

1. The party pays contributions to the LSC. This will happen where the party's income is not low enough to receive full funding under the means tests applied by the LSC, but is low enough to receive a limited amount of funding from the LSC.

2. An award of costs is made in favour of the assisted party (see below).

3. It is taken from any property recovered or preserved as a result of the proceedings. This is known as the statutory charge.

The statutory charge

Legal representatives applying for public funding on behalf of their clients must make them aware of the statutory charge. Failure to do so could result in a complaint about them or even affect the grant of LSC franchises.

Property recovered or preserved

Property is recovered or preserved if it has been at issue in the proceedings. If a claim is successful, the claimant will have recovered the property. If the claim fails, the defendant will have preserved the property.[24] "Property" includes money, so that, if damages are awarded to the assisted party, these should be paid to the LSC to cover the legal costs paid out of the fund on the assisted party's behalf. For example, Mr Wilkins, who receives legal funding, is awarded damages of £10,000. His legal costs amount to £2,000. He would have to pay £2,000 to the LSC and would be left with £8,000.

Where damages are awarded to a party, s/he will have been successful so the court will probably order the other party to pay the costs of the assisted party. However, even where costs are recovered, these usually do not cover all of the costs which the solicitor can claim from the LSC. For example, correspondence to and from the LSC and time spent filling in LSC forms will not be paid by the other party. Additionally, the court may accept that a solicitor is entitled to be paid for excessive amounts of time spent with a client who is particularly demanding or has special needs, but limit the amount which the unsuccessful party has to pay. If the assisted party's legal representative makes a claim to the LSC for these costs, there will be a shortfall in the costs recovered from the paying party. The statutory charge will apply to the shortfall.

The statutory charge is relevant to mortgage possession proceedings where an assisted party commonly preserves property. The charge arises[25] unless the defendant is awarded costs that are recovered; in which case a claim to the CLS public fund is not necessary. The same applies in many matrimonial cases where one party preserves the matrimonial

24 Hanlon v The Law Society (1980) 2 All ER 199, HL   25 Parkes v Legal Aid Board (1996) 4 All ER 271, CA

home. In these cases, the LSC is entitled to register a charge on the property in its favour. In matrimonial cases, the first £3,000 of property recovered is exempt from the statutory charge.[26]

The enforcement of the charge can be deferred where the property is the home of the assisted person or her/his dependants.[27] In cases of deferment, the LSC generally agrees not to enforce the charge until, for example, the property is sold.

Property is not preserved in possession proceedings relating to rented accommodation.

The unsuccessful party receives public funding

Where the assisted party is unsuccessful, s/he will usually be ordered to pay the costs of the unassisted party. However, the court might limit the amount of costs to pay and delay payments (see below). This is known as "costs protection".[28] Costs protection only applies if a party is in receipt of legal representation. Cases being funded by way of **help at court** or litigation support will not receive costs protection. If a party was receiving legal help and then later receives legal representation, s/he will receive costs protection throughout the time s/he receives both forms of funding.[29] Where a party receives legal representation later on in her/his case (this may be due to a change in financial circumstances), costs protection will only apply during the time that s/he is actually in receipt of funding by way of legal representation.

Legal representatives should be aware that costs protection only applies in limited circumstances. Many advice centres have been granted non-solicitor franchises. Costs protection does not apply to cases funded under these schemes.

When the court orders an assisted party to pay costs, section 11 of the Access to Justice Act 1999[30] limits costs that an assisted person can be made to pay to a reasonable amount taking into account the financial resources of both parties and their conduct during the case. The court can order that the assisted party pay a proportion of the successful party's costs, or even order that the costs are paid by instalments.

In addition to costs protection, where the court decides that the assisted party should pay the unassisted successful party's costs, it used to have the power to make a costs order postponing the date when the costs order was to be enforced. This would happen where the assisted party did not have the means to pay the costs at the date of the trial but might have acquired some funds in the future, eg. by winning the lottery. In this case, the court used to award the successful party her/his costs by adding words such as: 'not to go to detailed

26 see para 1D-023 of the Legal Services Commission Manual for further details
27 see para 1D-030 of the Legal Services Commission Manual for further details
28 covered by the Community Legal Service (Costs Protection) Regulations 2000 (SI 2000 No.824)
29 regs 3(1)&(2) of the Community Legal Service (Costs Protection) Regulations 2000 (SI 2000 No.824)
30 section 11(1)&(2) of the Access to Justice Act 1999; this is very similar to section 17 of the Legal Aid Act 1988

assessment without leave of the court'. Following the case of *R v Secretary of State for the Home Department ex parte Gunn and others*,[31] it appears that the courts no longer have the power to make this kind of order. The courts will have to order the assisted party to pay costs without postponing enforcement of the order. The assisted party, however, will still have costs protection as above.

The court can also order that the costs of the successful unassisted party are to be paid by the LSC.[32] This will happen only if *all* of the following apply:

- the assisted party has been ordered to pay the successful party's costs under section 11 of the Access to Justice Act 1999 (see page 200), and the amount that the assisted party is to pay does not cover all the costs of the successful party

- within three months of the section 11 costs order being made, the successful party makes a request for a hearing to determine the costs payable to her/him[33]

- the successful party is the defendant in the proceedings and will suffer severe financial hardship unless the order is made

- the court is satisfied that it is just and equitable in the circumstances to pay the costs out of **public funds**.

The successful party receives public funding

When costs are awarded to the party receiving public funding, these are paid to the party's **legal representative**. In such cases, the solicitor is entitled to charge the rates suggested by the Supreme Court Taxing Office (see above), and is not limited to claiming the amounts s/he would have been paid by the LSC.[34] S/he would be treated as if s/he were representing a private client. If these costs are recovered from the unsuccessful party, there will sometimes be no need for the assisted party's solicitor to make a claim for payment to the LSC.

Both parties receive public funding

When both parties are receiving public funding, generally the court will order that:

- there be 'no order as to costs'; this means that each party will bear their own costs and, effectively, that the LSC will pay the costs, or

- the successful party is awarded her/his costs but the order is 'not to be enforced without the leave of the court'.

The court will usually order the latter.

31 R v Secretary of State for the Home Department ex parte Gunn and others, CA, 14 June 2001
32 reg 5 of the Community Legal Service (Costs Protection) Regulations 2000 (SI 2000 No.824)
33 reg 10(2) of the Community Legal Service (Costs Regulations 2000 (SI 2000 No.441)
34 reg 107B of the Civil Legal Aid (General) Regulations and reg 4(4) of the Legal Aid in Civil Proceedings (Remuneration) Regulations

13.14 Conditional fee arrangements

This book does not cover conditional fee arrangements in full and anyone wishing to enter into them should check the rules that apply to them. The right to enter into conditional fee arrangements is given by section 58 of the Courts and Legal Services Act 1990.

Essentially, under a conditional fee arrangement, a party would not have to pay fees to her/his legal representative if s/he lost the case. However, if s/he was successful, s/he would have to pay the legal representative's fees plus a success fee out of the damages recovered. The party and the legal representative will have agreed the success fee before the case is taken on. This can be anything up to 100 per cent of the costs that the legal representative would have otherwise normally charged. The costs normally charged are known as the "base" costs. The success fee is known as the "percentage increase".

Although a party will not have to pay fees to the legal representatives if s/he loses, s/he will still probably be ordered to pay the other party's costs under the normal costs rules. There are insurance companies set up to cover this eventuality. A party should be advised to take out insurance.

Where a party wins and is awarded her/his costs, the other party may be ordered to pay the base costs of the winning party plus the percentage increase and insurance premium.[35]

The winning party can apply to have the costs charged by her/his legal representative and the percentage increase assessed by the court. The court has the power to reduce the percentage increase where it appears to be disproportionate, considering all the factors as they reasonably appeared to the legal representative when the conditional fee agreement was entered into.

CPR 48.9

35 Callery v Gray (2001) Legal Action, June 2001

14

Possession claims

Since 15 October 2001 virtually all new possession claims have been dealt with in accordance with the specialist procedure brought in by Part 55 of the CPR.

CPR 55.1(a)

Before the introduction of Part 55, possession claims sat uneasily within the CPR. The practice of fixing a date for the hearing at the time the claim was issued – the "fixed date action procedure" – meant that the Part 7 procedure was inappropriate. For this reason, before 15 October 2001, possession claims were included within those specialist proceedings assigned to the Part 8 procedure. However, the Part 8 procedure is primarily designed to deal with claims where there is no substantial dispute on the facts, which is rarely the case where possession claims are defended. To this extent Part 55 is welcome in that it provides a framework for possession claims.

This chapter outlines the procedure to be used for possession claims and the various options open to the claimant and the defendant after a possession order has been made. In addition, Case Study 3 provides examples of a possession action in practice.

14.1 Definitions

Before proceeding further, a few definitions should assist the reader in interpreting the Part 55 rules:

CPR 55.1

- "possession claim" means a claim for the recovery of possession of land (including buildings or parts of buildings)

- "possession claim against trespassers" refers to a claim against persons who either entered or remained on land without the permission of the person entitled to possession of the land. It does not include a claim against either tenants or sub-tenants, whether or not the tenancy or sub-tenancy has come to an end at **common law**, eg. by notice to quit

- "mortgage" includes a legal or equitable mortgage and a legal or equitable charge.

It is clear that the definition of a possession claim against trespassers does not include a claim against a sub-tenant, whether or not the sub-tenancy was lawfully granted. This reverses the position under the old rules for summary possession proceedings which could be brought against unlawful sub-tenants.[1]

---

[1] CCR Order 24 rule 1; RSC Order 113 rule 1; confirmed in Moore Properties (Ilford) Ltd v McKeon (1977), WLR 1278; 1 All ER 262

However, "trespassers" does include former licensees, for example where a notice to quit or reasonable notice, as the case may be, has been given.

14.2 When does Part 55 apply?

CPR 55.2

Part 55 applies to any of the following types of claim issued after 15 October 2001:

- a possession claim brought by a landlord (or former landlord), a licensor or a mortgagee
- a possession claim against trespassers
- a claim by a tenant seeking relief from forfeiture.

Part 55 and Order 24 proceedings

Many practitioners will recall Order 24 of the County Court Rules 1981, which provided a quicker and easier procedure for seeking possession against trespassers and former licensees. Part 55 applies to actions against these groups of occupier and Order 24 has largely been replaced by broadly equivalent provisions within Part 55. However, where possession proceedings are brought against trespassers and an interim possession order under the Criminal Justice and Public Order Act 1994 is sought, Part 55 does not apply. Advisers should consult the rarely used Part II of Order 24 for details of the procedure adopted for such cases.

14.3 Section I of Part 55 – general rules

Part 55 is divided into two sections. Section I provides general rules relating to possession claims while section II provides a different procedure to be adopted for accelerated possession claims. This part of the chapter examines the general rules.

Commencing a possession claim

CPR 55.3

Claims should be commenced in the county court for the district in which the land is situated, unless legislation provides otherwise or the circumstances of the case justify starting the claim in the High Court. The Practice Direction provides that commencing a claim in the High Court may be justified if one of the following apply:[2]

- complicated disputes of facts are involved
- there are important points of law
- the claim is against trespassers and there is 'a substantial risk of public disturbance or of serious harm to persons or property which properly require immediate determination'.

---

2 CPR PD 55 para 1.3

Although the value of the property and amount of financial claim may also be relevant circumstances, they will not usually be sufficient factors in themselves.[3]

CPR 55.3(2)
If a possession claim is brought in the High Court, the claimant should file a certificate verified by a **statement of truth**, giving reasons for starting the claim there.

Claimants should be reasonably certain that the claim is appropriate for bringing in the High Court, as the court may decide that it should have been brought in the county court and **strike out** the claim. Alternatively, the court may transfer the claim and disallow any claim for the costs of commencing the claim in the High Court.[4]

The claim form

A possession claim is commenced by filing a claim form in the prescribed form at the appropriate court. New claim forms are prescribed and these must be used by the claimant.[5] The forms are similar to those previously used and are:

- N5 – general claim form for possession

- N5A – claim form for relief from forfeiture.

See page 315 for an example of a completed Form N5.

CPR 16.2 & 22.1
As for other claims, the claim form must contain the information required by Part 16 and must be verified by a statement of truth (see page 23).

CPR 55.3(4)
If the claim is brought against trespassers, then the claimant should include the names of any of the defendants s/he can identify, as well as "persons unknown" where the names of any of the defendants are not known.

Particulars of claims

CPR 55.4
As before, the particulars of claim must be filed and served with the claim form. A number of revised forms are provided. These are tailored to the particular type of possession claim and are:

- N119 – claims in respect of rented residential property

- N120 – claims in respect of mortgaged residential property

- N121 – claims against trespassers.

Although the claimant is not required to use one of these forms, the particulars must include the detailed information outlined below. As the questions on the forms correspond with the content required, it is advisable to use the standard forms.

---

3   CPR PD 55 para 1.4
4   CPR PD 55 para 1.2

5   CPR PD 55 para 1.5

CPR 16.4

The general content required for particulars of claim, contained in Part 16 and outlined on page 25, apply equally to possession claims. There is, however, additional prescribed information which must be included depending on the type of possession claim.

GENERAL REQUIREMENTS

The particulars of claim for all possession claims must:[6]

- identify the land to which the claims relates, ie. in most cases, the full address for the property
- indicate whether the claim relates to residential property
- specify the ground on which possession is sought
- give full details about any tenancy or mortgage agreement
- provide details of all those occupiers known by the claimant to be in possession of the property.

RESIDENTIAL PROPERTY LET ON A TENANCY

Where a possession action is brought against tenants and the claim includes a claim for non-payment of rent, the particulars of claim must also set out:[7]

- the amount of rent arrears at the date the claim is issued
- a schedule of the rent due and paid, with dates of payments and a running total of arrears
- the daily rate of rent and any interest
- previous steps, if any, taken to recover rent arrears, eg. visits, letters, with full details of any court proceedings
- relevant information about the defendant's circumstances, in particular details of receipt of any social security benefits and whether direct payments from benefit are made to the claimant.[8]

If the claimant has knowledge of any person (including a mortgagee) entitled to claim relief against forfeiture as an underlessee,[9] the particulars of claim must also include the name and address of that person and a copy of the particulars must be filed at court for service on her/him.[10]

LAND SUBJECT TO A MORTGAGE

For possession claims brought by a mortgagee, the particulars of claim must also state a number of matters which are set out below.[11]

1. Details of the mortgage account. This includes:

---

6 CPR PD 55 para 2.1
7 CPR PD 55 para 2.2-2.3
8 ie. those made under the Social Security Contributions and Benefits Act 1992
9 under section 146(4) of the Law of Property Act 1925,

or in accordance with section 38 of the Supreme Court Act 1981 or section 138(9C) of the County Courts Act 1984
10 CPR PD 55 para 2.4
11 CPR PD 55 para 2.5

- the amount of the advance, any periodic repayment and payment of interest required to be made

- taking into account adjustment for early settlement, the amount required to be paid to redeem the mortgage as at a stated date, which must be not more than 14 days after the claim is started, and the amount of solicitor's costs and administration charges that are also payable

- if the loan secured by the mortgage is a regulated consumer credit agreement, the total amount outstanding under the terms of the mortgage agreement

- the rate of interest payable at the commencement of the mortgage, immediately before accrual of any arrears of periodic payments and at the commencement of the proceedings.

2. Relevant information about the defendant's circumstances; in particular, details of any social security benefits and whether direct payments from benefit are made to the claimant.

3. Details of any tenancy between the mortgagor and mortgagee.

4. Previous steps taken by the claimant to recover money secured by the mortgage, and details of any court proceedings.

5. Whether the loan secured by mortgage is a regulated consumer credit agreement and, if so, the date notice was given in accordance with section 76 (notice of intention to recover possession) or section 87 (default notice) of the Consumer Credit Act 1974. If appropriate, details should be included that show the property is not one to which section 141 of the Act applies.

6. Where the claim is brought as the result of a failure to meet periodic payments when due, the particulars must also include:

- a schedule of the dates when the arrears arose, all amounts due and paid, with dates of payments and a running total of arrears

- details of any other payments required to be made under the terms of the mortgage, eg. insurance premiums, default interest, legal costs, penalties and administrative charges

- details of any other sums claimed and whether payments of these are in arrears and whether they are included within any periodic payment.

7. If the claim relates to residential property, the particulars must state whether any of the following have been registered:

- a class F land charge under section 2(7) of the Matrimonial Homes Act 1967

- a notice under section 2(8) or 8(3) of the Matrimonial Homes Act 1983
- a notice under section 31(10) of the Family Law Act 1996.

If any of these have been registered, the particulars should state on whose behalf the notice or caution has been registered. If so, the claimant should confirm that the persons on whose behalf the notice or caution was registered has been served with notice of the claim.

POSSESSION CLAIM AGAINST TRESPASSERS

The particulars of claim must state the claimant's interest in land or other basis for the claim, together with the circumstances in which the property has been occupied without licence or consent.[12]

Defective particulars of claim

If the claimant fails to provide the appropriate information in the particulars, this is not automatically fatal to the claim. The court has the discretion to rectify the matter, or allow the claimant to amend the particulars of claim, and thus allow the case to proceed.[13] Much will depend on the extent of the defects and whether injustice would be caused to the defendant, having regard to the overriding objective.[14] A serious failure to comply may result in the claim being struck out (see page 74).

Issue of claim and hearing date

On issuing the claim the court will fix a date for the hearing. For possession claims, other than those against trespassers, the hearing date will be held not less than 28 days, and normally not more than eight weeks, from the date of issue.

CPR 55.5 (3)(a)

There is no standard period within which claims against trespassers will be heard. As before, the tendency will be to list such claims for hearing at an early date. This is reflected by the reduced time limits for service (see below).

Service of claim

The methods of service and dates of deemed service are the same as those for other claims (see page 30), with the exception that there are special rules for claims against unknown trespassers (see below).[15]

This should not be confused with service of the appropriate notice to quit or notice seeking possession, where other rules as to service apply.

CLAIM AGAINST TRESPASSERS

In the case of residential property, the defendant must be served with

---

12 CPR PD 55 para 2.6
13 ie. under its powers in CPR 3.10, 3.1 or 17.1
14 see Hannigan v Hannigan [2000] 2 FCR 650, CA, in which Brooke LJ refused to strike out a claim brought using the wrong form where the defendant was aware of the error and striking out would be 'wholly disproportionate'
15 see generally CPR Part 6

CPR 55.5(2)

the claim form, particulars of claims and any **witness statements** not less than five days before the hearing date. For other land the period is not less than two days before the date of the hearing.

CPR 55.6

Where the claim is issued against "persons unknown", the possession documents must be served on those persons in one of the following ways:

- by attaching copies of the documents to the main door or other part of the land, so that they are clearly visible; and, if practicable, inserting copies of the documents in a sealed transparent envelope addressed to "the occupiers" through the letter box

- by placing stakes in the land, which are clearly visible, and attaching to each stake copies of the documents in a sealed envelope addressed to "the occupiers".

ALL OTHER POSSESSION CLAIMS

CPR 55.5(3)(c)

The defendant must be served with the claim form and the particulars of claim not less than 21 days before the hearing date. In addition any **witness statements** the claimant wishes to rely on must be filed and served at least two days before the hearing.

CPR 6.3

CPR 6.7

For claims brought for possession of residential property, the claim form and particulars will generally be served by the court by first-class post (see page 31). They are deemed to have been served on the second day after posting (see page 30 for details of deemed service and calculation of time).

MORTGAGE POSSESSION CLAIMS – SPECIAL RULE

CPR 55.10

In the situation of mortgage possession claims, the claimant must send a notice addressed to "the occupiers" which gives details of the hearing not less than 14 days before the hearing. S/he is also required to produce a certificate of service of this notice at the hearing. This provision gives an opportunity for any other occupier to attend court to be joined as a party and, if appropriate, to provide a defence to the proceedings, eg. a spouse who is not the borrower, or sub-tenants of the mortgagor.

VARIATION OF THE TIME LIMITS

The court, in exercise of its case management powers in CPR 3.1, may extend or shorten the time limits for listing the hearing and for service of the possession documents on the defendant (see page 73). The Practice Direction provides that the court should consider exercising this power where the defendant or person for whom s/he is responsible has:[16]

16 CPR PD 55 paras 3.1-3.3

- assaulted or threatened to assault the claimant, member of claimant's staff or another resident in the locality, or there are reasonable grounds for fearing such an assault (eg. knowledge of violence perpetrated by the defendant in the past), or

- caused or threatened to cause serious damage to the property or that of another resident in the locality.

Responding to possession claims

The unique nature of possession claims is recognised further in Part 55 with significant departures from the normal rules governing the action which a defendant should take in response to the claim.

In addition to the claim itself, the defendant should be sent the following forms:

- N7 or N7A – notes for the defendant

- N11R (rented residential property) or N11M (mortgaged residential property) – these replace the "reply forms" used before Part 55 was introduced.

Acknowledgment of service

There is no requirement for the defendant to file an acknowledgement of service when s/he has been served with a claim for possession and particulars of claim.[17]

Defence to possession claims

The rules on filing a defence depend on whether the claim is against trespassers or any other type of occupier.

CLAIMS AGAINST TRESPASSERS

CPR 55.7(2)

Where the possession claim is brought against trespassers the defendant may, but does not have to, file a defence. This reflects the likely short time period between the issue of the claim and the hearing. It will be sufficient for the defendant(s) to turn up on the day of the hearing if they wish to raise a defence (see page 213).

ANY OTHER POSSESSION CLAIM

The defendant is required to file a defence within 14 days of service of the particulars of claim in the manner set out in Part 15 of the CPR, and described in Chapter 4 (see page 43).[18] As there is no provision for filing an acknowledgment of service in response to a Part 55 claim, it is not possible to effectively extend this time limit to 28 days as it is for other claims.

---

17 CPR 55.7(1), which disapplies Part 10 of the CPR in possession claims

18 CPR 55.7(3) & 15.4

The Practice Direction provides that the defence must be in the prescribed form.[19] The defence should contain all the information which s/he wishes the court to consider. This may include outright denials, and/or information in mitigation, and which may be relevant to the question of reasonableness where appropriate.

Advisers will note, however, that the defence form N11R for rented residential premises is largely geared towards rent arrears cases and requires the defendant to submit detailed financial information. The requirement for this information is clearly inappropriate in non-rent arrears cases. Moreover, some cases will require more technical and detailed defences and/or counterclaims to be pleaded.

It is unclear how strictly the courts will interpret the requirement to use the prescribed forms in every case. It is suggested that where a more detailed defence and/or counterclaim is required, then this should be attached to the prescribed form and referred to in the body of the form. Alternatively, an adviser could seek an order under the court's **case management** powers in CPR 3.1 that the defence need not be in the prescribed form.

In any event, the failure to use the prescribed defence form should be viewed in light of the comments made above with regard to defects in the claimant's particulars of claim and the court's powers to allow or remedy such defects under CPR 3.10.

CPR 55.7(3)   If the defendant fails to file any defence, this does not prevent the defendant taking part and defending the claim at the hearing. However, the court may take the failure into account when making an order on costs. For example, the court may award costs against a defendant in respect of a hearing which is adjourned because a defence is raised at the hearing when the defendant failed to file a defence, and gave the claimant no advance warning that s/he intended to raise the matter at the hearing.

CPR 55.7(4)   The claimant is not able to apply for default judgment where no defence is filed by the defendant before the hearing date.

CPR 15.5   Where compliance with the time limit is not possible, advisers should consider trying to agree an extension to the period within which the defence is to be filed (up to 28 days). In any event, the defence should be filed as soon as possible after the 14-day time limit so as to mitigate the consequences of the failure to meet the time limit and to minimise the risk on costs (see Chapter 13).

19 CPR PD 55 para 1.5

The hearing

CPR 55.8(1) At the initial hearing (or any adjourned hearing) the court may:

- make a decision on the claim, or

- give case management directions.

CPR 55.8(2) If the claim is 'genuinely disputed on grounds which appear to be substantial', the court may give **case management directions**, which will include allocating the claim to a track or directions which enable the case to be allocated to track. This does not mean that the court will give directions in every case where a proper defence is raised. Often the court will have sufficient evidence, written or oral, to enable the claim to be disposed of there and then. Other cases will need more detailed consideration; perhaps full legal submissions, an investigation into the position with regard to a housing benefit claim and/or the filing of further evidence.

Advisers will be familiar with the listing of claims in the court's "undefended possession" list. It is not unusual, in busy courts, for as many as 40 to 50 claims to be listed in a morning or an afternoon session, with many claims occupying little more than a few minutes' court time.

Many defendants, in particular tenants of residential property, do not attend the hearing. Of those that do attend, few are legally represented. The perception remains that a large number are deterred from attending by their landlord's assurances that a suspended, and not an outright, possession will be sought. Understandably, few tenants appreciate the fact that even a minor breach of the terms of a suspended order leads to a loss of their tenancies and the rights contained in them.

In every case, however, the claimant has to satisfy the court that a valid notice was served correctly, that the ground(s) for possession are made out and, where applicable, that it is reasonable for the court to make a possession order. However, in the absence of any written or oral evidence from the defendant, the court will not have a full picture of the circumstances of the case.

Allocation

CPR 55.9(1) If the court decides to allocate the claim to track, it will do so having regard to the usual factors (see page 77) and, in addition:

- the amount of any rent or mortgage arrears

- the importance to the defendant of keeping possession

- the importance to the claimant of obtaining vacant possession.

CPR 55.9(2)

The court will not allocate a possession claim to the small claims track unless all the parties agree to this.

If the case is allocated to the small claims track (ie. if the parties agree and the court considers this appropriate), for the purpose of costs the claim is treated as though it was proceeding in the fast track. The costs of the trial will be at the discretion of the judge, but, in any event, a party will not recover more than the amount normally recoverable in a fast track trial in which the value of the claim is up to £3,000. This means that the party will not recover more than £350 for the trial costs.[20]

CPR 27.14

Alternatively, where the parties agree, the court may, when allocating the claim, order that the rule on costs in the small claims track applies (see paragraph 13.8).

CPR 26.6

In practice, the majority of possession claims that are allocated by the court will proceed in the fast track. However, this will not be appropriate if the trial of the matter is likely to last more than one day, when the claim should proceed in the multi-track (see page 85). This is often the situation in nuisance cases where a large number of witnesses may be called to give oral evidence.

After allocation the claim will proceed as any other claim towards final hearing.

Evidence at initial or adjourned hearing

Wherever possible, the parties should include all the matters they seek to rely on in their statement of case.[21]

There is also a specific requirement on a defendant in a mortgage possession claim, where the loan is regulated by Consumer Credit Act 1974, to make an application for a time order under section 129 of the Act in her/his defence, or by an application notice in the proceedings (see page 125).[22]

CPR 55.8(3)

Where a claim has not been allocated or has been allocated to the small claims track then, unless the court orders otherwise, evidence of any fact may be proved in writing. This would allow a landlord to rely on her/his statement of case and any **witness statements** in support. However, if a claim has been allocated to track, or the court orders otherwise, the normal requirement that witnesses attend court and give oral evidence at trial applies.

CPR 32.1

In any event, it is likely that it will be appropriate for the court to hear an update on any developments in the matter since the written evidence has been filed and served, eg. level of rent arrears as at the date of the hearing, and so oral evidence is likely to be given.[23]

---

20 CPR 55.9(3) & 46.2
21 CPR PD 55 para 5.1

22 CPR PD 55 para 7.1
23 CPR PD 55 para 5.2

However, where the maker of a witness statement does not attend the hearing and the defendant disputes evidence that is material to the case, the court will normally adjourn the case so that the maker of the statement can attend and give oral evidence.

In practice, social landlords are likely to file witness statements to prove such matters as the service of notices and the level of arrears. However, there is a risk that the court will adjourn the matter where the maker of the statement does not attend court and the defendant disputes the evidence contained in the witness statement. This could include matters such as the service of an appropriate notice or other matters relevant to the question of whether it is reasonable to make a possession order.

EXAMPLE

Neil, a housing officer for Nirvana Housing Association, files and serves a witness statement in possession proceedings brought against Margaret on the discretionary ground that rent lawfully due has not been paid. In his statement, Neil addresses many of the matters relevant to the question of whether it is reasonable to make a possession order, including details of a conversation he had with Margaret during a visit to her house. He states that Margaret told him that she had 'made a claim for housing benefit ages ago'.

Neil is unable to attend the initial hearing as he is on holiday, and another housing officer attends to represent the association. At the hearing, Margaret denies that she said this to Neil and states that she completed a housing benefit claim form in the presence of Neil. She tells the judge that Neil told her he would 'pass the form to the housing benefit section as soon as I get back'. The judge could adjourn the case to enable Neil to attend court to give oral evidence and be cross-examined. Alternatively, the judge may accept Margaret's evidence and dismiss the claim.

Importantly, the rules pre-empt a familiar scenario encountered where possession proceedings are brought on the grounds of rent arrears when the "true" cause of the arrears is delays in processing benefit claims. Thus, the defendant should also be prepared to give evidence at the hearing, where appropriate, of:[24]

- any outstanding claims for housing benefit or other welfare benefits

- the status of any such claims where a decision has not been made on the claim

- details of any applications made to review or appeal the decision made on the housing benefit or other benefit claim where these have not been concluded.

24 CPR PD 55 para 5.3

The other general rules relating to evidence are contained in Parts 32-35 and are considered in Chapter 8.

The order

If a possession order is made then it will be in one of the following prescribed forms, depending on the nature of the claim and the order made:

- N26 – general order for possession

- N28 – order for possession (rented residential property) (suspended)

- N27 – order for possession (forfeiture).

One further important matter not addressed in the rules is that many orders for possession do not specify on which ground possession is ordered. This has particular relevance in assured tenancy cases. Often the claimant will base the claim on the mandatory ground for possession (ground 8, Schedule 2, Housing Act 1988) as well as the discretionary rent arrears grounds (grounds 10 and 11). If there is no indication of the ground on which the judge made an outright possession order, it is difficult to ascertain whether an application to vary the order to substitute a suspended order can be made.

In *Diab v Countrywide Rentals Ltd,*[25] the High Court emphasised that it was essential for a possession order which has been made on a mandatory ground to indicate this fact on the face of the order. Where this is not indicated on the order, then the court will consider that the possession order was made on uncertain grounds and will have jurisdiction to consider an application to vary the order and reconsider the matter.

If the judge does not make a possession order at all, for example, where the case is adjourned on terms with liberty to restore, or the action is dismissed, the order will be contained in the general form for judgments and Form N24 (see pages 323, 325, 335, 409, and 411 for examples of Form N24).

14.4 After the possession order

This section looks at the various options open to landlords and tenants after a possession order is made. These options will largely depend on whether the court made an outright or a suspended possession order.

An outright, also known as an absolute, possession order requires the defendant to give up possession of the property on a certain date. An absolute order may be made in the following circumstances:

25 Diab v Countrywide Rentals Ltd [2001] *Legal Action* April 2001, ChD

- The defendant has no statutory protection or has only the basic protection given by the Protection from Eviction Act 1977, eg. s/he is an unlawful sub-tenant.

- The claimant is entitled to recover possession against an assured shorthold tenant under section 21 of the Housing Act 1988.

- In the case of assured or Rent Act protected tenants, one or more of the mandatory grounds are made out.[26] In proceedings against assured tenants, the most common of the mandatory grounds encountered is where the court is satisfied that the tenant is more than eight weeks in rent arrears in respect of a weekly tenancy, or two months in respect of a monthly tenancy (ie. Ground 8, Schedule 2 of the Housing Act 1988).

- In the case of assured, Rent Act protected or secure tenants, one of the discretionary grounds is made out and the court considers that:

  – it is reasonable to make the order *or* is satisfied that suitable alternative accommodation is available, depending on the ground made out, or

  – it is reasonable to make the order *and* the court is satisfied that suitable alternative accommodation is available (this will apply where certain grounds are made out), and

  – the court does not exercise its discretion to suspend the possession order.

A suspended possession order does not require the tenant to give up possession on a definite date. The order is invariably suspended on terms, for example that the tenant pays the current rent when due plus a weekly or monthly amount towards the arrears, or refrains from committing certain anti-social behaviour.

In the case of assured and secure tenants, providing the tenant keeps to the terms of the suspended order then the tenancy and the rights attributed to the tenancy subsist. However, a breach by the tenant means that the order takes effect and the tenancy automatically comes to an end. The claimant may enforce the possession order by issue of a warrant of possession (see page 219).

Often the claimant will choose not to enforce the possession order immediately after a breach of the terms of suspension. In the case of former assured and secure tenants, the defendant becomes a "tolerated trespasser".[27]

26 grounds 1-8 of schedule 2 to the Housing Act 1988 (assured tenants); grounds 11 to 20 in Part II, Schedule 15 of the Rent Act 1977 and section 101 of the Rent Act 1977 (overcrowding)

27 Burrows v Brent LBC (1996) 29 HLR 167; 1 WLR 1448; 4 All ER 577, HL; Pemberton v Southwark LBC (2000) 32 HLR 784, CA

Claimant enforcing the possession order

A claimant may seek to enforce the possession order by requesting the court to issue a warrant of possession. This will occur when one of the following situations takes place:

- the tenant fails to comply with an outright possession order requiring her/him to leave the property on a date set by the court

- the tenant breaches a suspended order for possession so that the order comes into effect and the tenancy comes to an end.

The procedure to issue a warrant of possession in the county court is currently set out in Order 26 of the County Court Rules 1981, preserved in Schedule 2 to the CPR. Advisers should note, however, that reform of these rules is anticipated in the near future. This follows the comprehensive review of the enforcement of civil court judgments undertaken by the Lord Chancellor's Department (see paragraph 12.1). Advisers should check the current position with regard to the procedure for enforcement by a warrant of possession.

Normally, the claimant has only to file a request at court in the prescribed form (Form N235), certifying that the land has not been vacated in accordance with the possession order made by the court. It is not necessary for the claimant to give notice of the request to the defendant.[28]

An exception to this will be in cases where the possession order itself provided that no warrant should be issued without the leave of the court, in which case the claimant should apply on notice for permission to enforce the order. Any application should be made in accordance with the Part 23 rules (see Chapter 9).

Other exceptions where permission of the court is required to issue a warrant for possession include:[29]

- Six or more years have elapsed since the possession order was made.

- A change has taken place, by death or otherwise, in the parties entitled to enforce the possession order or those liable to have the possession order enforced against them.

Warrants of possession are executed by court bailiffs. The bailiffs are instructed to deliver a notice of the eviction, Form N54, addressed to all named defendants in the possession action and "any other occupants". Form N54 is a practice form which should specify when the execution will take place and tell the defendant that an application to court can be made to suspend the warrant (see page 220). It is important to note

---

28 Criticism of this aspect of the procedure was expressed by the Court of Appeal in Leicester CC v Aldwinkle (1992) 24 HLR 40, CA

29 CCR Order 26 rule 5 applies to warrants for possession by virtue of Order 26 rule 17(6)

that the instruction to bailiffs to deliver an N54 form does not confer a legal right for the defendant to receive one. It may, however, be a relevant factor in any application for a set aside of the warrant on the grounds that there has been "oppression" in its execution (see page 223).

When a warrant is issued, the claimant is entitled to ask that the defendant's goods be taken to satisfy any outstanding money judgment given with the order for possession, eg. a money judgment for rent arrears.[30] In practice this is rarely sought by claimants.

A warrant of possession is valid for a period of 12 months from the date it is issued, but may be renewed by the court.[31]

When the warrant is executed, the bailiffs may evict anyone they find on the premises including those who were not a party to the original possession proceedings.[32] In practice, it is sometimes possible to negotiate with the bailiffs for time to make an urgent application to the court to be joined as a party and for an application to be made to suspend the warrant. Whether such an application is worthwhile depends on the circumstances of the person concerned.

Defendant applies to set aside the possession order

In certain situations the defendant can apply to have the possession order itself set aside. If an order is set aside then the court may order a rehearing of the case and give appropriate directions. Alternatively, it may deal with the matter there and then and make any of the usual orders on a hearing for possession (see page 217).

Applications to set aside should be made in accordance with the Part 23 rules. This means it needs to be made using Form N244 with appropriate evidence in support, either on the application notice or by a witness statement (see Chapter 9; for an example of Form N244 see Case Study 3, page 329).

CPR 70.6

If the court sets aside the possession order then any outstanding warrant will also be set aside. However, a mere application to set aside a possession order does not mean the warrant is automatically suspended. If the execution of the warrant is due before the hearing of the set aside application, it will be necessary to apply to the court to suspend or stay the warrant.[33]

In any event, it is advisable to include an application to suspend the warrant pending the hearing of the application to set aside the possession order. This will enable the court to suspend the warrant or stay execution of the order on terms pending the hearing. Moreover, if the application to set aside the possession order fails, the warrant can

30 CCR 1981 Order 26 rule 17
31 CCR 1981 Order 26 rule 6
32 see R v Wandsworth County Court ex parte Wandsworth

LBC (1975) 3 All ER 390; 1 WLR 1314
33 CCR 1981 Order 37 rule 8

still be suspended on terms. If an application is not included on the Form N244, it may be made orally at court (see page 124).

A fee is payable; this is £50. If the application is made without notice then the fee is £25.

Failure to attend the trial

CPR 39.3

The most commonly used ground for an application is that the defendant did not attend the hearing when the judgment or order was made against her/him. Such an application can be made even after the possession order has been executed by a warrant of possession.[34]

CPR 39.3(5)

The court will look at three factors when deciding whether to set aside the possession order on this basis, and these should influence the decision as to whether such an application is appropriate. The factors the court will have regard to are that the defendant:

- has acted promptly after finding out that the possession order was made[35]

- had a good reason for not attending the trial, and

- has a reasonable prospect of success at the trial.

Other grounds

The court may set aside an order and direct that a rehearing is held where no error of the court is alleged and the application is made within 14 days of the original hearing.[36] Such applications are rare but may be appropriate where, for example, there has been a failure of service on the defendant.

CPR 3.10

Applications to set aside may also be made if there has been an error of procedure, such as a failure to comply with a rule or practice direction, where the court may make any order to rectify the error.

Applications to stay or suspend the possession order or postpone the date for possession

The courts have wide powers to suspend execution of an order or to postpone the date for possession under statutory provision. Applications should be made in accordance with Part 23 (see Chapter 9) and may be made by each of the following types of occupier:

- secure tenants by virtue of section 85(2) of the Housing Act 1985

- protected and statutory tenants by virtue of section 100(2) of the Rent Act 1977

---

34 Governors of the Peabody Donation Fund v Hay (1987) 19 HLR 145
35 see for example, Tower Hamlets LBC v Abadie

(1990) 22 HLR 264
36 CCR 1981 Order 37 rule 1 preserved by schedule 2 of the CPR

- assured tenants by virtue of section 9(2) of the Housing Act 1988. This does not apply where the possession order was granted on one of the mandatory grounds, including an order made against an assured shorthold tenant under section 21 of the Housing Act 1988.

Advisers should consult the substantive law, and in particular the case law which has arisen in the context of these applications. The powers enable the court to make a number of different orders, which include:

- varying an order to substitute a suspended possession order in place of an outright order (but only where the order was made on a discretionary and not a mandatory order)[37]

- varying the terms on which the original possession order was made, eg. the level of instalments made by the defendant under a suspended order or the date on which the defendant must leave the property

- varying the order so that the date of possession is postponed to a date in the future, such as 28 days from the date of the new hearing. This may have the effect of "reviving" a tenancy that has ended due to the breach of the terms of a suspended possession order.[38]

A fee is payable and is £50 for applications made on notice.

Applications to stay or suspend the warrant before execution

Applications to stay or suspend the warrant of possession are discussed above in the context of making applications to set aside the possession order (see page 220). Indeed such an application may also accompany an application to vary the possession order as stated in the previous section. However, the circumstances may be such that it is not appropriate to apply to set aside or vary the possession order. In these circumstances it is possible to make an application only to stay or suspend the execution of the warrant. This can properly be described as the final chance for a defendant to avoid eviction.

The court has the power to stay or suspend a warrant at any time before the execution of the possession order under the same statutory powers which enable the possession order to be suspended or the date for possession postponed (see the previous page). In addition, section 88 of the County Courts Act 1984 provides:

If at any time it appears to the satisfaction of the court that any party to any proceedings is unable from any cause to pay any sum recovered against him... or any instalment of any such sum, the court may in its discretion, stay any execution issued in the proceedings for such time until it appears that the cause of inability has ceased.

37 Ujima v Smith (2001) Legal Action 21, ChD; Greenwich v Grogan [2001] 33 HLR 140, CA. Although a case decided on an appeal, the principles for substituting a suspended order for an outright order apply

38 Burrows v Brent LBC (1996) 29 HLR 167; 1 WLR 1448; 4 All ER 577, HL and Lambeth v Rogers [2000] 32 HLR 784, CA

Applications should be made in accordance with Part 23 (see Chapter 9) on either Form N244 or Form N245, and supported by evidence. The evidence should be either on the form or by **witness statement.**

A fee of £50 is payable for applications made on notice or £25 for those made without notice. Applications should be made with notice of at least three **clear days.** Where an application is made at a very late stage then the court may abridge time.[39] If it is not possible to give formal notice to the other party, because, for example the warrant is about to be executed, the applicant should consider giving informal notice of the intended application and the time of the hearing; eg. by telephone.

Applications to set aside executed warrants

Once the warrant has been executed, tenants are unable to rely on any of the statutory provisions described in the previous pages which allow the court to stay or suspend the execution of the possession order or postpone the date for possession. Those powers are only available "before the execution of the order".

If appropriate, an application to set aside the possession order may be made. If the court sets aside the possession order then the warrant is also set aside.[40]

Often the circumstances of the case mean that it is not appropriate to apply for a set aside of the possession order. The only other way for an occupier to be reinstated into a property after the eviction is by making an application to set aside the warrant.

If the possession order itself cannot be set aside, a warrant of possession may only be set aside after execution where it was obtained by fraud, or there has been an abuse of process or "oppression" in the execution of the warrant. A detailed discussion of the case law is outside the remit of this book. Examples of "oppression" include where the occupier is deprived of the opportunity to apply to stay the warrant, before it is executed, due to being deterred from doing so by a housing officer.[41]

The "oppression" need not be as a result of the conduct of the claimant; it can include the conduct of a third party, such as the court.[42] However, the conduct itself must be unfair and "oppression" is not established simply because there is an unfair outcome in the case.[43] In *Southwark LBC v Sarfo,*[44] Roch, LJ. stated:

... oppression may be difficult if not impossible to define, but it is not difficult to recognise. It is the insistence by a public authority on its strict rights in circumstances which make that insistence manifestly

39 CPR 23.7(1); the court may abridge time under case management powers in CPR 3.1(2)(a)
40 Governors of the Peabody Donation Fund v Hay (1987) 19 HLR 145
41 see for example Hammersmith and Fulham LBC v Hill [1994] 27 HLR 40 & Lambeth LBC v Hughes [2001] 33 HLR 33, CA
42 Hammersmith and Fulham LBC v Lemeh [2001] 33 HLR 231
43 see for example Jephson Homes Housing Association v Moisejevs [2001] 33 HLR 594
44 Southwark LBC v Sarfo [1999] 32 HLR 602 at 609, CA

unfair. The categories of oppression are not closed because no-one can envisage all the sets of circumstances which could make the execution of a warrant for possession oppressive.

Applications should be made without delay on Form N244 with evidence in support. A fee of £50 is payable for all applications made with notice and £25 for applications made without notice.

Appeals

Although there is a right to bring an appeal against the order made by the judge, advisers should be aware that the courts have been extremely reluctant to disturb the decision of a judge made in exercise of her/his discretion, eg. in assessing the reasonableness of making a possession order. In *Kensington & Chelsea RLBC v Simmonds* in the Court of Appeal, the judge stated that:[45]

I would begin by noting the clearly established principle that this court will only interfere with the exercise of the trial judge's discretion in such a case, if it can be shown to be plainly and utterly wrong.

However, successful appeals are brought on the basis that the judge has made an error of law or has misapplied the law in making an order.

A brief outline of the procedure for bringing appeals is contained in paragraph 11.8.

14.5 Section II of Part 55 – accelerated possession claims

Since 2 October 2000 the accelerated procedure for possession has only been available for use against assured shorthold tenants.[46]

CPR 55.11-55.12

Under Part 55 of the CPR, the procedure may only be used to recover possession where the claim is brought following the expiry of the appropriate period of notice under section 21 of the Housing Act 1988, and the following conditions are met:

- both the tenancy and the agreement for the tenancy were entered into on or after 15 January 1989

- the tenancy is the subject of a written agreement or it is a statutory periodic tenancy which has followed the expiry of a fixed-term written tenancy (under section 5 of the Housing Act 1988)

- the claim is for possession only and no other claim is made, eg. for rent arrears

- the tenancy did not immediately follow a fully assured tenancy

45 Kensington & Chelsea RLBC v Simmonds [1996]; 3 FCR 246, p250, per Simon Brown LJ, case also reported at 29 HLR 507

46 CPR 55.11. CCR Order 49 rule 6 which applied to assured tenancies was revoked by SI 2000 No. 2092

- the tenancy fulfilled the statutory requirements of the Act for the creation of assured shorthold tenancies as at the date of the grant of the tenancy. A tenancy granted before 28 February 1997 is only an assured shorthold if it was initially for a fixed term of not less than six months, there was no power for the landlord to determine the tenancy earlier than six months from the beginning of the tenancy, and a valid section 20 notice was served on the tenant before the tenancy was entered into

- the appropriate notice was given to the tenant in writing in accordance with sections 21(1) or 21(4) of the Housing Act 1988.

Commencing the claim

CPR 55.13

A claim is brought by filing a claim form in the prescribed form (N5B) at court. The form combines a statement of case with the evidence in support of the claim. It must be completed so as to include all the information requested. This includes:

- the claimant's name and address and address for service (if different)

- the defendant's name and address

- the address of the property to which the claim relates

- confirmation that the conditions necessary to use the procedure are met (see above)

- details of the first and most recent written agreement (if applicable); the claimant should also attach these agreements to the claim form

- if appropriate, a copy of any section 20 notice of an assured shorthold, ie. for tenancies entered into before 28 February 1997

- details of the service of the notice requiring possession. Any proof of service, eg. recorded delivery slip, should also be attached to the claim form

- any further evidence in support of the application

- a **statement of truth.**

The claimant may also indicate on the claim form that s/he is content for the judge to postpone the date for possession for up to six weeks without a hearing (see page 226).

CPR 55.13

CPR 6.7

The claim form must be served by the court by first-class post. Service is deemed to be effected on the second day after the day it was posted.

Response by defendant

The defendant is required to file a defence within 14 days of service of the claim form. The defendant should use the prescribed form, which is N11B. This would be essential where either s/he wishes to oppose the claim for possession, or s/he wants the date for possession to be postponed on the grounds of exceptional hardship and in accordance with section 89 of the Housing Act 1980.

CPR 55.14

On receipt of the defence, the court will send a copy of the defence to the claimant and refer the claim and defence to a judge.

CPR 55.15(1)

If the defence has not been filed within 14 days of service of the claim form, the claimant may file a written request for a possession to be considered by a judge. If the defendant files a defence more than 14 days from service of the claim form but prior to a written request by the claimant, then the claim and defence will be referred to a judge.

CPR 55.15(2)

CPR 55.15(3)

Consideration of the claim

The judge considers the claim and any defence and, in the absence of the parties:

CPR 55.16

- makes an order for possession, or

- fixes a date for hearing and gives **case management directions**, or

- **strikes out** the claim where the claim form discloses no reasonable grounds for bringing the claim.

The judge will fix a date for a hearing if s/he is not satisfied that the claim form was served on the defendant or that the claimant is entitled to recover possession under section 21 of the Housing Act 1988.

CPR 55.16

The judge may also fix a date for a hearing where the defendant seeks a postponement of possession under section 89 of the Housing Act 1980. In this situation the judge will still make a possession order requiring the defendant to give up possession, usually on a date up to 14 days after the claim is considered. The date fixed for the hearing must be prior to the date on which possession must be given up, and the judge will direct how much notice is to be given to the parties.

CPR 55.18

CPR 55.18(2)

At the hearing, the judge may find that "exceptional hardship" will be caused to the tenant if s/he is required to leave the property on the date set. In this situation the judge will vary the possession order already made so as to postpone the date for possession. The judge can only delay possession by up to six weeks from the date of the original possession order.[47] Alternatively, the judge may find that the tenant will not suffer "exceptional hardship" and the possession order will take effect as previously ordered.

---

47 section 89(1) of the Housing Act 1980

Application to set aside or vary

The court may set aside or vary a possession order made under the accelerated possession procedure. The court may do this on its own initiative or on the application of a party. In any event, the order may not be varied so as to postpone the date for possession by more than six weeks from the date of the original possession order, and then only where the tenant shows "exceptional circumstances".[48] The order is only likely to be set aside where a procedural defect is shown and

CPR 3.10   subject to the court's powers to rectify any defect in procedure.

48 section 89(1) of the Housing Act 1980

Statutory homelessness appeals

Since 2 May 2000, statutory homelessness appeals under section 204 of the Housing Act 1996 must be brought in accordance with the procedure contained in Part 52 of the CPR. This chapter looks at the rules governing the conduct of a homelessness appeal from commencement to final order. This may be read alongside Case Study 2 which provides an example of a homelessness appeal in precedent form.

15.1 Applying the rules to homelessness appeals

Homelessness and other statutory appeals sit uneasily within Part 52. This is because the rules are predominantly drafted with appeals against decisions of the courts in mind. This is apparent from the wording of the rules throughout, as well as the information requested in the appellant's and the respondent's notices.

As a consequence, some difficulties have been experienced with certain county courts continuing to treat homelessness appeals as claims under either Part 7 or Part 8. One unhelpful aspect of this has been a tendency by some courts to list a **directions hearing.** This can substantially delay the hearing of the appeal, and is usually not necessary or appropriate.

Where such problems arise, advisers should refer the court to Section II of the Practice Direction to Part 52, which applies that part to statutory appeals, albeit with a number of amendments.[1]

15.2 Time limits

The time limit for bringing a homelessness appeal is 21 days from notification of the decision on review. This cannot be varied by agreement between the parties.[2] This is different from the usual time limit for appeals against court decisions, which is 14 days, and the general rule for statutory appeals, which is 28 days.[3]

Due to the changes contained in the Homelessness Act 2002 – which had not been implemented at the time of writing – it will be possible to seek the court's permission to bring a late appeal where good reason can be shown for the failure to bring an appeal in time.[4] This is examined in the later section on permission to appeal (see page 234).

With regard to the time limit, however, it is worth noting that the 21 days does not begin to run until the homeless applicant is actually notified of the review decision. Where, for example, a local authority

---

1 CPR PD 52 paras 17.1-17.2
2 section 204(2) of the Housing Act 1996
3 CPR 52.4(2) which is amended in the case of statutory appeals by PD 52 para 17.3

4 section 204(2A) of the Housing Act 1996, as inserted by paragraph 17, Schedule 1 of the Homelessness Act 2002

sends its decision letter by 2nd class mail, the applicant is not "notified" until receipt, which may be several days later. Many review decision letters indicate that the time limit for appeal is 21 days from the date of the letter. Quite simply this is incorrect. Nevertheless it is advisable to issue the appeal within 21 days of the letter, wherever possible, as it avoids having to prove the date on which the applicant received it.

15.3 Commencing a homelessness appeal

The appeal is commenced by filing the appellant's notice – with copies for the court and the respondent – at the county court.

The procedure adopts the "front loading" approach similar to that for Part 8 claims, and the appellant should file the following documents when s/he files the appellant's notice:[5]

- skeleton argument – this may, however, be filed within 14 days after filing the notice (see page 235)

- copy of the decision being appealed. This is the decision letter on review; or, where the respondent has failed to issue a review decision within the prescribed period, the initial decision on the applicant's homelessness application, ie. the section 184 letter

- any **witness statements** or **affidavits** in support of the appeal

- a bundle of documents in support of the appeal.

A fee is also payable. The courts can be inconsistent about which fee is applicable. The reason for this is that some courts do not consider statutory appeals as "appeals" for the purpose of deciding the fee. It is suggested that statutory appeals should be treated as other appeals but, until this is clarified, it is necessary to check the practice in the county court in which the appeal is to be brought. The court will treat the statutory appeal as one of the following:

- a claim "for something other than money", where the fee payable is £120

- an "appeal", in which case the fee is £100, unless permission to appeal is needed, ie. the appeal is brought outside of the 21-day time limit (see page 234), where the fee will be £150.

Appellant's notice

The appellant is required to complete the notice giving details of the parties, the decision being appealed against and the order sought by the appellant. Advisers will notice that the form is worded as if the

---

5   CPR PD 52 para 5.6

appeal relates to an order of a court and not a decision of a local authority. It is best to adopt a common sense approach to completion of the form and adapt it as required.

An example of a completed Form N161 is provided in Case Study 2 on page 286. The requirements for certain sections are highlighted below.

Grounds for appeal

The grounds for the appeal may be set out in section 7 of the form. However, the lack of adequate space usually means that it is necessary to set out the grounds on a separate document, which should be attached to the main body of the notice.

The grounds for the appeal should be put clearly and succinctly. It is important, however, to include each and every ground on which the appeal is based, as any ground not included cannot be relied upon at the hearing of the case unless the court gives permission.

CPR 52.11(5)

An appeal notice cannot be amended without the permission of the appeal court. If amendments do need to be made, an application will normally be heard at the beginning of the appeal hearing unless this would cause "unnecessary expense or delay". If this is likely to be the case, the appellant should ask the court to list the matter for an application hearing in advance of the final hearing.[5]

Where the proposed amendment to the appeal notice is significant, for example an additional ground of appeal, it is likely that the respondent will also wish to consider amending its notice. There is a danger in waiting until the appeal hearing to make the application as it may be necessary to adjourn the matter to allow the respondent to do this. The court could award a **wasted costs order** if an adjournment is necessary. It is suggested, therefore, that the appellant's advisers should seek to list the matter for an application hearing at the earliest opportunity. In any event, the respondent should be forewarned as soon as possible of the application to amend.

In contrast, amendments to a skeleton argument included on the notice may be made without permission from the court (see page 235).

Time estimate

The appellant is asked in section 4 to provide an estimate of how long the hearing of the appeal may last. Generally, this is likely to be between one half and one full day. If counsel is going to represent the appellant at the hearing and is familiar with the case, perhaps having been instructed to draft the grounds of appeal and the skeleton argument, s/he should be asked to provide an estimate.

5   CPR 52.8 & PD 52 para 5.25

Permission to appeal

Permission to appeal is not required as long as the appeal is brought within 21 days of notification of the decision on review. The reason for this is that the appellant has a right to bring the appeal under section 204(2) of the Housing Act 1996. In section 6, the appellant should tick the box indicating that permission is not necessary. Until the Homelessness Act 2002 is brought into force, an appeal brought outside of the 21-day time limit will not be allowed.

When the Homelessness Act 2002 is implemented, it will be possible to ask the court for permission to bring an appeal after the 21-day time limit. An application for permission to appeal will have to be made and will be granted if the court is satisfied that:[6]

- where permission is sought before the end of the 21-day time limit, the applicant has good reason for being unable to bring the appeal in time, or

- where permission is sought after the 21-day time limit, the applicant had good reason for failing to bring the appeal in time and for any delay in applying for permission.

Where permission is sought after the implementation date, this will be reflected in section 6 of the form. The appellant should outline the "good reasons" for failing to bring an appeal in time, together with the grounds for the appeal itself in section 7 or in a separate document attached to the form.

Alternatively, if it is not possible to file the grounds for appeal at that time, an application for permission to appeal may be brought alone. An application for permission may be made before or after the expiry of the 21-day time limit, but in any event should be brought as soon as practicable.

Other applications

It may be necessary to seek one or more court orders. This depends on the nature of the appeal and the appellant's circumstances. In addition to the quashing of the homelessness decision requested in section 9 of the form, section 10 of the form enables the appellant to outline those orders s/he seeks.

Examples of some of the possible applications are:

1. An order requiring the local authority to disclose the contents of the appellant's housing file, and any other document reasonably required for the appeal and held by the local authority.

---

6   section 204(2A) of the Housing Act 1996, as inserted by paragraph 17, Schedule 1 of the Homelessness Act 2002

2. A request for an expedited hearing.

3. When the Homelessness Act 2002 is brought into force, an order that the local authority exercise its discretion under section 204(4) to continue to provide accommodation pending the outcome of the appeal against the decision made on review, or the section 184 decision if no review decision has been made.[7] Before this time, any challenge against the decision of a local authority not to continue to provide accommodation pending the appeal must be brought by way of a judicial review.

These applications should be heard as soon as possible. The appellant should ask the court to list an interim hearing at the earliest opportunity.

Human Rights Act 1998

If the appellant seeks to rely on an aspect of the Human Rights Act 1998, the appeal notice must include certain additional information as required for all statements of case (see page 22).[8]

Skeleton argument

The skeleton argument is, in essence, a summary of the main facts and legal issues in support of the appeal. It should entail a list of numbered points. These need not be more than a few sentences, but should be sufficient to outline the areas of controversy between the parties.

Where appropriate, each point should refer to documentation relied on in support of the argument and set out the main statutory references and relevant case law.[9] Any references to case law or other relevant text should include the particular pages on which the principle concerned is discussed.

The appellant should also include a chronology of events and consider what other information would assist the court in making its decision, eg. a list of household members with dates of birth.[10]

The skeleton argument can be included within the appellant's notice at section 8. However, not surprisingly, there is little space on the form to do this, and in most cases it will be necessary to set it out on a separate document.

Amendments may be made to the skeleton argument without the court's permission. If amendments are made, then the amended skeleton argument should be filed at the court and served as soon as possible.[11]

Ideally the skeleton argument will be filed at the same time as the appellant's notice. This is particularly necessary where the quick resolution of the case is of the utmost importance to the appellant, eg.

---

7 section 204A of the Housing Act 1996, as inserted by section 11 of the Homelessness Act 2002
8 CPR PD 52 para 5.1A-5.1B & PD 16 para 16
9 CPR PD 52 para 5.10
10 CPR PD 52 para 5.11
11 CPR PD 52 para 5.9 & 7.6

s/he is street homeless. The reason for this is that the time limits for subsequent steps in the appeal, specified in Part 52, are governed by reference to the date on which the appellant's skeleton argument is filed, unless the court provides its own directions (see page 239).

If it is simply impracticable to file the skeleton argument with the appellant's notice, it must be lodged at court and served on each respondent within 14 days of filing the notice.[12]

If the appellant is not legally represented, then there is no requirement to file a skeleton argument. However, the unrepresented appellant is encouraged to do so in the interests of assisting the court in reaching a decision.[13] Where an appellant seeks legal representation after issuing the appeal, advisers should endeavour to file a skeleton argument within the time limit, or as soon as is practicable.

Witness statements in support

Invariably the appellant will provide a **witness statement** in support of her/his appeal giving the background to her/his homelessness, and information relevant to the issues which form the grounds of appeal. A **statement of truth** must be included.

CPR 22.1

Other witness statements may be appropriate in an individual case. For example, an adviser may wish to provide information about conversations s/he has had with an officer of the local authority, if this gives an insight into the manner in which the local authority reached an adverse decision.

It must be appreciated, however, that the court can only review the decision of the local authority on the information available at the date of the decision. Generally, the court will not usually consider any evidence that was not before the local authority when it made its decision.

CPR 52.11(1)-(2)

This is subject to an important qualification. It may be a fundamental part of the appellant's appeal that the local authority has failed to undertake necessary enquiries and that, had it done so, the information now provided would have been before it. An example is if the local authority failed to make enquiries of the appellant's GP or consultant in deciding whether that person is vulnerable and therefore in "priority need".

In such cases this argument should be made in the appellant's notice and skeleton argument, and the information should be provided in the **witness statement**. It is likely that the respondent local authority will resist the inclusion of the evidence or argue that the information is not relevant to the appeal. In this case the court will hear arguments by both sides either at the final hearing or at a separate prior hearing.

Bundle of documents in support

The bundle of documents in support should include copies of the following:[14]

- the appellant's notice

- the skeleton argument (if this is available)

- the decision appealed against

- any **witness statements** or **affidavits**

- any other documents which the appellant considers necessary to assist the court to reach a decision on the appeal.

The appellant's bundle of documents may form the basis for the trial bundle and must be indexed and paginated. The index should be as detailed as possible to assist the court and the parties at the appeal hearing. The appellant should update the bundle and the index, and file it at court not less than three days but not more than seven days
CPR 39.5 before the appeal hearing.

It is not possible to provide an exhaustive list of documents which may fall within the last category, but commonly these may include:

- if available, the relevant parts of the appellant's housing file. This may include correspondence, file notes or any document but only those which are relevant to the appeal

- the section 184 decision letter

- any relevant medical or other reports

- any relevant court order, eg. a possession order for intentionality decisions

- details of income and expenditure, eg. if relevant to an intentionality decision and where the local authority appears not to have considered the appellant's financial position in making its decision.

15.4 Disclosure

Advisers commonly encounter a problem in obtaining documents held by the local authority in relation to the homelessness application. Although such documents come within the ambit of the right to access under section 7 of the Data Protection Act 1998, the authority has 40

14 CPR PD 52 para 5.6

days in which to comply with its duty to provide the information requested. Obviously, this creates difficulties, given the strict time limit for filing the appellant's notice and supporting documents.

A useful approach is simply to inform the local authority, by letter, that the client is considering whether to bring an appeal, but that in order to properly advise her/him, it is necessary to have sight of the housing file. A sensible authority will comply with such a request.

Where an authority resists or ignores the request, an appeal should be lodged if the information available suggests that there are grounds to do so. So, if it appears from the review decision letter and other available paperwork that insufficient enquiries were made, this should be included as a ground for appeal. If it later transpires that the local authority had made sufficient enquiries and that this would have been evident from documents which have been unreasonably withheld, it can be strongly argued that the local authority should meet the costs of the proceedings, even if the substantive appeal is unsuccessful.

Equally, it may be necessary to apply to amend the appeal notice in advance of the hearing, following filing of evidence by the authority. The appellant can seek an order that the authority pay the costs of such an application.

For these reasons, the request for disclosure should include a reminder of the emphasis within the CPR of early disclosure, together with a warning that costs will be sought where non-disclosure has costs implications.

15.5 Respondent's notice

CPR 52.5(2)

The local authority rarely needs to file a respondent's notice. Such a notice would be required only where the local authority wished to ask the court to uphold a decision for different or additional reasons to those it gave to the appellant. If this is the authority's position, then it is suggested that it should withdraw the decision and agree to make a fresh one. This, in turn, will give rise to appeal rights.

CPR 52.5

If, however, the local authority does wish to file a notice, then it should do so within 14 days after the date on which the appellant's notice was served on it, unless the court directs otherwise.

Respondent's skeleton argument

The local authority must also file a skeleton argument in order to address its arguments to the court.[15] This may be included on the respondent's notice if one is filed by the local authority. In any event,

---

15 CPR PD 52 para 7.6

the skeleton argument must be lodged at court and served on the appellant no later than 21 days from the date that the local authority was served with the appellant's skeleton argument.[16]

The skeleton argument should be similar in style to that of the appellant, outlining the respondent's arguments while also addressing and responding to the appellant's arguments.

15.6 Listing for hearing

On the filing of the appellant's notice, the court notifies the parties of the hearing date, or the **listing window,** when the appeal will be heard. Some courts list the appeal for directions. This is not normally appropriate as the rules provide a comprehensive list of directions for each party to adhere to.

CPR PD 52 para 6

It will be vital to many appellants that the hearing is listed at the earliest opportunity. Many will be living on the streets or have other unsuitable living arrangements. For this reason, it is important to notify the court that the case should be expedited given the urgent nature of the appellant's situation. Ideally this should be requested in section 10 of the appeal notice (see page 234).

If an application for an expedited hearing has not been included in the appeal notice, then a request by letter accompanying the appeal documents may be made. In urgent cases, however, the appeal documents should be lodged in person and the request made in person and directly to the listing officer. The listing officer is likely to place the application or request before a judge for consideration.

Support for such requests can be found in the judgment of Lord Woolf in *R v Brighton and Hove Council ex parte Nacion:*[17]

While recognising the other problems which confront county courts, it is my hope that in this jurisdiction of homelessness, county courts will do their best to see that points of law ... are dealt with as promptly as possible.

CPR 3.1(2)(a)

In the most urgent cases, the court could be asked to abridge the time limits for the filing and serving of evidence outlined earlier.

The vast majority of appeals are listed for between a half and a full day. A time estimate should be entered on the appellant's notice.

15.7 Settlement

Many homelessness appeals do not reach the hearing stage. Often a local authority will seek an agreement whereby it will undertake a

---

16 CPR PD 52 para 7.7

17 R v Brighton and Hove Council ex parte Nacion (1999) 31 HLR 1095, CA

reconsideration of the case on the basis that an appeal is not issued or is withdrawn, as the case may be.

If such an approach is made, advisers need to be careful to protect the appellant's interests, in the light of the decision by the Court of Appeal in *Demetri v Westminster CC*.[18] A mere discretionary reconsideration by the authority will not give rise to fresh appeal rights. Therefore, it is imperative that the local authority agrees in writing that the outcome of its reconsideration will constitute a fresh review decision which can be appealed against. If the local authority will not give this guarantee, the appeal should be continued.

If settlement is reached, this will invariably mean that the local authority acknowledges that its decision was flawed. It should follow that the local authority meets the costs incurred where an appeal has been issued. Costs will normally follow the event. On the other hand the local authority may apply pressure on the appellant to accept an offer to withdraw the decision and undertake a further review on the basis that there is no costs order. If the appellant does not accept an offer on these terms then the local authority could decide to continue to fight the appeal.

If appropriate, the appellant should insist that the local authority provides temporary accommodation pending the new decision. If this is resisted then the appellant should normally continue with the appeal.

A consent order should be drafted to give effect to the agreement. This must be signed by the parties, or on their behalf, and sent to the court as far in advance of the final hearing date as possible.

15.8 The hearing

There is usually one circuit judge presiding over the appeal hearing.[19] The hearing usually proceeds in the following manner.

Any preliminary applications will be heard.

The appellant's advocate outlines the grounds of appeal, and may elaborate on the points set out in the skeleton argument. The judge may ask questions of the advocate to clarify issues.

The advocate for the respondent outlines the response to the appeal, and may elaborate on any of the points set out in the skeleton argument. The judge may ask questions.

The appellant's advocate makes a brief closing speech, followed by the closing speech of the respondent's advocate.

The judge retires to consider the matter, and returns to deliver judgment.

---

18 Demetri v Westminster CC [2000] 32 HLR 470, CA   19 see Crawley BC v B [2000] 32 HLR 636, CA

If the judge is unable to give judgment at this stage, then s/he may reserve judgment to a future date. This may occur where the issues involved in the appeal are particularly complex, the paperwork is bulky or simply that it is not convenient to give judgment on the day.

CPR 52.11(2) It will be rare for the court to hear oral evidence at the hearing. Indeed, this is allowed only if the court makes an order to this effect. Sometimes oral evidence will be appropriate in order to give the appellant the opportunity to clarify or amplify anything in her/his **witness statement**. This applies equally to an officer of the respondent local authority who has filed a witness statement in the case.

Advisers should not underestimate the importance of the fact that the client is unlikely to have to give oral evidence at the hearing. For many clients, the prospect of giving oral evidence is enough to put them off bringing an appeal in the first place.

15.9 Final order

Under section 204(3) of the Housing Act 1996, the court has power to 'confirm, quash or vary' the decision made by the authority. However, normally, the most realistic outcome for the appellant is a quashing of the decision. This means that the local authority has to make a further decision, having particular regard to the reasons given for the success of the appeal. For example, if the judgment includes a finding that the appeal is allowed on the basis that the local authority failed to undertake adequate enquiries into certain matters, it should make the enquiries before reaching a new decision. This new decision will itself give rise to the right to appeal under section 204 of the Act.

An order by the court to vary the decision, so as to compel the local authority to accept a duty, will only arise in cases where the authority cannot possibly reach an adverse decision on the available evidence. This is rarely the situation.

After appeal

If the decision which has been quashed is that made by the authority on review, the original section 184 decision stands. The local authority should be asked to provide temporary accommodation, pending the fresh review, in exercise of its discretionary powers.[20]

If, however, it is the section 184 decision which is quashed, the local authority will be under a duty to provide temporary accommodation until the fresh decision is made, whereupon it may exercise its discretion to continue providing accommodation pending the review.

20 this is under section 188(2) of the Housing Act 1996

Judicial review

When public bodies make an unlawful decision, eg. fail to process a homelessness application, it may be necessary to challenge this decision by making an application for judicial review to the High Court. Such applications are often made in housing law cases and, as a result, it is important to cover the procedure for judicial review in this book. This is the only chapter that will cover High Court procedures.

Judicial review is a large and complex area of law. In housing law cases alone, decisions reached in judicial review cases change the law frequently. This chapter does not deal with the merits of bringing a case for judicial review as this would be outside the scope of the book. The procedure for applying for judicial review is dealt with in this chapter. Case Study 1 is a case study of a judicial review application and can be read alongside this chapter.

In an application for judicial review, the court will consider the legality of a decision of a public body. The facts of a case will not be reconsidered as the court is only concerned with lawfulness of a decision. For example, where an authority has made a decision of "intentional homelessness" after considering all the facts in a case, an application for judicial review would be inappropriate where what is sought is simply an order to require the authority to look at the facts again and make a fresh decision.

16.1 Overview of the judicial review procedure

A brief overview of the judicial review procedure is given below. Each of the actions to be carried out is discussed under its individual heading following this section.

Judicial review is essentially a two-part procedure. The first stage is asking for permission to apply for judicial review. This stage includes:

• complying with the Judicial Review Pre-Action Protocol

• the claimant drafting, filing (with a fee) and serving the claim form, and compiling a bundle of documents to be used by the court in deciding whether to grant permission to apply for judicial review

• the defendant drafting, filing and serving the acknowledgment of service

• the court deciding whether permission to apply for judicial review will be granted. This can be done by paper, ie. where the court will make its decision based solely on the paperwork before it, namely the claim form and the acknowledgment of service. Alternatively, the application can be made orally, ie. where one or more of the parties make representations to the court.

Once permission is granted, the parties prepare for the hearing of the application for judicial review. This is the second stage of a judicial review application. It includes:

- the defendant drafting, filing and serving the response to the claim form

- both parties drafting, filing and serving their skeleton arguments

- the claimant compiling, filing and serving a bundle of documents. This is generally the bundle above with additions

- the court deciding the application.

Cases are often conceded after permission is granted. There are many reasons for this, eg. a party may decide that her/his case is not as strong as s/he initially thought, or the granting of an injunction at the same time that permission is given may obviate the need to continue the proceedings (see page 247). The remaining issue would then be one of costs (see page 252).

16.2 Types of orders

An application for judicial review is made using the procedure in Part 8 as modified by Part 54. This procedure must be used where the claimant is seeking:

CPR 54.2

- a mandatory order

- a prohibiting order

- a quashing order.

Mandatory order

A mandatory order used to be known as an order of mandamus. Such an order compels the performance of a public duty, eg. to make social services carry out an assessment of a child. Performance of a public duty also includes the duty to exercise discretion so as to make a decision, eg. make a housing authority consider a request to provide temporary accommodation pending the outcome of a review of a homelessness application.

Prohibiting order

A prohibiting order was previously known as an order of prohibition. This order prevents a public body from acting illegally, irrationally or improperly. It is not used very often in housing law as most orders sought require a positive action to be taken by the public body.

Quashing order

A quashing order used to be called an order of certiorari. The court makes this order to quash an invalid decision that has been made by a public body. An example of this is when a local authority makes an "intentional homelessness" decision, but has failed to make sufficient enquiries or give adequate reasons for it.

CPR 54.3 Part 54 can also be used where the claimant is seeking:

• a declaration

• an injunction

• damages.

Declarations

A declaration is when the court declares the law or the respective rights of the parties without making an order against the decision maker.

Injunctions

Injunctions are often granted as a form of interim relief at the permission stage of proceedings (see page 255). Injunctions prevent an illegal act or enforce the performance of a public duty. The outcomes they achieve are similar to the outcomes of mandatory and prohibition orders.

In most cases, injunctions are rare and tend to be used only as interim relief. However, injunctions are fairly common in homelessness cases. This is because a remedy is usually needed urgently. For example, a local authority might be ordered to provide temporary accommodation for someone pending its decision on a homelessness application.

Damages

A judicial review claim cannot seek damages alone. One of the above orders must also be sought. However, it should be noted that damages are not available for breach of most homelessness duties.[1]

16.3 Pre-action protocol for judicial review cases

The pre-action protocol for judicial review cases was introduced in March 2002. The protocol recommends a code of good practice and suggests the steps that parties should usually follow before making a judicial review claim.[2]

---

1 O'Rourke v Camden LBC (1997) 29 HLR 793, HL   2 Pre-Action Protocol for Judicial Review, para 5

The protocol does not compel a public body to disclose documents. This is because the duty to disclose under statute or common law is deemed to be sufficient. However, where a public body has failed to provide relevant documents and/or information, the court has a power to impose sanctions.[3]

All parties will normally be expected to comply with the protocol where it is appropriate. The courts have powers to impose sanctions on parties who do not comply, take into account any non-compliance when making costs orders and give directions for the case. Parties will not be expected to comply with the protocol if the case requires urgent action to be taken. However, it is suggested good practice to fax to the defendant the draft claim form which the claimant is going to issue, and to inform a defendant when an interim mandatory order is being sought.[4]

The letter before claim

The intention of the letter before claim is to identify the issues in dispute and ascertain whether litigation can be avoided. The claimant should send the letter to the defendant before s/he makes the claim.[5]

The protocol contains a suggested format for the letter before claim that should be used. The letter should include the following:[6]

- the name and address of the defendant. The letter should be sent not only to the address on the decision letter, but also to the public body's legal department

- the claimant's title, first and last name, and address

- reference details so that, when the letter is going to a large organisation, the person who has been dealing with the matter can be easily tracked

- details of the matter being challenged, ie. the decision of the public body

- details and date of the decision, act or omission being challenged, a brief summary of the facts and why it is thought to be wrong

- details of the remedy sought from the defendant including whether a review or any **interim remedy** is being requested

- the name, address and reference details of any legal advisers dealing with the claim

- details of any interested parties and confirmation that they have been sent a copy of the letter before claim

- details of any information that is being sought

---

3   Pre-Action Protocol for Judicial Review, para 6
4   Pre-Action Protocol for Judicial Review, para 7
5   Pre-Action Protocol for Judicial Review, para 8
6   Pre-Action Protocol for Judicial Review, paras 9-11 & Annex A

- details of any documents that the public body is expected to disclose and an explanation of why they are considered relevant. Where disclosure of the document is being sought under a statutory duty, this should be specified

- the address for reply and service of court documents

- the date by which the public body is to reply. This will vary according to the urgency of the case. Generally, 14 days is considered a reasonable time to allow for a reply.

The letter of response

The defendant will be expected to reply to the letter before claim by the date given in the letter. If it does not reply without good reason, the court may impose sanctions.

Where the defendant is unable to meet the claimant's deadline to reply to the letter, it should send an interim reply and suggest a reasonable extension within which to reply fully. Reasons why the extension is requested should be given and further information asked for if required. The claimant should note that an extension will not affect the three-month time limit for making a judicial review claim. The claimant need not agree to the extension if s/he considers it to be unreasonable. However, sanctions may be imposed by the court if it considers that a subsequent claim is made too early.[7]

The letter of response should use the format suggested by the protocol and include the following:[8]

- the claimant's title, first and last name and address

- the name and address of the defendant

- the public body's reference details for the matter in dispute

- details of the matter being challenged. This may include, where appropriate, a fuller explanation of the decision

- the response to the proposed claim (see below)

- details of any other interested parties who have not been included in the letter before claim. A copy of response letter should be sent to them

- the address for further correspondence and service of court documents.

Response to the proposed claim

If the claim is being conceded in full, the reply should say so in clear and unambiguous terms.[9]

7   Pre-Action Protocol for Judicial Review, para 14
8   Pre-Action Protocol for Judicial Review, para 13
9   Pre-Action Protocol for Judicial Review, para 15

The reply should also state in clear and unambiguous terms if the claim is being conceded in part or not being conceded at all and:[10]

- give a new decision, where appropriate, clearly identifying what aspects of the claim are being conceded and what parts are not, or give a date by which the new decision will be issued

- if appropriate, provide a fuller explanation for the decision

- address any points of dispute or explain why they cannot be addressed

- if relevant documents have been requested by the claimant, enclose them or explain why they are not being enclosed

- confirm, where appropriate, whether or not any application for an **interim remedy** will be opposed.

16.4 The claim form

Form N461 is used to issue judicial review proceedings. (For an example of a completed Form N461, see Case Study 1; page 267.) The form must include or be accompanied by:[11]

- details of other interested parties to the application (listed in section 2 of the form)

- a request for permission to proceed with a claim for judicial review (section 4)

- a time estimate for the hearing (section 5)

- a detailed statement of the claimant's grounds for bringing the claim for judicial review (section 6)

- any remedy (including any **interim remedy**) being sought (section 7). See "emergency injunctions" below

- a statement of the facts being relied on (section 8). These tend to be set out in a **witness statement** attached to the claim form

- any application to extend the time limit for filing the claim form (section 9)

- any application for directions (section 9).

The following should also be attached to the claim form:[12]

- any written evidence in support of the claim or application to extend time, eg. witness statements setting out the facts being relied upon

- a copy of any decision letter that the claimant seeks to have quashed

---

10 Pre-Action Protocol for Judicial Review, para 16   12 CPR 54.6(2) & CPR PD 54 para 5.7
11 CPR 54.6(1) & CPR PD 54 para 5.6

- where the claim for judicial review relates to a decision of a court or tribunal, its approved copy of the reasons for reaching that decision

- copies of any documents on which the claimant proposes to rely, eg. relevant correspondence

- copies of any relevant statutory material

- a list of essential documents for advance reading by the court.

The claimant needs to state which, if any, of the above documents are not being filed (in section 10 of the form) and the reason why they are not currently available.[13]

Essential documents list

The court will require a list of all the essential documents that need to be read before a decision can be reached on granting permission to apply for judicial review. The essential documents generally include:

- the judicial review claim form

- witness statements

- relevant correspondence

- relevant case law

- relevant statutory provisions.

Statement of truth

The claim form has a statement of truth in it that must be completed (see page 23).

Emergency injunctions

A common application in housing cases is one asking for a mandatory order (see page 246) to make a local authority continue housing the claimant pending the outcome of a homelessness review. This is just one example of a case in which the claimant may be imminently roofless. It, and others like it, would clearly require emergency action. The claimant, as well as applying for a mandatory order, should also apply for an injunction to order the local authority to continue housing her/him. This will be contained in the claim form in section 7.

In the case above, the claimant will most likely be seeking a remedy on the same day that the local authority makes the decision not to continue housing her/him. This situation is not unusual. **Legal representatives** should be aware that, if they are to take on such a

---

13 CPR PD 54 para 5.8

case, they will have little time for any other work for a day or two. There will be a large amount of work to do in a very short space of time, eg. drafting **witness statements**, applying for **public funding**, instructing a barrister, compiling bundles and completing the claim form. The court will expect all this work to be done before it will consider the application.

A party seeking an emergency injunction may not have time to serve the other party with all the papers. Nevertheless, this should be done wherever feasible. In some cases the court will insist on the papers being faxed to the other side at the very least. It may also require a letter from the party seeking the injunction confirming that s/he has served the papers on the other party. However, in some instances, it will not be possible to serve the other party with the papers because of time constraints. In this case, the party should still proceed with the application for an emergency injunction. If the court then grants the emergency injunction, it is likely to direct that the other party is served with the papers and that there will be a further hearing where the other party can make representations to the court as to why the emergency injunction should not be granted.

The court will consider whether or not to grant an **interim remedy** at an early stage of the judicial review application. This would be either at the permission stage or just before it. If the injunction is granted, there may be no point in proceeding with the judicial review application where the final outcome would be much the same as the outcome of the injunction application. In this case, the action should be discontinued, subject to dealing with costs, in accordance with Part 38 (see paragraph 5.4).

Costs where a case is concluded without a full hearing

Generally, where a party discontinues a case, that party will bear the costs of the proceedings. However, judicial review cases are often concluded, for a variety of reasons, without a full hearing. In the example above – of asking for a mandatory order to make a local authority continue housing the claimant pending the outcome of a homelessness review – if the local authority decides, or is ordered, to house following an application for an injunction, then there seems little point in the claimant continuing with the action if the ultimate aim of the proceedings has been achieved. In this case, it would be for the claimant to discontinue the proceedings; but it may be unjust for her/him to pay the costs. The overriding objective of the CPR would not then be achieved.

The leading case that courts refer to in deciding the costs order to make in judicial review cases that are concluded without a full hearing is *The Queen (on the application of Boxall and Boxall) v London Borough of Waltham Forest (2000)*.[14] The principles to apply in making a costs order were summarised as follows:

- The court has power to make a costs order where proceedings have been resolved without a trial, but the parties do not agree on costs.

- It is generally irrelevant that the claimant is legally aided. Courts should not refuse to make a costs order against a public body solely on the grounds that a public body (ie. the Legal Services Commission) is already paying the claimant's solicitor's costs.

- The overriding objective to do justice should be met without incurring unnecessary court time and, as a result, additional cost. If the cost involved in resolving the costs issue is likely to be disproportionate to the costs of the case, the court might decide to make no order as to costs (see Chapter 1).

- In some cases, it will be obvious who would have won had the case proceeded to trial. However, this will not always be clear. The depth that the court will look into the previously unresolved substantive issues will depend on the circumstances of the particular case, especially the amount of costs at stake and the conduct of the parties.

- Where the court cannot find good reason to make an order, it should make no order as to costs.

- Care should be taken by the court to ensure it does not discourage parties from settling judicial review proceedings, for example by a local authority making a concession at an early stage.

There is no bar on a party applying for costs on a case that is resolved before permission is granted or otherwise.[15]

Human rights

If the claimant wishes to raise an issue or seek a remedy under the Human Rights Act 1998, then the claim form must include the information required by CPR Practice Direction 16 para 16[16] (see page 22).

16.5 Filing and serving the claim form

Papers filed and served in High Court cases follow much the same procedure as papers filed in the county court. Any differences are pointed out below.

---

14 transcript available from the Smith Bernal website, www.casetrack.com. The case number is CO/3234/2000

15 R v Royal Borough of Kensington and Chelsea ex parte Ghrebregiosis (1994) 27 HLR 602, QBD

16 CPR PD 54 para 5.3

The Administrative Court in London deals with claims for judicial review.[17] There is also an option of making the claim in Wales where the claim or the remedy sought involves a Welsh public body.[18]

The claim form must be filed at the Administrative Court office[19] without delay, and in any event within three months after the grounds to make the claim first arose. Permission to apply for judicial review could be refused on grounds of delay even if the claim form is filed within three months. This might happen where an adviser has delayed unnecessarily in filing the claim form.

Two copies of the claim form and attached documents are sent to the court. The documents should be organised into paginated and indexed bundles[20] (see page 145). The court then issues the claim and returns the bundles to the claimant. Unlike the county court, the High Court will not serve the claim form on the defendant and all interested parties. It is the responsibility of the claimant to do this.[21] This must be done within seven days after the date of issue of the claim.

CPR 54.7

Certificate of service

Form N215 must be completed by the claimant to certify that s/he has served the claim form on the defendant. The form must then be lodged at the Administrative Court within seven days of serving all relevant parties with the claim form.

16.6 Fees

A fee of £30 is to be paid when filing the claim form asking for permission to proceed with judicial review (see page 255). A further fee of £120 is payable if permission is granted. This should be sent to the Administrative Court.

If the party is a **litigant in person** and on a low income, s/he may be entitled to a waiver of the fees. S/he should apply for a waiver from the High Court.

16.7 Acknowledgment of service

Once served with a claim form, the defendant has 21 days to file an acknowledgment of service in Form N462. The defendant must then serve this on the claimant and any other person named in the claim form within seven days of filing. These are strict deadlines and cannot be extended, even if the parties agree. However, the court has a power to extend this deadline under CPR 3.1(2)(a).

CPR 54.8(2)(a)

CPR 54.8(2)(b)

CPR 54.8(2)(c)

If the acknowledgment of service is not filed and served as above, then in an oral hearing to decide whether permission should be given to

---

17 CPR PD 54 para 2.1
18 CPR PD 54 para 3.1(2)
19 The address for London claims is Administrative Court Office, the Royal Courts of Justice, Strand, London WC2A 2LL. Documents for claims proceeding in the

Welsh administrative court should be filed at the Law Courts, Cathays Park, Cardiff, CF10 3PG
20 CPR PD 54 para 5.9
21 CPR PD 54 para 6.1

CPR 54.9(1)(a) apply for judicial review, the defendant can only take part if so allowed by the court.

The acknowledgment of service form is fairly straightforward. Page one simply asks whether or not the claim is being contested, and if a different remedy to that being asked for by the claimant is being sought. This does not tend to happen in housing cases as the defendant is unlikely to be applying for a remedy as well.

CPR 54.8(4)(a) Page two is the detailed part of the form. Grounds for contesting the claim must be given here. Although these need only be in summary, the grounds generally tend to be quite detailed. Relevant case law may be included in this section, but is more likely to be found in the skeleton argument (see page 257).

CPR 54.8(4)(b) In the final page of the form, the defendant can choose to apply for directions from the court.

16.8 Permission to apply for judicial review

CPR 54.4 This is the first stage of a judicial review case. The court's permission is needed to bring a claim for judicial review. The court decides whether to give permission after the claim form and acknowledgment of service have been filed. The purpose of this stage of the proceedings is for the court to assess whether there is an arguable case. It will usually deal with the issue of permission without a hearing,[22] but can direct that the parties attend.[23] This will usually be when the court is undecided on whether to grant permission based on the claim form and acknowledgment of service, and needs further representations from the parties.

CPR 54.11 When the judge has made a decision on the application, the court will serve an order granting or refusing permission on all relevant parties. The parties will also be informed of any directions that the court has given.

CPR 54.13 If permission is granted, the defendant cannot apply to set aside this decision.

CPR 54.12(1)-(2)
CPR 54.12(3) Where there has been no hearing and permission is refused, or it is granted but the claimant can only proceed subject to certain conditions or on certain grounds, then the court will give its reasons for making the decision at the same time as serving the order. The claimant is then able to ask that the decision be reconsidered at a hearing. At this hearing, s/he can make representations to try to persuade the court to come to a different decision. The request for a hearing has to be filed within seven days after the claimant receives the reasons for the CPR 54.12(4)
CPR 54.12(5) decision. All relevant parties will be given at least two days' notice of the hearing date.

22 CPR PD 54 para 8.4   23 CPR PD 54 para 8.5

If permission is refused at the hearing and the claimant still wants to go ahead with the action, s/he must appeal to the Court of Appeal. This must be done within seven days of the decision to refuse permission.

CPR 52.15(1)-(2)

16.9 Response

After a defendant receives the order giving permission, s/he has 35 days to file and serve a response. This response must contain detailed grounds for contesting the claim and any written evidence. This might already have been done in the acknowledgment of service form. In this case, the defendant need just refer to the acknowledgment of service.

CPR 54.14(1)

Where the defendant is relying on documents not already filed at the court, it must file a paginated bundle (see page 145) of those documents when filing the detailed grounds.[24]

The defendant can rely on grounds not already stated in the acknowledgment of service and response, but only if the court allows this. Notice of the application (see Chapter 9 on how to make an application) to rely on such grounds should be given to the court, and all relevant parties, no later than seven days before the hearing.[25]

CPR 54.18

Once the court has all the relevant papers in the case, it can decide the claim for judicial review without a hearing where all the parties agree. However, this is unlikely to happen in practice, as parties tend to prefer attending a hearing.

16.10 Preparing for the hearing

The court will inform all parties of the date of the hearing or it will inform them of a **warned date**. This is when the court has not allocated a specific date to the hearing but is able to state when it is likely to be. The court will let the parties know that the hearing might be, for example, in the week beginning 16 April. The parties will have to be ready for the hearing by 16 April even though it might not go ahead in that week. The purpose of a warned date is to give the parties enough time to prepare for the hearing. Courts are sometimes unable to say when a judge is available for a hearing. This might be because, for example, the judge is hearing a trial that is listed for five days but may finish in three days. Rather than have the judge out of court for the remaining two days, courts will try to fit in other hearings such as a judicial review.

The court will require two items from the parties before the hearing:

• skeleton arguments
• bundle of documents.

Skeleton arguments

A skeleton argument is simply an outline of the argument that the party is to present to the court. It has to include:[26]

- a time estimate of the complete hearing, which includes the court giving judgment at the end

- a list of issues

- a list of legal points to be taken. This should include any authorities being relied on, with page references to relevant passages

- a chronology of events referring to relevant pages in the bundle of documents (see below)

- a list of essential documents for the court to read before the hearing, referring to passages being relied on and a time estimate for that reading

- a list of persons referred to.

The claimant has to file and serve a skeleton argument 21 days before the date of the hearing of the judicial review or the warned date.[27]

The defendant has to file and serve its skeleton argument 14 days before the hearing or the warned date.[28]

Bundle of documents

The claimant has the responsibility of filing a paginated and indexed bundle (see page 145). This must be done when s/he files her/his skeleton argument. The bundle must contain documents that the defendant wants included as well as those being relied on by the claimant.[29]

16.11 Hearing and appeals

The next step in the judicial review proceedings is the hearing. This will follow much the same procedure as that outlined in Chapter 10. However, there is unlikely to be any oral evidence (other than exceptionally), and so the hearing will consist entirely of speeches/legal argument by the advocates and questions from the judge.

Only certain advocates will have **rights of audience** in the High Court. These are barristers, solicitors with higher court advocacy rights and **litigants in person**. No other person will be able to present a case to the High Court.

26 CPR PD 54 para 15.3
27 CPR PD 54 para 15.1
28 CPR PD 54 para 15.2
29 CPR PD 54 paras 16.1-16.2

Once judgment is given, any party wishing to appeal the decision should ask for permission from the court to do so immediately. If this is not done at the hearing, then the party should make an application to seek leave to appeal from the Court of Appeal Civil Division within 14 days.

CPR 52.3(3)

Where permission to appeal is refused by the High Court, a further application for permission to appeal may be made to the Court of Appeal Civil Division as above.

Judicial review

Background

Maryam Farah is a Somalian refugee who was granted exceptional leave to remain on 28 June 2002. She has three children, aged 3, 7 and 8. She arrived in the United Kingdom in 1999 and, until 24 July 2002, was provided with accommodation by Othertown Social Services. The accommodation provided was actually situated in a neighbouring borough, Anywhere. Mrs Farah wishes to stay in this area. Her children are at school there and she has formed many associations in the neighbourhood.

Due to her new immigration status, Mrs Farah is eligible for housing assistance. She is interviewed by an officer of Othertown Council's Homeless Persons Unit. At the interview she is accompanied by a friend who speaks some English. During the course of the interview she tries to explain her wish to continue to live in Anywhere. However, her wishes are misunderstood and the Othertown Council officer completes a homelessness application form on her behalf.

Subsequently, Mrs Farah withdraws the homelessness application to Othertown Council and attempts to make an application to Anywhere Council. Despite the intervention of her adviser, Salma Hayek, at the local Refugee Support Centre, Anywhere Council will not accept her homelessness application. Anywhere Council contend that she cannot withdraw her application to Othertown Council, who are required to process her application.

On 24 July 2002, Othertown Council withdraw the accommodation provided to Mrs Farah. With the assistance of her adviser, Anywhere Social Services agree to provide the family with bed and breakfast accommodation under the Children Act 1989. However, they have indicated that this accommodation will end on 5 August 2002. Mrs Farah seeks help from a solicitor.

Points to note

(1) From October 2000, the correct titles to use for the respective parties to a judicial review claim are Claimant, Defendant and Interested Parties. This is reflected in the case study.

(2) The list of essential reading, which should be filed when the claim commences and is usually prepared by counsel, is not included here. The list of essential reading will include many of the documents included in the bundle of documents – ie. the **claim form, witness statements** – together with correspondence and any other documents of particular importance to the case.

Homeless Persons Unit
Housing Department
Anywhere Council
Anywhere

29 July 2002

Your Ref: HPU123
Our Ref: Home/Farah

By fax and 2nd class post

Dear Sir or Madam

URGENT – LETTER BEFORE ACTION
MRS MARYAM FARAH – 16, THE BEECHES, ANYWHERE

We refer to the telephone conversation earlier today between Mr Jackson of this office and Ms Roberts of your department, in relation to your refusal to accept and process our client's application for accommodation under Part VII of the Housing Act 1996.

We confirm our understanding of the background to this matter.

1. Mrs Farah is a refugee originally from Somalia. She was granted exceptional leave to remain in the United Kingdom on 28 June 2002. She has care of her three children aged 3, 7 and 8 years.

2. Prior to 24 July 2002, Mrs Farah and her children were accommodated under asylum support arrangements by Othertown Council. This accommodation was withdrawn on this date, as Mrs Farah is now eligible for housing assistance. Mrs Farah is currently being provided with emergency bed and breakfast accommodation by your own Social Services Department.

3. On 19 July 2002, Mrs Farah approached your authority to make a homelessness application, where she was interviewed by an officer of your Homeless Persons Unit. During the course of the interview, she informed the officer that she had unwittingly made a prior homelessness application to Othertown Council. She explained that she had been interviewed by an officer of Othertown's Homeless Persons Unit. She used a friend to interpret as she speaks very little English. She had attempted to explain to her friend that she wished to be referred to your authority, but this was lost in translation.

4. On 24 July 2002, Mrs Farah again approached your authority and was interviewed by a different member of the Homeless Persons Unit. She informed the officer that she had withdrawn the application to Othertown

Council and produced a letter from that authority (dated 24 July 2002) confirming that they are treating the application as withdrawn.

5. After the interview Mrs Farah was handed a letter from your Council's Housing Department dated 24 July 2002. This informed her that the Council will not process her application as she has an outstanding claim with Othertown Council. We understand that the basis for this is that it is your authority's view that an application under Part VII cannot be withdrawn. You contend, therefore, that Othertown Council remains under a duty to make necessary enquiries and reach a decision on Mrs Farah's application while providing interim accommodation pursuant to section 188 of the Housing Act 1996.

We confirm our view that we believe that your authority has misdirected itself as to the law, and that the decision not to accept and process our client's homelessness application is unlawful for the following reasons.

1. There is nothing in Part VII of the Housing Act 1996 to support your view that an application, once made, cannot be subsequently withdrawn by the applicant. Your contention, if correct, would mean that local housing authorities would have to undertake detailed enquiries at public expense, even though the applicant has indicated that she does not wish to pursue the application for housing assistance. This cannot have been the intention of Parliament.

2. The Code of Guidance, at para 10.3, specifically allows for multiple applications to be made, and requires the authorities involved to agree among themselves which authority should make the necessary enquiries. Your contention would mean that an authority approached first would, in every instance, be responsible for processing the application, thereby rendering para 10.3 illogical and redundant.

3. The definition of applicant in section 183(2) is "a person making an application". The use of "making" implies an ongoing process. If a person wishes to remove herself from this process, s/he can clearly do so.

We consider therefore that your authority is under a duty to consider our client's application for housing assistance under Part VII of the Housing Act 1996. Furthermore, your authority is under a duty to provide interim accommodation under section 188 of the Act, pending enquiries made into the application.

If you do not contact us by 4pm on 1 August 2002 indicating that you will process our client's application and provide interim accommodation, we are instructed to apply for permission to apply for judicial review against your decision. Within these proceedings, we shall seek an interim injunction requiring you to provide accommodation until the proceedings are resolved.

In the meantime, we would be grateful if you could provide a copy of each document contained on our client's file in relation to her application for housing. It may be necessary for these documents to be used in evidence to support any claim by our client for judicial review. We would ask you to disclose these documents as soon as possible in the interests of furthering the Overriding Objective contained in Part One of the Civil Procedure Rules 1998.

If you do not wish to comply with this request then, if necessary, we shall draw this to the attention of the court. In any event, we enclose a formal written request by our client for access to personal data held by you pursuant to the Data Protection Act 1998. We also enclose a cheque for the sum of £10 to cover your reasonable expenses for providing the information requested.

We trust that this will not be necessary and look forward to hearing from you shortly.

Yours faithfully

Samuel Jackson
Solicitor
Yourclaim Solicitors

cc. Legal Department, Anywhere Council

Legal Department
Anywhere Council
Anywhere

By fax and 2nd class post

2 August 2002

Our Ref: Home/Farah

Dear Sir or Madam,

MRS MARYAM FARAH – 16, THE BEECHES, ANYWHERE

We refer to our letter before action of 29th July 2002 and note that we have not yet heard from you in response.

Our client has been granted legal funding to seek permission for judicial review and we enclose notice of issue as appropriate.

We also enclose a draft Form N461 together with draft witness statements of Mrs Farah and Ms Hayek, adviser at the Anywhere Refugee Support Group. It is our intention to lodge these papers at the Crown Office on the morning of 5 August 2002. However, if you contact us by 4pm today indicating that you are willing to accept and process our client's application for housing assistance and provide interim accommodation, then this action will not be necessary.

We look forward to hearing from you later today.

Yours faithfully

Samuel Jackson
Solicitor
Yourclaim Solicitors

IN THE HIGH COURT OF JUSTICE
ADMINISTRATIVE COURT

IN THE MATTER OF AN APPLICATION BY MRS MARYAM FARAH FOR
PERMISSION TO APPLY FOR JUDICIAL REVIEW

AND IN THE MATTER OF A DECISION OF THE ANYWHERE COUNCIL
BETWEEN:

REGINA

and

ANYWHERE COUNCIL

Defendant

Ex Parte

MRS MARYAM FARAH

Claimant

INDEX TO BUNDLE OF DOCUMENTS

Document	Date	Pages
1. Form N461	05.08.02	1-6
2. Witness Statement of Salma Hayek	01.08.02	7-15
3. Witness Statement of Maryam Farah	02.08.02	16-21
4. Bundle of Correspondence		22-31

Date	Document	
24.07.02	Letter: Othertown Council to Mrs Farah	22
24.07.02	Letter: Anywhere Council to Mrs Farah	23-24
25.07.02	Letter: Anywhere Refugee Support Centre to Anywhere Council	25
25.07.02	Letter: Anywhere Refugee Support Centre to Anywhere Council	26-27
26.07.02	Letter: Othertown Council to Mrs Farah	28
29.07.02	Letter: Yourclaim Solicitors to Anywhere Council	29-30
02.08.02	Letter: Yourclaim Solicitors to Anywhere Council	31

Form N461 Judicial review claim form

| JUDICIAL REVIEW CLAIM FORM | In The High Court Of Justice Administrative Court |

Administrative Court
Reference No.:
Date Filed:

Section 1 Details of claimant(s) and defendant(s)

Claimant(s)   MARYAM FARAH

Address: c/o   Yourclaim Solicitors,
Anywhere.   Tel:
Fax:

Defendant(s)

ANYWHERE COUNCIL

Section 2 Details of other interested parties

N/A

Section 3 Details of the decisions to be judicially reviewed

Court/Tribunal Person or body who made the decision to be reviewed	(1) Anywhere Housing Department	Date of decision: On or about 24 July 2002	Refusal to entertain the applicant's application for Housing Assistance under Part VII Housing Act 1996

Section 4 Permission to proceed with a claim for judicial review

I am seeking permission to proceed with my claim for Judicial Review.

Are you making any other applications?   **Yes**
If Yes, complete Section 9.

Is the Claimant in receipt of a Community   **Yes**
Legal Service Fund (CLSF) certificate?

Does the claim include any issues arising from   **No**
the Human Rights Act 1998?

Section 5 Time estimate for judicial review hearing

How long do you estimate the hearing will take? **20 minutes**
(permission stage)

Who will represent you at the hearing? **Counsel**

Section 6 Detailed Statement of Grounds **Attached**

Section 7 Details of remedy (including any interim remedy) being sought

1. An order quashing the said decision.

2. A mandatory order, requiring the said Local Authority to consider the applicant's application for housing assistance under Part VII of the Housing Act 1996.

3. An interim injunction to secure that accommodation is made available for the applicant and her family until the final determination of this matter.

4. An order that the Anywhere Council do pay the costs of this application.

5. Such further relief as this Honourable Court may see fit in the exercise of its discretion to grant.

THE APPLICANT SEEKS AN URGENT HEARING OF THIS APPLICATION FOR LEAVE.

Section 8 Statement of facts relied on

The salient facts are contained in the grounds for judicial review attached to Section 6 and in the witness statements of Salma Hayek dated 1 August 2002 and the Claimant's witness statement dated 2 August 2002.

Section 9 Other applications

I wish to make an application for:

An interim injunction that the proposed Defendants do secure accommodation for the Claimant and her children pending final determination of these proceedings.

Statement of Truth

~~I believe~~ (the Claimant believes) that the facts stated in Section 9 are true.

Full name _____

Date:

Name of Claimant's solicitor's firm: Yourclaim Solicitors, Anywhere.

Signed: Position or office held:

Claimant('s solicitor)   (If signing on behalf of firm or company)

Section 10 Supporting documents

If you do not have a document that you intend to use to support your claim, identify it, give the date when you expect it to be available and give reasons why it is not currently available in the box below

Please tick the papers you are filing and any you will be filing later.

✓	Statement of grounds		Included	✓	attached
✓	Statement of facts relied on		Included	✓	attached
	Application for extending time limit for filing the claim form		Included		attached
	Application for directions		Included		attached

	Any written evidence in support of the claim or application to extend time
	Where the claim for judicial review relates to a decision of a court or tribunal, an approved copy of the reasons for reaching that decision
✓	Copies of any documents on which the Claimant proposes to rely
✓	A copy of the legal aid or CSLF certificate *(if legally represented)*
✓	Copies of any relevant statutory material
✓	A list of essential documents for advance reading by the court *(with page references to the passages relied upon)*
Reasons why you have not supplied a document and date when you expect it to be available	
Signed Claimant('s solicitor)	

Section 6 Detailed statement of grounds

The contention advanced by the proposed Defendant that a homeless applicant cannot withdraw an application under Part VII because the Act does not specifically state that this can be done is wrong for the following reasons.

i. There is nothing in the wording of Part VII to justify the restrictive interpretation contended for by the proposed Defendant nor can it be justified having regard to the purposes nor spirit of the Act. On the contrary, the correct approach is that there is nothing in the Act to state that a Part VII application cannot be withdrawn.

ii. The interpretation advanced by the proposed Defendant is manifestly absurd in that, if correct, it would require local housing authorities to carry out the detailed enquiries required under Part VII despite the fact that the applicant does not wish to pursue her application. If Parliament had intended that local housing authorities should carry out such a pointless exercise at public expense, it would have used clear wording to indicate such an intention.

iii. "Applicant" in Part VII is defined in Section 183 (2) in the following terms:

'applicant means a person making an application'.

"Making" envisages a continuing state of affairs which must presuppose that an application once made can be withdrawn.

iv. Paragraph 10.3 of the Code of Guidance states that multiple applications can be made to different authorities who should then agree among themselves which authority should make the statutory enquiries. This would be unnecessary if, as a matter of law, responsibility passes to the first authority to whom an application had been made. The relevant passage states:

Authorities need to be alert to instances where an applicant has applied as homeless to other local authorities at the same time. Multiple applications are not unlawful. Authorities can ask the applicant at the initial interview if s/he has applied to another local housing authority and, if so, contact the other authorities to agree which authority will take responsibility for carrying out enquiries.

v. The approach adopted by the proposed Defendant is contrary to the spirit of co-operation urged by Parliament as indicated, for example, in paragraph 10.3 Code of Guidance. It exacerbates inter-departmental disputes and inter-authority disputes over which an applicant, who is likely to be homeless and vulnerable, has no control. In this case, the applicant and her children would have spent the night of the 24 July 2002 on the street had not the manager of their hostel taken pity on their plight.

Urgency

The application is urgent as the accommodation secured for the applicant and her children is precarious in that Anywhere Social Services are anxious to cancel the accommodation and cannot guarantee for how long they are willing to continue to provide it.

Section 8 Statement of facts relied on

The facts are set out in the witness statements of Salma Hayek dated 1 August 2002 and of the Claimant dated 2 August 2002.

The Claimant is a single woman with three young children, aged 3, 7 and 8 respectively. She is a Somalian refugee who came to the United Kingdom in 1999. Housing was secured for her and her children by Othertown Social Services within the area of Anywhere where she has lived for the last two years. The children attend local schools and such ties as the family has are all in this area. On 28 June 2002, she was granted exceptional leave to remain by the Home Office, and so became entitled to income support and to apply for housing assistance under Part VII of the Housing Act 1996. Othertown Social Services cancelled her temporary accommodation with effect from 24 July 2002 and referred her to Othertown Homeless Persons Unit who duly interviewed her with an interpreter. She made an application to Othertown Council for Part VII housing which appears to have been a misunderstanding as it is common ground between her and Othertown Council that her local connections are in the Anywhere area. She withdrew her application with Othertown Council on 24 July 2002, as confirmed by them in a letter of the same date. She then applied to Anywhere Council for housing assistance on the same day but they refused to entertain her application on the grounds that she could not withdraw her application with Othertown Council. Anywhere Council have maintained their stance with the Claimant's solicitors to whom the Claimant turned for advice, leaving her with little option but to bring these proceedings. The family is currently being accommodated by Anywhere Social Services (it is understood that this is pursuant to the provisions of the Children Act 1989).

IN THE HIGH COURT OF JUSTICE
ADMINISTRATIVE COURT

IN THE MATTER OF AN APPLICATION BY MRS MARYAM FARAH FOR
PERMISSION TO APPLY FOR JUDICIAL REVIEW

AND IN THE MATTER OF A DECISION OF THE ANYWHERE COUNCIL HOUSING
DEPARTMENT

BETWEEN:

REGINA

and

ANYWHERE COUNCIL

Defendant

Ex Parte

MRS MARYAM FARAH

Claimant

WITNESS STATEMENT OF MARYAM FARAH

1. I am the claimant in this matter and I wish to seek a judicial review of the decision of Anywhere Council not to take a homeless person's application from me. I am also seeking an injunction to the effect that the Anywhere Council take an application from me and provide temporary accommodation until they make a decision on my application.

2. I am at present accommodated at 16, The Beeches, Anywhere, together with my three daughters aged 3, 7 and 8 respectively.

3. The accommodation at 16, The Beeches, Anywhere, has been provided by the Social Services Department of Anywhere Council under the Children Act 1989. It is of a temporary nature and will be withdrawn on 5 August 2002. I understand that my advisers have had to renegotiate with Social Services several times in order to preserve this accommodation. Without this accommodation I would have nowhere for myself and my daughters to live.

4. I speak and read in the Somali language. I do not speak any English and I am reliant upon somebody translating for me when dealing with anybody who does not speak Somali.

5. I arrived in the United Kingdom, as an asylum seeker, from Somalia on 28 August 1999. I was immediately accommodated by the Social Services

Department of the Othertown Council at a hostel 'Ivy House', 3 George Road, Anywhere.

6.   On 28 June 2002 I was granted exceptional leave to remain. I am advised that this means I am now eligible for housing assistance under the homelessness legislation.

7.   On 10 July 2002 I was interviewed by a social worker, from the Othertown Council. I was advised that now that I had become eligible for housing my accommodation at 'Ivy House' would be cancelled with effect from 24 July 2002. I was advised to make a homelessness application to Othertown Council's Housing Department. I explained that the children were at school or nursery and I had now become established in the Anywhere area and wished to stay locally. The social worker advised me that I could make a homelessness application to the Anywhere Council, but that I would need to explain what my intentions were to Othertown's Housing Department.

8.   At 11.00am on 19 July 2002 I had an appointment with an officer from the Homeless Persons Unit at the Othertown Council. I went along with a friend who speaks some English, but not very much. I tried to explain, through my friend, that it was my intention to apply to the Anywhere Council for housing. The housing officer completed a form. I did not really know what this form was for. I was of the understanding, because of my friend's translation, that the form was something to do with a transfer to the Anywhere Council. I signed the form and was then told to go.

9.   Shortly afterwards on the same day, I went to the Homeless Persons Unit at Anywhere Council, where I was seen by a tall male officer. I am afraid I do not remember his name. I explained to him that I wished to apply to Anywhere Council for housing and about my contact with the Othertown Council. The man made some telephone calls and then told me that he could not help me because I had made an application at Othertown Council. I remember being upset and I did not understand why he was saying this. I again explained to him about my circumstances in Anywhere. He then said that I would need a letter from Othertown Council. He told me to go back to Othertown Council's Housing Department to explain that I never had the intention of making an application for housing in Othertown and that it was my intention to apply for housing in Anywhere.

10. On 24 July 2002 I returned to the Housing Department at Othertown Council. This time I had a different friend whose English is good. Through this person I was able to explain my situation about not wanting to apply for housing to Othertown Council but instead to Anywhere Council. The officer who interviewed me gave me a letter dated 24 July 2002. This letter was headed Notification under Section 184 of the Housing Act 1996 (Part VII – "Homelessness"). A copy of this letter is attached as exhibit

"MF 1". I understand that it referred to me withdrawing my application for housing from Othertown Council.

11. On the same day, 24 July 2002, I returned to the Homeless Persons Unit at Anywhere Council. I arrived at 12.30pm and I was seen by a woman. Again, I do not remember her name. I was not interviewed but I did give the woman the letter that I had been received from Othertown Council. I was asked to wait and I sat in the offices until approximately 4.00pm. The female officer then gave me a letter dated 24 July 2002 which was headed, 'Re: Housing Act 1996, Part VII'. A copy of this letter is attached as exhibit "MF 2". My friend translated the letter and I understood that it detailed how the Housing Department at Anywhere Council would not help me with housing. I explained that I now had no accommodation for the night, because my accommodation provided by Othertown's Social Services had been withdrawn. I was told to go to Othertown Council and that Anywhere Council would not help me.

12. At 5.00pm the same day, 24 July 2002, I went to seek help from the Refugee Support Centre. My adviser, Ms Hayek, spoke to the hostel manager at 'Ivy House' hostel, on my behalf. The manager agreed that I could stay one more night. It was made clear to me that I had to leave the next morning.

13. On the morning of 25 July 2002 I returned to the Refugee Support Centre. Ms Hayek sent a letter by fax on my behalf to Anywhere Housing Department. I understand that the letter was a notification to Anywhere Council that I wished to make a formal homelessness application.

14. I understand also that Ms Hayek spoke to a man at the Anywhere Homeless Persons Unit called Mr Robbins. I understand that Mr Robbins would not entertain any discussion about the matter with her and refused to take a homelessness application from me.

15. As a consequence of the Homeless Persons Unit not taking an application from me and not providing any form of interim accommodation, I was faced with not having a place for myself and children to stay that night.

16. I understand that Ms Hayek then faxed a letter to Anywhere Council's Social Services Department, seeking assistance for me under the Children Act 1989. As a consequence of this, I was provided with bed and breakfast accommodation at my current address, 16 The Beeches, Anywhere. I have been informed that this accommodation will be withdrawn on 5 August 2002. I do not know yet what will happen after that date.

17. My adviser at the Refugee Support Group referred me to a solicitor. My solicitor has advised me that I should be provided with housing assistance by Anywhere Council.

I believe that the facts stated in this witness statement are true.

Dated 2 August 2002

....

I certify that I, Amina Badawi, Co-ordinator of The Refugee Support Centre, Anywhere, have well and faithfully interpreted the contents of this witness statement and the declaration of truth to the witness who appeared to understand (a) the statement and approved its content as accurate and (b) the declaration of truth and the consequences of making a false witness statement, and who has signed the document in my presence.

Dated 2 August 2002

....

Case update

On 5 August 2002, Mrs Farah's solicitors lodge the application at the High Court. Due to the urgency of Mrs Farah's situation, the court list the matter for a short hearing later that morning to consider the application for permission and application for an **interim injunction**. Although there is insufficient time to serve the application on proper notice, the solicitors immediately inform Anywhere Council of the time of the hearing by telephone and send the application papers by fax.

At the hearing Mrs Farah is represented by counsel. No representative from Anywhere Council attends. The Judge makes the order (see attached) granting permission for judicial review and also an injunction requiring Anywhere Council to provide accommodation until the judicial review is determined by the court. Yourclaim Solicitors immediately fax the order to Anywhere Council's Legal Department and the housing department to secure accommodation for Mrs Farah and the children.

Subsequently, the final hearing is listed for 13 September 2002. However, the Legal Department of Anywhere Council contact Mrs Farah's solicitors indicating that they are willing to process a homelessness application and provide interim accommodation under section 188 of the Housing Act 1996. This agreement is confirmed by the parties in writing and a **consent order** is prepared and sent to the court. The consent order confirms that the claim for judicial review is withdrawn on the basis of the council's agreement to process the application and provide interim accommodation. The consent order also provides that Anywhere Council meet Mrs Farah's costs on the application.

[HIGH COURT SEAL]

In the High Court of Justice   **Crown Office Ref:**
Queens Bench Division
Crown Office List

In the matter of an application for judicial review

The Queen v Anywhere Council

Ex parte Maryam Farah

Application for permission to apply for judicial review following an oral hearing.

NOTIFICATION of the Court's decision.

IT IS ORDERED by Ms Susan Sarandon QC sitting as a deputy judge that:

1. Permission be granted

2. There be expedition and an Injunction requiring Anywhere Council to ensure that accommodation is made available for the Applicant and her children pending the final determination of these proceedings

3. There be a detailed assessment of the Applicant's costs in accordance with Regulation 107 of the Civil Legal Aid (General) Regulations 1989

Ms K Winslett of Counsel for the Claimant

(This matter occupied the time of the court from 11.50am to 12.01pm)

Date: 5 August 2002

BY THE COURT

Where permission to apply has been granted, claimant's and their legal advisers are reminded of their obligation to reconsider the merits of the application in the light of the Defendant's affidavit.

Claimant's solicitors: Yourclaim Solicitors, Anywhere
Defendant's solicitors: Legal Department, Anywhere Council

Case study 2: **Homelessness appeal**

Background

James Brown, his partner and three children, are facing eviction from accommodation provided by Anytown Borough Council following a previous homelessness application in March 2000. The council sought a possession order due to a number of allegations of anti-social behaviour and nuisance, but did not have to prove grounds for possession as the tenancy was non–secure. A possession order was granted to expire on 25 January 2002.

Soon after the original possession hearing, James Brown made a fresh homelessness application to Anytown Borough Council. In its decision letter, the council informs James Brown that he has been found to be intentionally homeless, citing the alleged nuisance. With the assistance of his local Citizens Advice Bureau (CAB), James Brown sought a review of that decision, but the council confirmed its decision by letter dated 23 January 2002.

The CAB refer the case to a firm of solicitors who decide that there are grounds to appeal the decision. They send a **letter before action** (not attached) indicating that, unless the local authority agree to withdraw the review decision and issue a fresh decision on review, an appeal will be brought in the county court under section 204(3) of the Housing Act 1996.

They also ask the council to exercise its discretion, under section 204(4), to continue to provide accommodation to the Browns during the period for filing the appeal, and thereafter until the outcome of the appeal. The local authority refuse to withdraw the review decision, but confirm that the Browns can remain at the property until the outcome of the appeal.

The solicitor with conduct of the case, in exercise of the firm's devolved powers, grants emergency legal funding to James Brown. A witness statement from James Brown is prepared and another witness statement of one of his neighbours, Martha Reeves, is also prepared in support of the appeal. The solicitor instructs counsel to prepare the appeal papers.

Points to note

(1) Although the skeleton argument (see page 296) is filed at the same time as the Appellant's notice, it may be filed within 14 days if it cannot be filed on the date of issue.

(2) In the letter from Mr Brown's solicitors to Anytown County Court, dated 11 February 2002 (see page 285), the issue fee is referred to as being £100. However, the court fee varies between different courts and also may depend on whether permission to appeal is being sought.

(3) As Mr Brown's solicitors exercised devolved powers to grant emergency legal funding, there is no certificate at the time the appeal is issued. However, if a certificate is available, ie. where a faxed emergency application was made, a copy of the emergency certificate should accompany the notice of issue of emergency funding.

The Court Manager
Anytown County Court
Anytown

Our ref: Home/Brown

11 February 2002

Dear Sir or Madam,

Re: James Joe Brown v Anytown Borough Council
Statutory homelessness appeal pursuant to section 204(3) Housing Act 1996

We act for the Appellant, Mr Brown, in this matter, which is a statutory appeal against a decision by the Respondents that our client is intentionally homeless. The appeal is brought in accordance with Part 52 CPR 1998.

Please find enclosed:

1. Appellant's Notice in triplicate (with attached copy of decision letter issued by Respondent dated 23 January 2002)

2. Appellant's Skeleton Argument

3. Witness Statements of James Brown and Martha Reeves

4. Bundle of documents in support of appeal

5. Notice of Issue of Emergency Funding Certificate

6. Issue fee of £100 payable to HMPG.

As the Part 52 Rules provide for the filing and service of evidence for such appeals, we respectfully suggest that this matter should be listed for final hearing without the need for a directions hearing, thus saving court time and costs. Should either party require additional directions on any matter, an application can be made in the appropriate manner.

We would ask you to list the matter for three hours before a Circuit Judge at the earliest convenience.

As regards service of the Appellant's Notice and Skeleton Arguments, we request you to return the sealed copies to us as soon as possible, as Rule 52.4 CPR 1998 and paragraph 17.5 of the Practice Direction require the Appellant to serve these documents on the Respondent within seven days of filing.

Yours faithfully

Ms D Ross
Anyclaim Solicitors

Appellant's Notice

In the ANYTOWN COUNTY COURT

Notes for guidance are available which will help
you complete this form. Please read them
carefully before you complete each section.

For Court use only	
Appeal Court Reference No.	
Date filed	

Seal

Section 1	Details of the claim or case

Name of court _____

Case or claim number _____

Names of claimants/ applicants/ petitioner

James Joe Brown

Names of defendants/ respondents

Anytown Borough Council

In the case or claim, were you the
(tick appropriate box)

☐ claimant ☐ applicant ☐ petitioner

☐ defendant ☐ respondent ☑ other *(please specify)* HOMELESS APPLICANT

Section 2	Your (appellant's) name and address

Your (Appellant's) name James Joe Brown

Your Solicitor's name Ms Ross, Anyclaim Solicitors *(if you are legally represented)*

Your (your solicitor's) address

1 Church Lane
Anytown
Anycounty

reference or contact name DR/000/01

contact telephone number

DX number

1

N161 Appellant's Notice (4.00)

Printed on behalf of The Court Service

Section 3	Respondent's name and address

Respondent's name   Anytown Borough Council

Solicitor's name   Mr Wilson   *(if the respondent is legally represented)*

Respondent's (solicitor's) contact address

Civic Offices
Green Street
Anytown

reference or contact name	
contact telephone number	
DX number	

Details of other respondents are attached ☐ Yes   ☐ No

Section 4	Time estimate for appeal hearing

Do not complete if appealing to the Court of Appeal

	Days	Hours	Minutes
How long do you estimate it will take to put your appeal to the appeal court at the hearing?		3	

Who will represent you at the appeal hearing?   ☐ Yourself   ☐ Solicitor   ☑ Counsel

Section 5	Details of the order(s) or part(s) of order(s) you want to appeal

Name of Judge

NOT APPLICABLE

Date of order(s)

NOT APPLICABLE

If only part of an order is appealed, write out that part (or those parts)

Was the case allocated to a track? ☐ Yes   ☐ No   **N/A**

If Yes, which track was the case allocated to? ☐ fast track   ☐ multi-track

Is the order you are appealing a case management order?   ☐ Yes   ☐ No   **N/A**

2

Section 6	Permission to Appeal

Has permission to appeal been granted?

Yes ☐   complete box **A**   No ☑   complete box **B**

if you are asking for permission or it is not required

A

Date of order granting permission _____

Name of Judge _____

Name of Court _____

B

☑ I do not need permission

☐ I _____
Appellant('s solicitor) seek permission to appeal the order(s) at **section 5** above.

Are you making any other applications?   Yes ☐   No ☑
If Yes, complete section 10

Is the appellant in receipt of legal aid certificate or a community legal service fund (CLSF) certificate?   Yes ☑   No ☐

Section 7	Grounds for appeal

I (the appellant) appeal(s) the order(s) at **section 5** because:

Please refer to attached grounds of appeal.

| Section 8 | Arguments in support of grounds |

My skeleton argument is:-

☐ set out below   ☑ attached   ☐ will follow within 14 days of filing this notice

I (the appellant) will rely on the following arguments at the hearing of the appeal:-

4

| Section 9 | What decision are you asking the appeal court to make? |

I (the Appellant) am (is) asking that:-

(tick appropriate box)

☐ the order(s) at **section 5** be set aside

☑ the order(s) at **section 5** be varied and the following order(s) substituted :-

> The Appellant asks this court to exercise its power under section 204(3) of the Housing Act 1996 to quash or vary the decision at section 5 that the Appellant is intentionally homeless.

☐ a new trial be ordered

☐ the appeal court makes the following additional orders :-

5

Section 10	Other applications

I wish to make an application for additional orders

☐ in this section

☐ in the Part 23 application form (N244) attached

Part A
I apply (the appellant applies) for an order (a draft of which is attached) that :-

because :-

Part B
I (we) wish to rely on :

☐ evidence in Part C
☐ witness statement (affidavit)

Part C

I (we) wish to rely on the following evidence in support of this application:-

Statement of Truth

I believe (the appellant believes) that the facts stated in Section 10 are true.

Full name _____

Name of appellant's solicitor's firm _____

signed _____ position or office held _____

Appellant ('s solicitor)   (if signing on behalf of firm or company)

Section 11	Supporting documents

If you do not yet have a document that you intend to use to support your appeal, identify it, give the date when you expect it to be available and give the reasons why it is not currently available in the box below.

Please tick the papers you are filing with this notice and any you will be filing later.

☑ Your skeleton argument *(if separate)*

☑ A copy of the ~~order~~ DECISION being appealed

☐ A copy of any order giving or refusing permission to appeal together with a copy of the reasons for that decision

☐ Any witness statements or affidavits in support of any application included in this appellant's notice

☑ A copy of the legal aid or CLSF certificate *(if legally represented)*

☑ A bundle of documents for the appeal hearing containing copies of your appellant's notice and all the papers listed above and the following:-

    ☐ a suitable record of the reasons for the judgment of the lower court;

    ☐ any statements of case;

    ☑ any other affidavit or witness statement filed in support of your appeal;

    ☐ any relevant transcript or note of evidence;

    ☐ any relevant application notices or case management documents;

    ☐ any skeleton arguments relied on by the lower court;
       relevant affidavits, witness statements, summaries, experts' reports and exhibits;

    ☐ any other documents ordered by the court; (give details)

    _____

    ☐ in a second appeal, the original order appealed, the reasons given for making that order and the appellant's notice appealing that original (first) order

    ☐ if the appeal is from a decision of a Tribunal, the Tribunal's reasons for that decision, the original decision reviewed by the Tribunal and the reasons for that original decision

Reasons why you have not supplied a document and date when you expect it to be available:-

CLSF CERTIFICATE NOT YET RECEIVED. IT WILL BE FILED AS SOON AS IT IS AVAILABLE WHICH WE EXPECT TO BE WITHIN 14 DAYS

Signed _____*D Ross*_____ Appellant ('s Solicitor)

IN THE ANYTOWN COUNTY COURT   <u>Claim No:</u>

BETWEEN:

JAMES JOE BROWN

Appellant

and

ANYTOWN BOROUGH COUNCIL

<u>**Respondent**</u>

GROUNDS OF APPEAL

**The decision is wrong in law and Wednesbury perverse for the
following reasons:**

<u>Inadequate inquiries</u>

1. The respondent has failed to carry out proper or adequate inquiries either
    at the decision stage or at the review stage into the allegations of
    nuisance made against the Appellant. There is an apparent admission in
    the review letter dated 23 January 2002 that the reviewing officer did
    little more than review the Appellant's housing file held at the relevant
    housing management office. As such the Respondent has failed to
    properly consider whether the Appellant is intentionally homeless.

2. The authority do not appear to have given any or any real consideration
    to the new material advanced in the letter from the Citizens Advice
    Bureau, dated 11 January 2002, namely,

    (a) the possibility that that the allegations made by neighbours against
    the Appellant were not genuine but founded on racial prejudice

    (b) the fact that the Appellant lives in an area where many of the
    residents are elderly and that the allegations of nuisance may reflect no
    more than their susceptibility to the normal behaviour and noise of the
    Appellant's young children

    (c) the fact that a number of the Appellant's neighbours corroborated the
    Appellant's version of events in relation to the alleged nuisance.

3. It follows that the section 184 letter and the review decision letter are
    based upon a failure to undertake obvious inquiries and are tainted with
    unfairness and illegality.

Natural justice

4. Both at the decision stage and at the review stage, the authority has failed to put specific allegations to the Appellant in order to afford him the opportunity to refute them or explain any relevant circumstances surrounding an incident. It is established law that natural justice requires that any fact that the authority considers to be of substance in reaching its decision on intentionality and which is adverse to the Appellant should be put to him in order that he may have an opportunity to put his version of events.

Inadequate reasons

5. Both at the decision stage and the review stage the Respondent has failed to identify and detail the specific acts which led it to conclude that the Appellant is intentionally homeless.

6. Insofar as the Respondent has considered any of the matters raised by the CAB in its letter dated 11 January 2002, and referred to in paragraph 2 above, it has failed to give adequate reasons as to why the contentions raised by the CAB in its letter have been rejected by the Respondent.

7. The failure to give adequate reasons precludes an understanding of the factors which influenced the decision maker and prevents the Appellant from assessing whether the decision is flawed.

Gil Scott-Heron
Counsel

IN THE ANYTOWN COUNTY COURT   <u>Claim No:</u>

BETWEEN:

JAMES JOE BROWN

<u>**Appellant**</u>

and

ANYTOWN BOROUGH COUNCIL

<u>**Respondent**</u>

APPELLANT'S SKELETON ARGUMENT

Brief factual background

1. The Appellant, his partner and his dependent children were provided with temporary accommodation by the Respondent in March 2000. The accommodation consisted of a three-bedroom house at 24 Upper Street, Anytown and was provided pursuant to the Respondent's housing duties under Part VII of the Housing Act 1996. This tenancy would necessarily be non-secure by virtue of Schedule 1, Paragraph 4 of the Housing Act 1985. As such the tenancy could be determined by simple notice to quit.

2. The Respondent alleges that the Appellant and/or his children were guilty of anti-social behaviour and, in particular, of causing noise nuisance to his neighbours. These allegations are denied by the Appellant.

3. The Respondent brought possession proceedings against the Appellant by issuing a claim form and particulars of claim on 11 October 2001. The matter was listed in the undefended possession list on 14 December 2001. At the hearing an outright possession order was made.

4. Although the allegations of nuisance were cited in the particulars of claim by the Respondent as its reason for bringing possession proceedings, these were not particularised. Moreover, the allegations would not have been tested in court because the judge would have had no option but to make an outright order provided the tenancy was duly determined by a valid notice to quit.

5. The Appellant duly applied as a person threatened with homelessness. By a decision letter dated 20 December 2001, the Appellant was found to be threatened with homelessness, in priority need but intentionally homeless. In the section 184 letter the full extent of the reasons given is:

You are deemed to be intentionally homeless due to your anti-social behaviour at your accommodation, namely noise nuisance to your neighbours.

6. On behalf of the Appellant, a review was requested by the Citizens Advice Bureau (CAB) in a letter dated 11 January 2002. The letter contained representations in support of the review and invited the reviewing officer to consider a number of factors.

7. By letter dated 23 January 2002, the Respondent notified the Appellant that it had completed the review. The letter confirmed the original decision that the Appellant was intentionally homeless.

8. The Appellant and his family are currently being housed by the Respondent in exercise of its discretion under section 204(4) of the Housing Act 1996 pending the outcome of this appeal.

Inadequate inquiries

1. There has been a failure to carry out necessary inquiries into the allegations that the Appellant and his family were guilty of anti-social behaviour and nuisance. In the review letter dated 23 January 2001 the Respondent's reviewing officer states that:

    Having reviewed the housing management file relating to your occupancy at 24 Upper Street, Anytown, I am satisfied that you made yourself intentionally homeless from that address and I confirm the decision made on your homelessness application.

    This statement represents an admission that the homelessness department carried out few, if any, of its own inquiries into the allegations of anti-social behaviour and nuisance.

2. In the letter dated 11 January 2002, the CAB invited the Respondent to carry out its own investigations as to whether the Appellant or his family were guilty of nuisance. Specifically, the letter asked the Respondent to consider the following factors in the review:

    (a) whether the complaints of the neighbours relating to the alleged anti-social behaviour were genuine or founded on racial prejudice

    (b) whether the fact that many residents in the immediate area were elderly may have caused them to be disturbed by the natural play and boisterousness of young children

    (c) the fact that the Appellant's denials of the allegations were supported by a number of other residents in the area.

    The review letter fails to address any of these matters and no reasons are given by the Respondent as to why such factors were not considered to be relevant to the question of intentionality.

3. It may be that the Respondent was under the same mistaken belief as the Appellant's CAB adviser, namely that there would have been some findings of nuisance by the court when the possession order was made. Be that as it may, there has been a failure to make independent or adequate inquiries into whether or not the Appellant is intentionally homeless both at the decision stage and at the review stage **(section 184 Housing Act 1996; R v Woodspring DC ex p Walters (1984) 16 HLR 73).**

4. The duty of the local authority to make appropriate inquiries is summarised in the judgment of Simon Brown J in **R v Gravesham Borough Council ex p Winchester (1986) 18 HLR 208 @214:**

    This burden lies upon the local authority to make appropriate inquiries... in a caring and sympathetic way... These inquiries should be pursued rigorously and fairly albeit the authority are not under a duty to conduct detailed CID-type inquiries... the applicant must be given an opportunity to explain matters which the local authority is minded to regard as weighing substantially against him.

Natural justice

5. The Appellant was not interviewed for the purpose of the review process and was not afforded an opportunity to refute specific allegations that were being levelled against him. An earlier request by the Appellant to see a copy of a petition that had allegedly been received complaining about his family's conduct was refused.

6. The failure to put specific allegations to the Appellant in order to afford him the opportunity to refute them, or explain any relevant circumstances surrounding an incident, is clearly wrong. It is established law that natural justice requires that any fact that the Respondent considers to be of substance in reaching its decision on intentionality, and which is adverse to the Appellant, should be put to him in order that he may have an opportunity to put his version of events. This is also set out in paragraph 15.6 of the Code of Guidance on Housing Act 1996 Parts VI and VII, which states:

    The act or omission referred to in paragraph 15.2 must be deliberate. An appellant should always be given an opportunity to explain an act or omission.

    R v LB Hackney ex p Decordova (1994) 27 HLR 108 @ 113 per Law J:

    In my judgment where an authority lock, stock and barrel is minded to disbelieve an account given by an Appellant for housing where the circumstances described in the account are critical to the issue whether the authority ought to offer her accommodation in a particular area, they are bound to put to the Appellant in an interview, or by some appropriate means, the matters that concern them. This must now surely be elementary law. If the authority is minded to make an adverse decision because it does not believe the account given by the Appellant, it has to give the Appellant an opportunity to deal with it.

Reasons

7. The section 184 decision letter and the review letter are manifestly defective in that each fails to give reasons for the finding of intentionality against the Appellant. The Respondent does not identify the incidents of nuisance which it is satisfied were intentional acts and which led to Appellant losing his accommodation.

8. The failure to identify specific acts which it has found caused the Appellant to lose his home is a failure to give adequate reasons. Moreover, if the further contentions raised by the CAB in their letter requesting a review were taken into account, there is a general failure to give reasons in that the review letter does not identify why these contentions have been rejected. In **R v LB Croydon ex p Graham (1993) 26 HLR 286: @291** Sir Thomas Bingham MR. held:

There is, nonetheless, an obligation under the Act to give reasons and that must impose on the council a duty to give reasons which are intelligible and which convey to the Appellant the reasons why the application has been rejected in such a way that if they disclose an error of reasoning the Appellant may take such steps as may be indicated.

@ 292 Steyn LJ. added:

Nevertheless, it seems to me that if the reasons are insufficient to enable the court to consider the lawfulness of the decision the obligation of furnishing reasons has been breached and in that event the decision itself will be unlawful.

A similarly defective decision letter was quashed in **R v Camden LBC ex p Adair (1996) 29 HLR 236 @ 247.**

IN THE ANYTOWN COUNTY COURT   <u>**Claim No:**</u>

BETWEEN:

JAMES JOE BROWN

<u>**Appellant**</u>

and

ANYTOWN BOROUGH COUNCIL

<u>**Respondent**</u>

WITNESS STATEMENT OF JAMES JOE BROWN

---

1. I am James Joe Brown of 24 Upper Street, Anytown, Anycounty. I am the Appellant in this matter and make this statement in support of my appeal.

2. I made an application to Anytown Borough Council as a homeless applicant in March 2000. Following this application the council offered a three-bedroom house at 24 Upper Street, Anytown, Anycounty. I accepted the offer and the tenancy began on 27 March 2000. I have occupied this property with my partner, Mary Brown, and our three children now aged 10, 12 and 13 years ever since that date.

3. I received a letter from the council dated 15 July 2000 indicating that they had received complaints of alleged anti-social behaviour involving myself and members of my family. This letter is attached as exhibit "JB1".

4. The first allegation made was that I held a party that continued until four o'clock in the morning. The council did not specify in the letter when it was alleged that there was a party at my house.

5. The second allegation concerned the behaviour of my children, namely that they had caused a nuisance by climbing on bungalow roofs; using skateboards and cycles in a reckless manner down slopes in an area where elderly and frail people predominantly live; trespassing in gardens; allowing rubbish to be strewn about and sliding down steps on various 'sledges' made of old doors and other items.

6. I heard nothing more about these allegations until some eight months later when I received a further letter from the council dated 13 March 2001. This letter is attached as exhibit "JB2". The letter stated that the council wanted to interview me about the allegations of anti-social behaviour.

7. I attended an interview at the council offices on 16 March 2001. I told the council officer present that I categorically denied the allegation that I had

held a late night party at any time. I also denied that my children had used skateboards or cycles in the manner alleged and further that they had not trespassed in neighbouring gardens or allowed rubbish to be strewn about. I did admit, however, that there was an incident when my children had climbed on a few roofs and used old doors as slides. I informed the council that the children had been reprimanded for this behaviour which they had not repeated since. No new complaints were made known to me at this meeting.

8. I received a letter from the council dated 17 May 2001, which stated that they had received a complaint of excessive noise from my house over the course of the previous weekend. This letter is attached as exhibit "JB3". Shortly afterwards, I attended a further meeting at the council at which I denied these further allegations. I cannot remember the exact date of the meeting.

9. The council contacted me further by letter dated 7 August 2001. This letter is attached as exhibit "JB4". The letter informed me that the council had received complaints that I held a party over the weekend of 28-29 July 2001. I informed the council that these allegations were false and that, in fact, the family and myself stayed with friends that weekend. After this meeting the friends who we stayed with that weekend sent a letter to the council confirming this fact. The council's response to this was to accuse us of allowing others to use the house whilst we were away. I flatly denied this. There was no one in the house over the weekend of 28-29 July.

10. On one occasion I was told by a housing officer that a petition had been given to the council, signed by seven local residents, asking me to be removed from the area. I asked if I could see the petition, but the officer refused, stating that he had to protect the residents involved.

11. I received a possession summons on 13 October 2001 informing me that the council was seeking a court order to evict us from our home. The court hearing took place on 14 December 2001. I attended the hearing, but was not allowed to speak so that I could deny the allegations of nuisance referred to by the council. The court made a possession order requiring us to leave the property by 25 January 2002.

12. During the week after this court hearing, one of my neighbours indicated to me that he was surprised that I was living in the house. He asked why I was still there and remarked that I did not belong in the area. He also suggested that I would be better off living in town with my "other friends". This man does not know any personal details about me and certainly does not know any of my friends. Because of this and his overall tone and manner, I took his reference to "my friends" to mean other black

people. There is a large Asian and Afro-Caribbean population living in and around the town centre of Anytown.

13. After the court hearing on 14 December 2001, I made another homelessness application to Anytown Borough Council. I received the council's decision by letter on or about 2 January 2002, though the letter was actually dated 20 December 2000. This letter is attached as exhibit "JB 5". The decision was that I was homeless and in priority need but that I had made myself intentionally homeless due to the alleged anti-social behaviour, and specifically noise nuisance against my neighbours.

14. Soon after receiving the decision letter, I contacted my local borough councillor, who put me in touch with the Citizens Advice Bureau (CAB). I informed my adviser at the CAB that I suspected a degree of racial discrimination amongst some of the older residents in the area and confirmed that the allegations against my family were untrue.

15. The CAB on my behalf requested a review of the council's decision that I was intentionally homeless. The council confirmed its decision that I was intentionally homeless by letter dated 23 January 2002. This letter is attached as exhibit "JB6". Between the date when the request for review was made and the date of the council's decision on review, I had not been told in any detail the allegations made against me, nor have I been given the opportunity to refute them.

16. The CAB referred me to a solicitor. My solicitor contacted the council to inform them that I wished to appeal to the county court against its review decision. She also asked the council to continue to provide me and my family with accommodation until the appeal has been resolved. The council has agreed to this.

I believe that the facts stated in this witness statement are true

Signed *James Brown*

Dated *11th February 2002*

Case update

James Brown's solicitors lodge the appeal papers by taking them in person to the court on 11 February 2002. The request not to list the matter for directions is accepted and the case is listed for final hearing for one half day on 17 April 2002. The appeal papers are served personally on Anytown Borough Council at the Civic Offices on 12 February 2002.

On 28 February 2002, the council lodges a Respondent's notice and its skeleton argument. In addition it files a witness statement by Ms Knight, the Housing Needs Manager who made the decision on review. The witness statement (not shown here) details dealings with James Brown during the course of his tenancy at 24 Upper Street and at previous accommodation also provided by Anytown Borough Council. It contains numerous allegations of anti-social behaviour provided by other residents in the area. In view of this, the parties agree that James Brown can file a second witness statement detailing his response to the alleged incidents in Ms Knight's witness statement. James Brown's second witness statement (not shown here) is filed at court on 7 March 2001.

Point to note

As mentioned in Chapter 15 (see page 238), it is unusual for local authorities to file a Respondent's notice. The reason that the local authority has filed a notice in this case is that it is asking the court to uphold the finding of intentionality, not only on the basis of the reasons given in the review decision letter, but also for additional reasons. In this situation, local authorities will often agree to withdraw the review decision and undertake a fresh reconsideration of the case which will give rise to fresh appeal rights under section 204 of the Housing Act 1996.

IN THE ANYTOWN COUNTY COURT   <u>Claim No:</u>

BETWEEN:

JAMES JOE BROWN

<u>**Appellant**</u>

and

ANYTOWN BOROUGH COUNCIL

<u>**Respondent**</u>

RESPONDENT'S NOTICE

---

1. The Respondent's Case, and answer to the arguments set out in the Appellant's Skeleton Argument, is contained in the Respondent's Skeleton Argument dated 7 March 2002.

2. The Respondent further wishes to ask the Court to uphold the decision that the Appellant was intentionally homeless for reasons additional to those contained in the decision letter dated 23 January 2002.

3. The reasons given in the letter of 23 January 2002 were:

    (i) you have, over a considerable period of time, been the subject of many complaints from the areas surrounding your accommodation;

    (ii) many requests for moderation in your behaviour have been made;

    (iii) you have been informed of the consequence of continuing nuisance;

    (iv) possession proceedings were continued as you failed to comply with requests.

4. The additional reasons on which the Respondent also wishes to rely are:

    (v) no other decision could reasonably and/or properly have been reached on the available evidence;

    (vi) the result of a further review would inevitably, or virtually certainly, be the same and, following the case of **Barty-King v Ministry of Defence (1979) 2AER** 80 the Court should not, in those circumstances, intervene even if it considers there to have been any procedural irregularities;

(vii) any other decision would have placed the Respondent in breach of its covenants of quiet enjoyment in favour of neighbouring tenants and/or in breach of its obligations and/or responsibilities to other tenants generally.

James Wilson

J Wilson
Solicitor, Anytown Borough Council

Dated this 28th day of February 2002

IN THE ANYTOWN COUNTY COURT   <u>Claim No:</u>

BETWEEN:

JAMES JOE BROWN

Appellant

and

ANYTOWN BOROUGH COUNCIL

<u>**Respondent**</u>

RESPONDENT'S SKELETON ARGUMENT

<u>Appeal based on law or on fact?</u>

1. The right of appeal under section 204 of the Housing Act 1996 does, of course, only arise on questions of law. The grounds of appeal are put forward accordingly. However, an examination of the evidence, including the two witness statements filed at court on behalf of Mr Brown, will demonstrate that at the heart of this appeal are issues of fact and not law and, further, that exploration of the supporting evidence of Mrs Reeves would inevitably take the court into an extensive inquiry on matters of fact. Stripped to its bare essentials the council's case is that Mr Brown had caused serious nuisance to neighbours. The council was entitled to make a finding of intentionality and accordingly not to offer further accommodation. Mr Brown has consistently denied most of the allegations. He makes limited admissions at paragraph 7 (see page 301) of his witness statement dated 2 February 2002 but, those admissions apart, there is a substantial conflict of fact.

2. That the real issue is fact and not law is clearly demonstrated by the witness statement of Mrs Reeves. She states at paragraph 11, 'It is my opinion that the council has been seriously misinformed'. Much of what she says in her statement is contentious and, if it were to be admitted, the council would want to call evidence in rebuttal. However, the court is not supposed to receive either oral evidence or evidence that was not before the council (CPR Rule 52.11(2)). Mrs Reeves's evidence was not before the council and it follows that her statement should not have been filed.

3. While Mr Brown naturally does not like the decision which has been reached, the council's case is that it has endeavoured faithfully to discharge its statutory duties in a context of:

- serious complaints against Mr Brown of persistent anti-social behaviour at successive addresses;

- no adequate explanation for, or diminution of, that behaviour, despite repeated oral and written warnings;

- no fewer than 2,237 homelessness applications to the council in the nine months from April to December 2001;

- approximately 603 households at present in temporary accommodation in the Borough, including some in overspill bed and breakfast accommodation, and the need in those circumstances to be satisfied as to any Appellant's entitlement to the assistance for the accommodation which he or she seeks.

The history of Mr Brown's dealings with the council's homelessness section

4.   The council housed Mr Brown in March 2000. Its involvement with him had, in fact, commenced on 5 November 1999 when he made his first homelessness application. Ms Knight has set out a detailed account of the council's dealings with Mr Brown from paragraph 6 onwards in her witness statement. Ms Knight was exceptionally well informed on the matter upon which she had been called upon to decide. Mr Brown had had numerous opportunities to redeem his situation and possession proceedings in respect of the temporary accommodation at 24 Upper Street had only commenced in September 2001 when repeated warnings had fallen on apparently deaf ears and much distress had been caused to others. Ms Knight was entitled to take account of that credible, and well-documented, history and it would have been perverse and irresponsible had she not done so.

Inevitability of decision

5.   The case of **Barty-King and Another v Ministry of Defence (1979) 2AER 80** is authority for the proposition that a decision by a body, such as a housing authority, will not be quashed, despite obvious procedural irregularities, if it is inevitable that the same decision would in any case have been reached. That case was concerned with the review of a decision by the Defence Council, an Administrative Tribunal. May J. deals in some detail with the entitlement of a court to review the determination of an inferior tribunal holding that entitlement to exist only where it is demonstrated beyond doubt that the tribunal's decision was a perverse decision which no reasonable tribunal, on the material before it, could have reached.

6.   It is the council's case in this matter that it was inevitable that, on a proper consideration of the evidence, the decision which Ms Knight made would be made. Far from her decision being one which no reasonable tribunal could have reached, on the material of repeated nuisance available to her, and the applicable law as to intentional homelessness

and acts or omissions of an Appellant, no other conclusion was open to her. The guidance available to her at paragraph 15.7(d) of the Homelessness Code of Guidance lends support to that view. The Code advises that *'acts or omissions which may be regarded as deliberate could include the following examples:*

(d) where someone is evicted because of anti-social behaviour such as nuisance to neighbours, harassment etc.'

Inadequate inquiries?

7. Ms Knight's witness statement details the extensive inquiries made between March 2000 and January 2002 when Mr Brown had been the council's tenant. There was an intimate knowledge of what had occurred at, and around, 24 Upper Street. There had been various complaints direct to the Homelessness Section and reports from the Estate Management Section to the Homelessness Section. There had been many letters to Mr Brown, and interviews with him on, at the very least, the following dates:

    (a) 16 March 2000

    (b) sometime after the letter dated 17 May 2000 (statement of Mr Brown paragraph 8)

    (c) 26 September 2000.

8. On the basis of the substantial information already available to it, the council applied its mind to the further homelessness application from November 2001. There is no substance to the assertion of inadequate inquiry.

Natural justice

9. Throughout his tenancy of 24 Upper Street, Anytown, there were numerous occasions when the allegations of nuisance were put to Mr Brown. He ignored or denied most of these. There had been numerous letters to him and meetings in March, May and September 2001.

10. It is clear from the note of the meeting of 26 September 2001 that the real difficulty was not a failure to put specific allegations to Mr Brown, but rather a difference of opinion as to the truth of those allegations. Over a period of 18 months he failed to refute a variety of allegations or to give an adequate explanation. He had had every opportunity, including in a number of interviews, to respond to the matters which had caused the council continuing concern.

11. Ms Knight deals with this at paragraph 41 of her witness statement. Inter alia she makes the point that the content of the 150 paragraphs contained in the three exhibits to her statement represented 'far more

than 150 specific allegations'. To have gone through each and every allegation, and listened on each point first to the complainants and then to Mr Brown, would have taken many hours. There is no requirement that she should have embarked on such a detailed quasi-judicial process.

12.   Reference is made in the Appellant's skeleton argument to paragraph 15.6 of the Code. This states that 'an Appellant should always be given an opportunity to explain an act or omission'. The council contends that Mr Brown had that opportunity on many occasions.

Failure to give specific reasons?

13.   Ms Knight responds to this allegation at paragraph 40 of her statement. As Sir Thomas Bingham MR held in **R v LB Croydon ex p Graham (1993) 26 HLR 286**, to which reference is made at paragraph 4 of the Skeleton Argument, the obligation on the council is an obligation to give reasons which are intelligible and which convey to the Appellant the reason why the application has been rejected in order to enable him, and his advisers, to see whether those reasons might be challengeable in law. In the judgment he implies that a "nit-picking" approach to the decision letter would not be appropriate, saying that 'a pedantic exegesis of letters of this kind would be inappropriate'. The question is whether Ms Knight got the matter broadly right, and stated the essentials, in her letter of 23 January 2002. She is not to be criticised for omitting minor details if she has given an adequate statement of her overall reasons.

James Wilson

J Wilson,
Anytown Borough Council

Dated this 1st day of March 2002

Case update

The appeal hearing is heard before a circuit judge. The judge considers submissions made on behalf of James Brown and the council and delivers judgment allowing the appeal and quashing the decision made on review dated 23 January 2002.

The judge gives as his reasons the failure by the council to properly consider the matters raised by the Citizens Advice Bureau on review, in particular the possibility that the allegations made by other residents were racially motivated. The judge notes that a number of residents living in close proximity to the Browns, including Mrs Reeves, had not been approached to comment on the allegations.

The judge also orders the council to pay the Appellant's costs.

The council undertakes to conduct fresh inquiries by a senior officer not involved in the case previously and to provide accommodation pending the fresh review of James Brown's homelessness application.

Background

Denise Lewis is 26. She is a full-time nursing student living with her three year old son, Carl, in council accommodation. She receives an annual bursary award of £8,500 and child benefit. Denise also receives housing benefit as a lone parent student, but this is subject to the student restriction and she is expected to pay nearly all of her weekly rent liability. During term-time, Denise pays £70 in nursery fees. As her bursary is not classed as remuneration from employment for housing benefit purposes, she is not eligible for the child care disregard for housing benefit or working families tax credit.

This case study falls into two unrelated parts. In the first part, Denise seeks advice having just received a **claim form** and **particulars of claim** from the council.

In the second part, Denise approaches her solicitor after a possession hearing when an absolute possession order has been made against her.

Part 1

Denise Lewis approaches her solicitor, Roger Black, having received a **claim form** and **particulars of claim** (which are shown on the following pages) from the council on the previous day. She cannot recall whether or not she received a notice seeking possession.

Denise explains the background to the matter. She states the financial hardship she has suffered and which has led to the rent arrears upon which the claim form and particulars of claim are based. However, she informs her solicitor that her situation has now improved as her brother is now caring for Carl during term-time, and her mother has lent her £500.

Her solicitor drafts a full defence, which is shown on page 320. However, he is mindful of the Practice Direction to Part 55 which provides that Form N11R must be used for the defence. To ensure compliance with this, the full defence is attached to a completed Form N11R and both are filed at court (Form N11R is not shown here).

The defence is supported by **witness statements** from Denise and her brother. These are not produced here but would be similar to those provided for part 2 at pages 332 and 334.

In the meantime, Roger Black advises Denise to pay the £500 borrowed from her mother to reduce the rent arrears. In addition he suggests that she pays a minimum of £2.70 and the current rent weekly.

At the hearing on 25 October 2002, the judge finds that it would not be reasonable to make a possession order, given the change in Denise's circumstances, the reduction in the arrears and the ongoing weekly payments she has been making. He adjourns the case on terms (see page 323).

Claim form for possession of property

In the
ANYTOWN COUNTY COURT

Claim No.	ABC 123

Claimant
(name(s) and address(es))

ANYTOWN DISTRICT COUNCIL
CIVIC OFFICES
MEDAL WAY
ANYTOWN

SEAL

Defendant(s)
(name(s) and address(es))

DENISE LEWIS
12 OLYMPIC STREET
ANYTOWN

The claimant is claiming possession of :

12 OLYMPIC STREET
ANYTOWN

which (includes) (does not include) residential property. Full particulars of the claim are attached.
(The claimant is also making a claim for money).

This claim will be heard on: 25TH OCTOBER   20 0**2** at 10.30   am/~~pm~~

at ANYTOWN COUNTY COURT
   THE LAW COURTS
   SILVER ROAD
   ANYTOWN

At the hearing
• The court will consider whether or not you must leave the property and, if so, when.
• It will take into account information the claimant provides and any you provide.

What you should do
• Get help and advice immediately from a solicitor or an advice agency.
• Help yourself and the court by **filling in the defence form** and **coming to the hearing** to make sure the court knows all the facts.

Defendant's name and address for service

DENISE LEWIS
12 OLYMPIC STREET
ANYTOWN

Court fee	£ 120.00
Solicitor's costs	£ 74.50
Total amount	£ 194.50

Issue date	17 AUGUST 2002

N5 Claim form for possession of property (10.01)   *Printed on behalf of The Court Service*

| Claim No. | ABC 123 |

Grounds for possession

The claim for possession is made on the following ground(s):

- ☑ rent arrears
- ☐ other breach of tenancy
- ☐ forfeiture of the lease
- ☐ mortgage arrears
- ☐ other breach of the mortgage
- ☐ trespass
- ☐ other *(please specify)* _____

Anti-social behaviour

The claimant is alleging:

- ☐ actual or threatened assault
- ☐ actual or threatened serious damage to the property

See full details in the attached particulars of claim

Does, or will, the claim include any issues under the Human Rights Act 1998?   ☐ Yes ☑ No

Statement of Truth

*(I believe)(The claimant believes) that the facts stated in this claim form are true.
* I am duly authorised by the claimant to sign this statement.

signed __*[signature]*__   date **16 AUGUST 2002**

*(Claimant)(Litigation friend *(where the claimant is a child or a patient)*)(Claimant's solicitor)
delete as appropriate

Full name   **FRAZER RICHARDSON**

Name of claimant's solicitor's firm **ANYTOWN DISTRICT COUNCIL, LEGAL DEPARTMENT**

position or office held **ASSISTANT SOLICITOR**
   (if signing on behalf of firm or company)

Claimant's or claimant's solicitor's address to which documents or payments should be sent if different from overleaf.	AS OVERLEAF		*if applicable*	
		Ref. no.	
		fax no.	
		DX no.	
		e-mail	
	Postcode	Tel. no.	

Particulars of claim
for possession
(rented residential premises)

In the
ANYTOWN COUNTY COURT

ANYTOWN DISTRICT COUNCIL

DENISE LEWIS

Claim No.

ABC 123

Claimant

Defendant

1. The claimant has a right to possession of:

    12 OLYMPIC STREET
    ANYTOWN

2. To the best of the claimant's knowledge the following persons are in possession of the property:

    DENISE LEWIS (THE DEFENDANT)
    AND
    CARL LEWIS (THE DEFENDANT'S SON – AGED 3 YEARS)

About the tenancy

3. (a) The premises are let to the defendant(s) under a(n)   SECURE   tenancy
    which began on 15TH SEPTEMBER 1998   .

    (b) The current rent is £57.62   and is payable each (week) (fortnight) (month).
    (*other*   )

    (c) Any unpaid rent or charge for use and occupation should be calculated at £ 7.41   per day.

4. The reason the claimant is asking for possession is:

    (a) because the defendant has not paid the rent due under the terms of the tenancy agreement.
    (Details are set out below)(Details are shown on the attached rent statement)

    AS AT 6TH AUGUST 2002, THERE WERE OUTSTANDING ARREARS OF RENT IN THE SUM OF £2,148.35
    [SEE ATTACHED SCHEDULE OF RENT ACCOUNT]

    (b) because the defendant has failed to comply with other terms of the tenancy.
    Details are set out below.

    (c) because: (including any (other) statutory grounds)

5. The following steps have already been taken to recover any arrears:

VARIOUS WRITTEN AND VERBAL REMINDERS THAT RENT ACCOUNT IN ARREARS
LETTER ADVISING DEFENDANT OF LEVEL OF RENT ARREARS AND OF CLAIMANT'S INTENTION TO ISSUE
POSSESSION PROCEEDINGS SENT BY FIRST CLASS MAIL ON 6TH AUGUST 2002.
VISIT TO DEFENDANT'S HOME ON 7TH AUGUST 2002.

6. The appropriate ~~(notice to quit)~~ ~~(notice of breach of lease)~~ (notice seeking possession)
~~(other~~ ————————) was served on the defendant on 9 JULY   20 02 .

About the defendant

7. The following information is known about the defendant's circumstances:

THE DEFENDANT HAS ONE DEPENDENT CHILD AGED 3 YEARS
THE CLAIMANT UNDERSTANDS THAT THE DEFENDANT IS A FULL-TIME NURSE AND RECEIVES AN
ANNUAL BURSARY AND CHILD BENEFIT. SHE IS IN RECEIPT OF HOUSING BENEFIT BUT THIS IS
RESTRICTED TO £11.67 PER WEEK

About the claimant

8. The claimant is asking the court to take the following financial or other information into account when making
its decision whether or not to grant an order for possession:

CLAIMANT IS A LOCAL AUTHORITY RESPONSIBLE FOR THE EFFECTIVE AND EFFICIENT MANAGEMENT OF
ITS HOUSING STOCK

Forfeiture

9. (a) There is no underlessee or mortgagee entitled to claim relief against forfeiture.

or   (b)   of

is entitled to claim relief against forfeiture as underlessee or mortgagee.

What the court is being asked to do:

10. The claimant asks the court to order that the defendant(s):

    (a) give the claimant possession of the premises;

    (b) pay the unpaid rent and any charge for use and occupation up to the date an order is made;

    (c) pay rent and any charge for use and occupation from the date of the order until the claimant recovers possession of the property;

    (d) pay the claimant's costs of making this claim.

Statement of Truth

*(I believe)(The claimant believes) that the facts stated in these particulars of claim are true.
* I am duly authorised by the claimant to sign this statement.

signed _____ date **16 AUGUST 2002**

*(Claimant)(Litigation friend(where claimant is a child or a patient))(Claimant's solicitor)
delete as appropriate

Full name **FRAZER RICHARDSON**

Name of claimant's solicitor's firm **ANYTOWN DISTRICT COUNCIL, LEGAL DEPARTMENT**

position or office held **ASSISTANT SOLICITOR**
                    (if signing on behalf of firm or company)

IN THE ANYTOWN COUNTY COURT   <u>Claim No:</u> ABC 123

BETWEEN:

ANYTOWN DISTRICT COUNCIL

<u>Claimant</u>

and

DENISE LEWIS

<u>Defendant</u>

DEFENCE

---

1. Save that it is denied that the Claimant is entitled to possession of 12 Olympic Street, Anytown, paragraphs 1, 2 and 3 of the Particulars of Claim are admitted.

2. No admissions are made as to any arrears of rent or level of the same and the Claimant is put to strict proof of the existence or level of any arrears.

3. No admissions are made as to the service, form or effect of any Notice of Seeking Possession.

4. Further and in the alternative the Defendant claims the protection of section 84 of the Housing Act 1985 and denies that in all the circumstances it would be reasonable for an Order of Possession to be made.

PARTICULARS

(i)   The Defendant moved into the property in September 1998. Until the birth of her son in January 1999 she worked full-time and paid the rent from her wages.

(ii) From January 1999 until September 2001 the Defendant was in receipt of income support and her weekly rent was paid in full by direct housing benefit payments to her landlords. Up to September 2001, there were no significant rent arrears on the Defendant's rent account.

(iii) In September 2001, the Defendant commenced a nursing diploma course. She receives a bursary of £8,500.00 per annum in respect of the course. She also receives child benefit at a weekly amount of £17.55.

(iv) As a lone parent student, the Defendant has been entitled to housing benefit since the nursing course began in September 2001. However, she is subject to the "student rent reduction", which reduces by a set amount the weekly rent eligible for housing benefit. In the academic year 2001-2002 the Defendant's eligible rent was reduced by £27.75 per week.

(v) The Defendant, until recently, was paying £70.00 in respect of nursery charges for her three-year-old son. Prior to commencing her course, the Defendant believed that in calculating her housing benefit, the full amount of the charges would be disregarded from her income. However, as the bursary she receives is not classified as "remuneration from employment" this income is not disregarded.

(vi) As a consequence of the circumstances outlined in paragraphs (iv) and (v), the Defendant has been entitled to housing benefit of only £11.67 per week towards total rent liability of £57.62 per week.

(vii) The Defendant has applied to the relevant Housing Benefit Department for Discretionary Housing Payments on the grounds that her circumstances are exceptional. The Housing Benefit Department has turned down this request. The Defendant is appealing against this decision with the assistance of her local Citizens Advice Bureau. If the appeal is successful the rent arrears will be reduced substantially.

(viii) The Defendant's financial situation has now improved in that she has removed her son from the nursery. She has made arrangements for her brother to look after her son at no charge. Consequently, the Defendant has an additional £70.00 per week with which to pay the full amount of her rebated rent.

(ix) Since 2nd August 2002, the Defendant has paid the weekly rent due in full together with weekly payments of £2.70 towards the rent arrears. The Defendant will continue to make these payments weekly. She has also made a lump sum payment of £500.00 towards her rent arrears. This sum represents a loan received from her mother to be repaid once the Defendant is in full-time employment.

Statement of truth

I believe that the facts stated in this Defence are true

Denise Lewis
....

Denise Lewis

Dated this 20th day of August 2002

ROGER BLACK, solicitor, Torch Solicitors, 46 Ring Street, Anytown.
Solicitors for the Defendant who will accept service at the above address.

To the District Judge and to the Claimant

General Form of Judgment or Order

In the	
	Anytown Court Court

Claim No.	
Claimant (including ref)	Anytown District Council
Defendant (including ref)	Denise Lewis

To [Claimant] [Defendant] ['s Solicitor]

Ms Denise Lewis
12 Olympic Street
Anytown

SEAL

TO THE DEFENDANT:

Before DISTRICT JUDGE THOMPSON sitting at Anytown County Court, Anytown,

Upon hearing the Solicitor for the Claimant,

IT IS ORDERED THAT:

The Claimant's claim for possession be adjourned generally with permission to restore on terms that the Defendant do pay the current rent plus £2.70 per week towards the arrears of £2,200.50, the first payment towards the arrears to be made on or before 1st November 2002.

There be permission to the Claimant to restore this action in the event that the Defendant fails to comply with the terms set out in paragraph 1 of this order.

There be no order as to costs save that there be detailed assessment of the Defendant's costs in accordance with the Access to Justice Act 1999 and the Community Legal Service (Funding) Order 2000.

DATED: 25th OCTOBER 2002

Note: If judgment is for £5,000 or more, or is in respect of a debt which attracts contractual or statutory interest for late payment, the claimant may be entitled to further interest

The court office at

is open between 10 am and 4 pm [4.30pm]Monday to Friday. When corresponding with the court, please address forms or letters to the Court Manager and quote the case number.

N24 -w3 General form of judgment or order (4.99)

Part 2

On 14 November 2002, Denise seeks advice from her solicitor, Roger Black, and explains to him that on 25 October 2002, she attended a possession hearing brought against her by her landlord, Anytown District Council, due to rent arrears amounting to around £2,600. She brings the **claim form**, **particulars of claim** (see pages 315 and 317) and a copy of the court order; (this is shown on the next page). The order requires her to give up possession by 22 November.

Denise explains that the judge who granted possession commented, when making the order, that he could not see how Denise could continue to meet her rent liability as long as she was training to be a nurse.

Denise informs her solicitor that, since the court hearing, her financial situation has improved because she has made arrangements with her brother to look after her son, Carl, during term-time. This will save her £70 per week, and enable her to meet her weekly rent plus make payments towards the outstanding rent arrears. She has also borrowed £500 from her mother which she can pay to the council, and thus reduce the arrears significantly.

On this basis, her solicitor obtains CLS emergency **public funding** for Denise to make an application to vary the absolute possession order. As the date for giving up possession has not yet passed, no **warrant** has yet been issued.

The solicitor sends a letter to the landlord.

General Form of Judgment or Order

In the	
	Anytown Court Court

Claim No.	ABC 123
Claimant (including ref)	Anytown District Council
Defendant (including ref)	Denise Lewis

To [Claimant] [Defendant] ['s Solicitor]

Ms Denise Lewis
12 Olympic Street
Anytown

SEAL

TO THE DEFENDANT:

Before DISTRICT JUDGE THOMPSON sitting at Anytown County Court, Anytown,

Upon hearing the Solicitor for the Claimant,

IT IS ORDERED THAT:

The court has decided that you should give the Claimant possession of 12 Olympic Street, Anytown.

This means you must leave the property by 22nd November 2002.

You must also pay to the Claimant £2,650.20 for unpaid rent, use and occupation of the property together with £120.00 for the Claimant's cost of making the application for possession.

You must pay the total amount of £2,770.20 to the Claimant on or before 22nd November 2002.

IF YOU DO NOT LEAVE THE PROPERTY AND PAY THE MONEY OWED BY THE DATES GIVEN, THE CLAIMANT CAN ASK THE COURT BAILIFF TO EVICT YOU AND REMOVE YOUR GOODS TO OBTAIN PAYMENT.

This is called "enforcing the order and money judgment".

Payments should be made to the Claimant at the place where you would normally pay your rent. If you need more information about making payments you should contact the claimant. The court cannot accept any payments.

AND IT IS ORDERED:
The Defendant do pay the Claimant £7.41 per day for use and occupation until possession is given.

DATED: 25TH OCTOBER 2002

Note: If judgment is for £5,000 or more, or is in respect of a debt which attracts contractual or statutory interest for late payment, the claimant may be entitled to further interest

The court office at

is open between 10 am and 4 pm [4.30pm]Monday to Friday. When corresponding with the court, please address forms or letters to the Court Manager and quote the case number.

N24 -w3 General form of judgment or order (4.99)

Anytown District Council
Legal Department
Civic Offices
Medal Way
Anytown

Our Ref: RB/poss/lewis

14 November 2002

Dear Sir or Madam,

Ms Denise Lewis – 12 Olympic Street, Anytown.

We act for Ms Lewis who is a tenant of the council at the above address, in connection with her current housing situation.

We understand that on 25 October 2002 an absolute possession order was made against her at Anytown County Court. We understand that our client is required to leave the property on or before 22 November 2002, failing which we assume that you will issue a bailiff's warrant to have her evicted.

Having taken instructions from our client, we consider that there are good grounds to make an application to vary the possession order made on 25 October. We intend to seek a variation so as to postpone the date for possession and suspend the order on terms that our client pays the current rent plus a weekly amount of £2.70 towards the rent arrears.

To this end our client has obtained emergency legal funding to pursue the application and we enclose notice of issue of legal funding as appropriate.

The grounds to request a variation of the possession order are that Ms Lewis's financial situation has improved to the extent that she is now able to meet her weekly rent liability and make contributions to the rent. The details are as follows:

1. Ms Lewis has withdrawn her son from nursery and made arrangements for her brother to look after him during term-time. This will result in a weekly saving of £70.00 per week.

2. Ms Lewis's mother has lent our client £500.00 to use to reduce her rent arrears.

Ms Lewis's nursing course will be completed in April 2003, whereupon she has an excellent opportunity of employment, given the need in the NHS for qualified nurses. Consequently her income is set to rise significantly, enabling her to reduce her arrears more quickly after April 2003.

We would be grateful if you could let us know what your position is in relation to our application to vary the possession order.

As an urgent request, we would ask you to agree not to issue a warrant to execute the said possession order until our application is heard and the outcome known.

We look forward to your response in the near future.

Yours faithfully

Roger Black
Solicitor
Torch Solicitors

Case update

On the following day, Ms Lewis's solicitor receives confirmation from the council that a warrant would not be issued until the application to vary the possession order has been heard by the court. However, the council indicates that they will contest the application to vary the possession order.

Roger Black prepares the application form (with draft order attached) together with **witness statements** in support by the client and her brother; these are on the following pages. He files these documents at Anytown County Court on 20 November 2002 with the appropriate fee and the CLS emergency funding certificate. The court lists the matter for 22 November and the application paperwork is served on the council.

At the court hearing both sides make representations. The judge orders that the possession order be varied on the terms proposed in the application to vary.

Application Notice

- You must complete Parts A **and** B, **and** Part C if applicable
- Send any relevant fee and the completed application to the court with any draft order, witness statement or other evidence; and sufficient copies of these for service on each respondent

In the	ANYTOWN COUNTY COURT
Claim no.	ABC 123
Warrant no. (If applicable)	
Claimant (including ref.)	ANYTOWN DISTRICT COUNCIL
Defendant(s) (including ref.)	DENISE LEWIS
Date	20TH NOVEMBER 2002

You should provide this information for listing the application

1. Do you wish to have your application dealt with at a hearing?

    Yes ✔   No ☐   If Yes, please complete 2

2. Time estimate _____ (hours) __30__ (mins)

    Is this agreed by all parties? ☐ Yes ✔ No

    Level of judge   DISTRICT JUDGE

3. Parties to be served: ANYTOWN DISTRICT COUNCIL

Part A

1. Enter your full name, or name of solicitor

I ~~(We)~~[1]   ~~(on behalf of)(the claimant)~~(the defendant)

DENISE LEWIS

2. State clearly what order you are seeking and if possible attach a draft

intend to apply for an order (a draft of which is attached) that[2]

THE POSSESSION ORDER DATED 25TH OCTOBER 2002 BE VARIED SO AS TO POSTPONE THE DATE FOR POSSESSION AND SUSPEND THE ORDER ON THE TERMS ON THE ATTACHED DRAFT ORDER because[3]

3. Briefly set out why you are seeking the order. Include the material facts on which you rely, identifying any rule or statutory provision

I AM NOW ABLE TO PAY THE CURRENT RENT PLUS £2.70 TOWARDS THE ARREARS AS DETAILED IN THE ATTACHED WITNESS STATEMENT.

Part B

I ~~(We)~~ wish to rely on: *tick one box*

the attached (witness statement)~~(affidavit)~~ ✔   my statement of case ☐

4. If you are not already a party to the proceedings, you must provide an address for service of documents

evidence in Part C in support of my application ☐

Signed   *Denise Lewis*   **Position or office held** (if signing on behalf of firm or company) N/A

(Applicant)~~('s solicitor)('s litigation friend)~~

Address to which documents about this claim should be sent (including reference if appropriate)[4]

		if applicable
MR ROGER BLACK TORCH SOLICITORS 46 RING STREET ANYTOWN	fax no.	
	DX no.	
Tel. no. Postcode	e-mail	

The court office at

is open from 10am to 4pm Monday to Friday. When corresponding with the court please address forms or letters to the Court Manager and quote the claim number.

N244 - w3 Application Notice (4.99)   *Printed on behalf of The Court Service*

Part C

Claim No.

I (We) wish to rely on the following evidence in support of this application:

PLEASE REFER TO ATTACHED WITNESS STATEMENT

Statement of Truth

*(I believe)(The applicant believes) that the facts stated in this application are true

Signed _Denise Lewis_

(Applicant)('s solicitor)('s litigation friend)

Position or office held
(if signing on behalf of firm or company)

N/A

Date 20/11/2002

*delete as appropriate

IN THE ANYTOWN COUNTY COURT <u>**Claim No:**</u>

ANYTOWN DISTRICT COUNCIL

<u>**Claimant**</u>

and

DENISE LEWIS

<u>**Defendant**</u>

DRAFT ORDER

It is ORDERED that:

The possession order dated 25 October 2002 be varied so as to postpone the date for possession to 22 November 2002 and suspended thereafter in accordance with the following terms:

1. That the Defendant do pay the current rent plus £2.70 per week towards the arrears.

2. The Defendant do continue in occupation as a secure tenant of the Claimants, subject to the terms of this order.

3. That the costs of this application be provided for.

Dated...

IN THE ANYTOWN COUNTY COURT <u>**Claim No:**</u>

BETWEEN

ANYTOWN DISTRICT COUNCIL

<u>**Claimant**</u>

and

DENISE LEWIS

<u>**Defendant**</u>

WITNESS STATEMENT OF DENISE LEWIS

1. I am the Defendant in this action and I make this statement in support of my application to vary the possession order made on 25 October 2002.

2. I have lived at 12 Olympic Street, Anytown since September 1998. I have one three-year-old son, Carl, who lives with me at the property. Before my son's birth in January 1999, I worked full-time and paid the rent from my wages. After Carl was born, I received income support and my full weekly rent was paid by housing benefit. My rent account was nearly always up to date until September 2001.

3. I commenced a nursing diploma course in September 2001. The course does not entitle me to apply for student loans, working families tax credit and other benefits. My main source of income is a student bursary of £8,500.00 per year. In addition, I receive child benefit currently at the rate of £17.55 per week.

4. Immediately after starting the course, I advised the Housing Benefit Department of my change in circumstances. Although I am entitled to receive housing benefit as a lone parent in full-time education I became subject to the student restriction for housing benefit. This rule reduces by a set figure the amount that students are paid towards their rent. It means that only a small proportion of my rent is paid by housing benefit – currently £11.67 per week – and I am expected to pay the rest from my income. This has resulted in my rent arrears accruing.

5. One of the main reasons that I have struggled financially is the cost of child care. Carl attended a local nursery for which I have had to pay £70.00 per week. My bursary is not counting as income from employment, which would entitle me to a disregard on my income. Before starting the nursing

course, I was under the impression that the disregard would be applied. As a result, I had calculated that I would be able to afford to meet the cost of my essential living needs, including my weekly rent. I attach as exhibit "DL1" a financial statement detailing my current income and expenditure.

6. Once I realised how little housing benefit I was to receive, I took advice from my local Citizens Advice Bureau (CAB). With the assistance of the CAB I applied to the Housing Benefit Department for extra help to pay my rent on the basis that my circumstances are exceptional. They refused my application.

7. The CAB are currently assisting me with an appeal to the Appeal Tribunal against the Housing Benefit Department's refusal to award me discretionary housing payments. If this appeal is successful I am hoping that a much higher proportion, and possibly all, of my rent will be covered by housing benefit.

8. Since the possession order hearing on 25 October my financial situation has improved. I have taken my son out of the nursery to save on these child care costs and my brother has volunteered to take care of him when I am at college. My brother does not work as he receives incapacity benefit. He has always taken a keen interest in Carl's welfare and has baby-sat for me on a number of occasions.

9. As a result I now have £70.00 per week available income to pay towards the current rent which I did not have when the possession order was made.

10. My mother has offered to lend me £500.00 to reduce my rent arrears significantly.

11. In the meantime, I respectfully request the court to vary the possession order made on 25 October 2002 and suspend it on terms that I pay the current rent plus £2.70 per week towards the arrears. I shall arrange for direct debit payments to be made directly from my bank account to guarantee that the payments are received by the Claimants.

I believe that the facts stated in this statement are true.

Signed *Denise Lewis*

Denise Lewis

Dated *20th November 2002*

IN THE ANYTOWN COUNTY COURT   <u>Claim No:</u>

BETWEEN

ANYTOWN DISTRICT COUNCIL

<u>Claimant</u>

and

DENISE LEWIS

<u>Defendant</u>

WITNESS STATEMENT OF JONATHAN LEWIS

---

1. I am the Defendant's brother in this action and I make this statement in support of her application to vary the possession order made on 25 October 2002.

2. I confirm that my sister, Denise Lewis, has asked me to look after her three-year-old son, Carl, during the term-time of her nursing diploma course.

3. I am disabled and paralysed on the left side of my body after I suffered a stroke. I am therefore currently unable to work and I am at home during the day and likely to be at home for the foreseeable future. Although I am partially paralysed I am able to look after Carl and have baby-sat him on many occasions.

4. I am happy to look after my nephew whilst my sister is studying at college. I understand that my sister cannot afford to pay the nursery charges because she needs this money to pay her rent.

5. I confirm that I will not be charging my sister for looking after her son. She has agreed to supply a packed lunch and snacks for the days that I look after him.

I believe that the facts stated in this statement are true.

Signed......................................

Jonathan Lewis

Dated... 19th November 2002

General Form of Judgment or Order

To [Claimant] [Defendant] ['s Solicitor]

Ms Denise Lewis
12 Olympic Street
Anytown

In the	
Anytown Court Court	

Claim No.	
Claimant (including ref)	Anytown District Council
Defendant (including ref)	Denise Lewis

TO THE DEFENDANT:

Before DISTRICT JUDGE THOMPSON sitting at Anytown County Court, Anytown,

Upon hearing the Solicitor for the Claimant and the solicitor for the Defendant,

IT IS ORDERED THAT:

(1)The possession order dated 25th October 2002 be varied so as to postpone the date for possession to 31st December 2002 on the following terms:

(a) The possession order is suspended on terms that the Defendant do pay the current rent plus £2.70 per week towards the arrears.

(b) The Defendant do continue in occupation as a secure tenant of the Claimant's subject to the terms of this order.

(2) There be no order as to costs.

AND IT IS ORDERED:
The Defendant do pay the Claimant £7.41 per day for use and occupation until possession is given.

DATED: 22nd November 2002

Note: If judgment is for £5,000 or more, or is in respect of a debt which attracts contractual or statutory interest for late payment, the claimant may be entitled to further interest

The court office at

is open between 10 am and 4 pm [4.30pm]Monday to Friday. When corresponding with the court, please address forms or letters to the Court Manager and quote the case number.
N24 -w3 General form of judgment or order (4.99)

Background

Ms Povey moved into local authority accommodation with her two children in January 2000. She did not have a chance to inspect the property before she moved in. Once she did so, she realised there was damp which meant that plaster was falling off the walls in many parts of the house, the roof was leaking in many places and the sash windows would not stay open.

Ms Povey complained to her housing officer about the state of the property. Her housing officer stated that the problem would be dealt with; but nothing happened. Over time, Ms Povey complained to her landlord by letter and in person on a number of occasions about the disrepair; but always to no avail. Two years after her first complaint, the house had still not been repaired.

She finally sought advice from Anywhere Law Centre in January 2002, who took on her case. The law centre initially advised her under the **Help at Court** scheme. The law centre subsequently applied for full **public funding** from the Legal Services Commission to start a county court claim against the landlord.

Ms Povey receives income support.

Pre-action protocol for disrepair cases

The pre-action protocol for disrepair cases is presently in draft form. What follows in this section is taken from the draft pre-action protocol.

The aims of pre-action protocols are to:[1]

- encourage the exchange of early and full information about the prospective legal claim
- enable parties to avoid litigation by agreeing a settlement of the claim before commencement of proceedings
- support the efficient management of proceedings where litigation cannot be avoided.

The specific aims of the pre-action protocol for disrepair cases are to:

- promote the speedy and appropriate carrying out of repairs
- ensure that tenants receive any compensation to which they are entitled as speedily as possible
- promote good pre-litigation practice, including the early exchange of information and to give guidance about the instruction of experts
- avoid unnecessary litigation
- keep down the costs of resolving disputes.

The protocol does not apply to counterclaims and set offs for disrepair.[2] The protocol should be followed wherever possible but it is recognised that an expert might need to be instructed earlier than the protocol suggests in urgent cases. These cases might include:[3]

- where the tenant considers that there is a significant risk to health and safety
- where an interim injunction is being sought by the tenant
- where it is necessary to preserve evidence.

Early notification letters

These are letters sent to the landlord notifying her/him of the disrepair problem. An early notification letter should be sent to the landlord before sending a letter that contains the full details of the claim (known as a letter of claim; see page 341). The following information should be in the early notification letter:[4]

- the tenant's name, the address of the property and tenant's address if different

---

1   Draft pre-action protocol for disrepair, para 2
2   ibid. para 3.1(a)

3   ibid. para 3.6(j)
4   ibid. para 3.2

- details of the defects, including any defects outstanding
- details of any notification previously given to the landlord of the need for repair
- a request for disclosure of relevant documents, which should include an authorisation form and £10 to cover costs
- proposals for the instruction of an expert (see below).

The landlord should reply within 21 days enclosing all relevant documents.[5]

Letter of claim

This should be sent as soon as possible. It should contain all the information above, if not already provided, plus:[6]

- a history of the defects
- information as to any emergency work which has been carried out
- the effect of the defects on the tenant
- details of any special damages
- details of costs incurred to date.

Once again, the landlord should normally reply within 21 days.[7] The reply should contain all the information requested if not already provided. In relation to the tenant's claim, the following should also be included:[8]

- whether liability is admitted and if so, for which defects and/or reasons why liability is not admitted
- any allegation regarding lack of notice or access
- a full schedule of intended works, including anticipated start and completion dates and a timetable for the works
- any offer of compensation
- any offer in respect of costs.

Experts

Parties should bear in mind that the use of an expert is not always necessary in a disrepair action. The use of video footage and/or photographs before and after works might be adequate.[9]

The protocol encourages the use of a single joint expert. If instructions to the expert cannot be agreed, both parties can send their own instructions.[10] Each party should pay one half of the cost of the report.[11] The joint expert should send a copy of her/his report to both parties within 14 days of the inspection.

5   Draft pre-action protocol for disrepair, para 3.5.1
6   ibid. para 3.3(a)
7   ibid. para 3.5.2
8   ibid. para 3.5.2(a)
9   ibid. paras 3.6(a) & 4.6(d)
10 ibid. paras 3.6(d) & 4.6(b)
11 ibid. para 3.6(m)

Either party can ask the expert questions; the expert should send the answers separately and directly to each party.[12]

Where a joint expert cannot be agreed, both parties should aim to arrange a joint inspection of the property.[13] Each party pays for their own expert's report.[14] The experts should produce a schedule of works within 14 days of the joint inspection with details of:[15]

- the defects and required works which are agreed
- the areas of disagreement and the reasons for disagreement.

The terms of appointment of the expert should be agreed when s/he is instructed. Points to decide upon should include:[16]

- the expert's charges, eg. whether there is to be a daily/hourly rate or a fee for the services
- any relevant expenses, eg. for travel
- rates for court attendance if this becomes necessary
- time for delivery of the report
- time for making the payment
- whether fees are to be paid by a third party
- arrangements for dealing with questions for experts and discussions between experts and for providing for the cost involved.

Limitation period

Where a limitation period is about to expire, the tenant may need to issue proceedings immediately. However, before doing this, the tenant should write to the landlord requesting that s/he agree to an extension of the limitation period. The extension should normally be up to six months. If the landlord does not agree to this, it will be for the court to decide whether s/he has acted unreasonably and whether there are to be any **sanctions** imposed.[17]

---

12 Draft pre-action protocol for disrepair, paras 3.6(g) & 3.6(n)
13 ibid. paras 3.6(e) & 4.6(b)
14 ibid. para 3.6(m)

15 ibid. para 3.6(h)
16 ibid. para 3.6(l)
17 ibid. para 3.4 & 4.8

Anywhere Borough Council
Town Hall
Anywhere

6 January 2002

Dear Madam/Sir

Re: Stephanie Povey, 23 Old Street, Anywhere

We are instructed by your above-named tenant. We are providing our client
with advice and assistance under the Community Legal Service Legal Help
Scheme. We are using the disrepair pre-action protocol. We enclose a copy
of the protocol for your information.

Repairs

Your tenant complains of the following defects at the property:

• water leaking through various parts of the roof affecting all the
  rooms upstairs

• damp in various parts of the house

• plaster falling off the walls in various parts of the house

• broken sash windows.

Please arrange to inspect the property as soon as possible. Please let us know
what repairs you propose to carry out and the anticipated date for completion
of the works.

Disclosure

Please also provide within 21 days of posting, the following:

1. All records or documents in any file relevant to the disrepair claim including:
   • copy of the tenancy agreement including tenancy conditions
   • tenancy file
   • documents relating to notice given or disrepair reported
   • any other file of other documentation likely to be relevant (see below).

2. Examples of other relevant files or documentation might be:
   • inspection file
   • property file
   • works record
   • heating and mechanical records.

We enclose a signed authority form from our client for you to release this information to ourselves and a cheque for the sum of £10.

<u>Expert</u>

If agreement is not reached about the carrying out of repairs within 21 days, we propose to instruct as a single joint expert, Mr Tushar Bala of Bala Surveyors, 29 Whitecross Street, Anywhere, to carry out an inspection of the property and provide a report. We enclose a copy of his CV, plus a draft letter of instruction. Please let us know if you agree to his appointment. If you object, please let us know your reasons within 21 days.

If you do not object to the expert being appointed as a single joint expert but wish to provide your own instructions, you should send those directly to Tushar Bala within 21 days. Please send to ourselves a copy of your letter of instruction. If you do not agree to a single joint expert, we will instruct Tushar Bala to inspect the property in any event. In those circumstances if you wish your expert to attend at the same time, please let ourselves and Tushar Bala know within 21 days.

<u>Claim</u>

Our client's disrepair claim requires further investigation. We will write to you as soon as possible with further details of the history of the defects and of the notice relied on, along with details of our client's claim for general and special damages.

Yours faithfully

Anywhere Law Centre

Anywhere Borough Council
Town Hall
Anywhere

27 January 2002

Dear Madam/Sir

Re: Stephanie Povey, 23 Old Street, Anywhere

We write further to our letter of 6 January 2002 regarding our client's disrepair claim. We have now taken full instructions from our client.

Repairs

The history of the disrepair is as follows:

- water leaking through various parts of the roof affecting all the rooms upstairs

- damp in various parts of the house causing mould growth

- plaster falling off the walls in various parts of the house

- broken sash windows.

You received notice of the defects as follows:

- On 21 January 2000, Ms Povey gave a list of the disrepair in the property to her housing officer at the housing estate office. She was told that a re-plastering order would be put out and that someone would visit her to assess the damage to the roof and windows.

- In June 2000, Ms Povey complained that the re-plastering had still not been done and no-one had visited her regarding the roof and windows.

- In September 2000, Ms Povey complained about the disrepair again.

- In November 2000, another complaint about the disrepair was made.

- In March 2001, Ms Povey reported damp patches in the ceiling in the front bedroom.

- In April 2001 an employee of Anywhere Borough Council inspected the premises.

- In June 2001, Ms Povey wrote to the Head of Anywhere Borough Council and was advised to open her windows.

The defects at the property are causing our client distress, inconvenience and embarrassment. She feels unable to invite friends to visit as the damp causes an unpleasant smell.

Ms Povey has stopped using her front bedroom where the roof leaks particularly badly. This has caused damp throughout the bedroom and plaster to fall off the walls. She has been unable to keep the sash window open in this room and the other bedroom because the cords are broken. Ms Povey sleeps in the living room while her daughters sleep in the other bedroom. However, there is also damp in their bedroom caused by a leak in the roof and, in the summer months, Ms Povey's daughters slept with her in the living room because the smell caused by the damp caused the bedroom to be unusable. There is also plaster falling off the walls in this bedroom and the sash window does not stay open due to broken cords.

The bathroom does not have a window. There is a slight leak in the roof in this room causing damp but there is no plaster falling off the walls yet. Ms Povey believes this is because she keeps the extractor fan in the bathroom continuously switched on. There is mould growth in the bathroom and both the bedrooms.

The sash windows in both the kitchen and the dining room do not stay open due to broken cords. There is slight damp in both of these rooms.

The living room is the least affected room and the damp is very slight here. There is, however, an unpleasant smell throughout the house caused by the damp.

Please forward to us within 21 days of this letter a full schedule of works together with the anticipated date for completion of the works proposed.

Claim

We take the view that you are in breach of your repairing obligations. Please provide us with your proposals for compensation. Our client also requires compensation for special damages. We attach a schedule of the special damages claimed.

The costs of this claim to date are £90.27 plus £15.80 VAT totalling £106.07. We attach a schedule of costs.

Yours faithfully

Anywhere Law Centre

SPECIAL DAMAGES FORM

	ITEM	DATE PURCHASED	WHERE PURCHASED	PRICE	RECEIPTS YES/NO	HOW DAMAGED
1	LEATHER JACKET	SUMMER 1996	ANYWHERE MARKET	£220	NO	ROTTEN WITH DAMP
2	BOOTS	15/10/99	ANYWHERE SHOE SHOP	£50	YES	ROTTEN WITH DAMP
3						
4						
5						
6						
7						
8						
9						
10						

Statement of Costs

Description of fee earners*
(a) (name) (grade) (hourly rate claimed)
(b) (name) (grade) (hourly rate claimed)

| SARAH LUND, GRADE 2, £53.10 |
| |

Attendances on   *(party)*

| STEPHANIE POVEY |

(a) (number)	1.5	Hours at £	53.10	£	79.65
(b) (number)		Hours at £		£	

Attendances on

(a) (number)		Hours at £		£	
(b) (number)		Hours at £		£	

Attendances on

(a) (number)		Hours at £		£	
(b) (number)		Hours at £		£	

Site inspections

(a) (number)		Hours at £		£	
(b) (number)		Hours at £		£	

Work done on negotiations

(a) (number)	0.2	Hours at £	53.10	£	10.62
(b) (number)		Hours at £		£	

Other work, not covered above

(a) (number)		Hours at £		£	
(b) (number)		Hours at £		£	

Work done on documents

(a) (number)		Hours at £		£	
(b) (number)		Hours at £		£	

| | Subtotal £ | 90.27 |

Statement of Costs

Brought forward £ | 90.27

Other expenses

**Others
(give brief description)**

Total | 90.27

Amount of VAT

Claimed

On solicitor's fees | 15.80

On other expenses |

Grand total | 106.07

Date | | Signed |

Name of firm of solicitors
[partner] for the (party) | **ANYWHERE
LAW CENTRE**

---

*3 grades of fee earner are suggested: (1) solicitors with over 4 years' post qualification experience (2) Other solicitors and legal executives and fee earners of equivalent experience. "Legal Executive" means a Fellow of the Institute of Legal Executives. Those who are not Fellows of the Institute are not entitled to call themselves legal executives and in principle are therefore not entitled to the same hourly rate as a legal executive. In respect of each fee earner communications should be treated as attendances and routine communications should be claimed at one tenth of the hourly rate.

Case update

Anywhere Law Centre receives a telephone call from the council informing them that the council will be sending its own expert to the property to carry out a survey. The council representative states that he will contact Mr Bala to arrange for the inspection of the property to take place with both the council's expert and Mr Bala present.

Anywhere Law Centre instructs Mr Bala to carry out the inspection.

31 January 2002

Dear Mr Bala

Re: Stephanie Povey, 23 Old Street, Anywhere

We act for the above named in connection with a housing disrepair claim at the above property. We are using the disrepair pre-action protocol. We enclose a copy of the protocol for your information.

Our client complains of the following defects:

- water leaking through various parts of the roof affecting all the rooms upstairs

- damp in various parts of the house causing mould growth

- plaster falling off the walls in various parts of the house

- broken sash windows.

Please carry out an inspection of the above property by 22 February and provide a report. The landlord is Anywhere Borough Council. The landlord will contact you to confirm that their expert will attend at the same time as you to carry out a joint inspection.

Please provide a report within 14 days of the inspection. Please contact us immediately if there are any works which require an interim injunction.

If the case proceeds to court, the report may be used in evidence. In order to comply with court rules we would be grateful if you would insert above your signature a statement that the contents are true to the best of your knowledge and belief. We refer you to Part 35 of the Civil Procedure Rules which specifies experts' responsibilities, the contents of any report and the statements experts must sign. We enclose a copy for your information. [not attached]

[Insert details as to costs and payment]

Yours sincerely

Anywhere Law Centre

Case update

Tushar Bala's report concludes as follows:

'Dampness and mould growth are important threats to the health of the tenant. They can cause inconvenience and discomfort and damage to possessions.

The damp is caused by leaks in the roof due to roof tiles becoming loose. Consequently, the damp has caused mould growth in both the bedrooms.

The sash windows do not stay open due to broken sash cords.

To bring the house to a satisfactory standard, it is necessary to carry out appropriate works to remedy the defects as set out in the Schedule of Works attached [this is attached to the Particulars of Claim].

In my opinion:

1. the landlord is in breach of the repairing covenant implied into the tenancy agreement by section 11 of the Landlord and Tenant Act 1985

2. the landlord is in breach of the duty of care owed by virtue of section 4 of the Defective Premises Act 1972.'

The experts do not agree on the cause and extent of the disrepair. Anywhere Borough Council's expert believes the repairs suggested by Tushar Bala are not necessary. He believes that all Ms Povey has to do is open the windows and put the heating on more often. The mould just needs to be cleaned with a specialised mould cleaning and prevention kit. He accepts that the broken cords in the sash windows should be repaired by the council, but claims that the first that the council heard of them was when Anywhere Law Centre wrote to the council in January 2002.

Anywhere Law Centre write a **letter before action** on Ms Povey's behalf. This puts the council on notice that Ms Povey will be starting court action if a settlement is not reached. The council does not reply.

Ms Povey's solicitor, Sarah Lund, recommends that court proceedings are started as it is unlikely that negotiations will resolve the issues of disrepair. **Public funding** is applied for and granted by the Legal Services Commission.

Ms Povey's solicitor drafts the Particulars of Claim and puts the court and Defendant on notice that Ms Povey is receiving legal funding from the Legal Services Commission.

Anywhere Borough Council receive the Particulars of Claim. A solicitor in its legal team, Aisha Begum, takes on the case. Ms Begum serves an acknowledgement of service on behalf of the council that gives her another 14 days to file the defence (see page 42).

16 March 2002

The Court Manager
Anywhere County Court
Anywhere

Dear Madam/Sir

Re: Povey v Anywhere Borough Council

Please find enclosed:

1. Claim form N1 plus one copy for the defendant

2. Particulars of Claim plus one copy

3. Notice of Issue of Funding Certificate plus one copy

4. Funding certificate in respect of the claimant

5. Court issue fee of £120.

Please issue and serve the papers on all relevant parties.

We look forward to hearing from you.

Yours faithfully

Sarah Lund
Solicitor
Anywhere Law Centre

Claim Form

Claimant

STEPHANIE POVEY

SEAL

Defendant(s)

ANYWHERE BOROUGH COUNCIL

Brief details of claim

AN ORDER FOR SPECIFIC PERFORMANCE AND DAMAGES

Value

OVER £5,000 BUT LIMITED TO £15,000

Defendant's name and address			£
ANYWHERE BOROUGH COUNCIL TOWN HALL ANYWHERE	Amount claimed		TBE
	Court fee		£120
	Solicitor's costs		TBA
	Total amount		TBE
	Issue date		

The court office at

is open between 10 am and 4 pm Monday to Friday. When corresponding with the court, please address forms or letters to the Court Manager and quote the claim number.

N1 Claim form (CPR Part 7) (10.00)   *Printed on behalf of The Court Service*

Claim No.

Does, or will, your claim include any issues under the Human Rights Act 1998? ☐ Yes ☑ No

Particulars of Claim (attached)(to follow)

SEE ATTACHED

Statement of Truth
*(I believe)(The Claimant believes) that the facts stated in these particulars of claim are true.
* I am duly authorised by the claimant to sign this statement

Full name   STEPHANIE POVEY

Name of claimant's solicitor's firm   ANYWHERE LAW CENTRE

signed _____   position or office held   SOLICITOR

*(Claimant)(Litigation friend)(Claimant's solicitor)   (if signing on behalf of firm or company)

*delete as appropriate

ANYWHERE LAW CENTRE
CITY STREET
ANYWHERE

Claimant's or claimant's solicitor's address to which documents or payments should be sent if different from overleaf including (if appropriate) details of DX, fax or e-mail.

IN THE ANYWHERE COUNTY COURT   **Claim No:**

BETWEEN:

STEPHANIE POVEY

Claimant

and

ANYWHERE BOROUGH COUNCIL

Defendant

PARTICULARS OF CLAIM

---

1) The Claimant is the secure tenant of premises known as 23 Old Street, Anywhere (the premises) and the Defendant is the Claimant's landlord. The tenancy commenced on 14 January 2000. The current weekly rent is £40. The premises consist of a house with two storeys comprising a kitchen, living room and a dining room on the ground floor and two bedrooms and a bathroom on the first floor. The Claimant lives at the premises with her two daughters aged 8 and 6.

2) Clause 4 in the tenancy agreement states that the landlord is 'responsible for all repairs to the structure and exterior of the dwelling and to the installations for the supply of water, gas and electricity and for sanitation, including sanitary fittings, and for space and water heating, except where repairs are caused by the tenant's use of the dwelling in an untenant-like manner'.

3) The terms implied by section 11 Landlord and Tenant Act 1985 apply to the tenancy.

4) At all material times the Defendant owed the duties imposed by section 4 of the Defective Premises Act 1972 to the Claimant.

5) The Defendant has been in breach of the aforesaid express and implied terms and duties since the tenancy began.

PARTICULARS

a) There is dampness and mould growth in numerous parts of the premises.

b) Plaster is falling of the walls in numerous parts of the premises.

c) The roof is leaking water in various places.

d) The sash windows in the premises have broken cords and do not stay open.

e) The defects are set out in the report of Tushar Bala, a professionally qualified environmental health and housing consultant, dated 17 February 2002 attached hereto.

6) The Claimant has made the Defendant aware of the aforesaid breaches on numerous occasions and in any event as and when each defect arose.

PARTICULARS

a) On the 21 January 2000 the Claimant visited her housing officer at the housing estate office and gave him a list of her complaints about the state of the premises.

b) The Defendant's response was to order workmen to re-plaster and to state that someone would visit the premises to inspect the disrepair. This has still not been done.

c) In June 2000 the Claimant complained by telephone that the re-plastering had still not been done.

d) In September 2000 the Claimant complained again by telephone about the disrepair.

e) In November 2000 the Claimant complained by telephone about the disrepair.

f) In March 2001 the damp patches in the ceiling in the front bedroom were reported by telephone.

g) In April 2001 an employee of the Defendant inspected the premises.

h) In June 2001 the Claimant wrote to the Head of Anywhere Borough Council complaining once again about the disrepair. Particular reference was made to the damp. The Defendant replied to the Claimant advising her to open the windows.

i) On 6 January 2002 Anywhere Law Centre wrote to the Defendant on behalf of the Claimant setting out the complaints.

j) On 27 January 2002 Anywhere Law Centre wrote to the Defendant again.

k) On 17 February 2002 the Defendant's surveyor inspected the premises.

7) Notwithstanding the aforementioned complaints the Defendant has failed to carry out any or any sufficient repairs.

8) As a result of the Defendant's aforesaid breaches the Claimant has suffered loss, distress, damage, inconvenience, and embarrassment.

PARTICULARS OF SPECIAL DAMAGES

a) The Claimant's jacket valued at £100 and her boots valued at £50 have been ruined beyond economic repair by damp.

PARTICULARS OF GENERAL DAMAGE

a) The premises have been damp, cold and unpleasant to live in.

b) There has been a pervading smell of damp in the premises and they have been unsightly.

c) The Claimant has been unable to use one of her bedrooms throughout the period of her tenancy due to the damp.

d) The Claimant has been unable to use the other bedroom during the summer months due to the smell of damp.

e) The Claimant has felt too embarrassed to invite friends to visit due to the smell of damp and the unsightliness of the plaster on the walls.

f) As a result of the foregoing the Claimant has been placed under considerable stress.

The Claimant reserves the right to add to these particulars upon discovery of further defects.

9) The Claimant claims interest pursuant to section 69 of the County Court Act 1984 on damages awarded at such rate and for such period as to the court appears just.

AND THE CLAIMANT CLAIMS:

a) An order requiring the Defendant to carry out works set out in the schedule of works annexed hereto.

b) Damages exceeding £5,000 but not more than £15,000.

c) Interest.

d) Costs.

Dated: 16 March 2002

Statement of truth of the Claimant

I believe the facts stated in these Particulars of Claim are true.

Full name: Stephanie Povey

Name of Claimant's solicitor's firm: Anywhere Law Centre, City Street, Anywhere

Signed:..

IN THE ANYWHERE COUNTY COURT   **Claim No:**

BETWEEN:

STEPHANIE POVEY

Claimant

and

ANYWHERE BOROUGH COUNCIL

Defendant

SCHEDULE OF WORKS

---

1. Replace loose roof tiles.

2. All mould-affected services need to be cleaned with a fungicidal solution and re-decorated as necessary.

3. Hack off and renew all damp ceiling and wall plaster which has lost its integrity or is becoming unkeyed or loose.

4. Replace cords in the sash windows.

IN THE ANYWHERE COUNTY COURT   **Claim No: AN54321**

BETWEEN:

STEPHANIE POVEY

Claimant

and

ANYWHERE BOROUGH COUNCIL

Defendant

DEFENCE

---

1) Paragraph 1 of the Particulars of Claim is admitted save that the ages of the Claimant's children are not known and therefore not admitted.

2) Paragraph 2 of the Particulars of Claim is admitted.

3) Paragraph 3 of the Particulars of Claim is admitted.

4) Paragraph 4 of the Particulars of Claim is admitted.

5) It is an implied term of the tenancy agreement that the Claimant would use and treat the property in a tenant-like manner.

6) As to paragraph 5 of the Particulars of Claim:

   a) it is admitted that the premises have been affected by dampness and mould growth, but it is not admitted that this amounts to a breach, by the Defendant, of the tenancy agreement for the reasons set out in paragraphs 7 and 8 below;

   b) it is not admitted that the roof is leaking and that the sash windows have broken cords. The Defendant will respond to these allegations substantively once they have received their own maintenance report about the conditions of the premises;

   c) the alleged defects contained in the report of Tushar Bala dated 17 February 2002 are not admitted, and the Defendant will also respond to these allegations as soon as the maintenance report has been received.

7) It is contended that the Claimant is in breach of the implied term of the tenancy agreement to use and treat the premises in a tenant-like manner.

PARTICULARS OF BREACH

The Claimant is in breach of the implied term as follows:

   a) failing to open the windows of the premises adequately or at all so as to prevent damp;

b) failing properly to heat the premises or to use the heating system in a reasonably effective manner as advised by the Defendant so as to prevent damp; and

c) failing to clean areas of mould despite being offered by the Defendant a specialised mould clearing and prevention kit by letter of 23 June 2001.

8) It is denied that the Defendant is liable for any disrepair that has arisen as a result of the Claimant's breach of tenancy or which has otherwise been caused by the mode of occupation and the acts or omissions of the Claimant.

9) It is denied that the Defendant has received a number of complaints from the Claimant, or her agents, regarding the condition of the property save that the Defendant received a letter from the Claimant in June 2001 complaining of mould growth in the premises.

10) It is not admitted that this complaint was justified or that it arose from a breach of the terms of the tenancy on the part of the Defendant.

11) As to paragraph 8 of the Particulars of Claim:

a) it is not admitted that the Claimant's belongings have been ruined by damp since this is a matter outside the Defendant's knowledge;

b) the Particulars of General Damage are not admitted, as these are matters outside the Defendant's knowledge, and the Claimant is put to proof as to each.

12) No admissions are made to the claim for interest contained in paragraph 9 of the Particulars of Claim.

13) The Defendant is unable to agree or dispute the statement of value contained in the claim form.

Statement of truth

The Defendant believes that the matters contained in this Defence are true.

Signed:...

Full Name: Aisha Begum

Position held: Solicitor to the Defendant

Dated 12 April 2002

TO the Court
AND to the Claimant

Case update

The parties receive and complete allocation questionnaires (see page 77).

The court sends notice of a case management conference. Both parties agree directions (see paragraph 6.2) for the case and send notice of these by letter to the court. In their letters, they ask the court to excuse them for not being at the hearing. The reason they give for not attending is that they have agreed the directions and that they will be saving costs if they do not attend.

The court will not necessarily grant agreed directions if it does not consider them adequate. If parties want the court to grant their agreed directions, they should send the agreed directions to the court well in advance of the case management conference, if possible, and ask the court, simply by letter, to approve them. If the court does agree them, there will be no need to attend the case management conference unless the court instructs otherwise. If the directions are sent to the court quite late, such that the court does not have enough time to approve them, it will be up to the parties as to whether they attend the case management conference but they may be criticised for not doing so.

The court does not grant the agreed directions. It considers that there has been too much time allowed to carry out each direction, and this would be unjust to the Claimant, if there is disrepair, as she would have to live with it for much longer. The court gives the following directions.

1. The case is allocated to the fast track.

2. There is standard disclosure by 23 May 2002 by list. Any request for copies shall be made by 30 May 2002.

3. There is exchange of all witness statements by 4 July 2002.

4. The Defendant shall inform the Claimant by no later than 4pm on 9 May 2002 that they either:

    *   agree with the report of Tushar Bala, or

    *   wish to ask any questions of him pursuant to CPR 35.6 (in which case the questions shall be put to him by no later than 23 May 2002 and answered by him no later than 20 June 2002), or

    *   do not agree the report and wish expert evidence to be given by another expert. In this case, the expert evidence in the case shall be limited to the evidence of a single environmental health expert, agreed by both parties and jointly instructed by no later than 23 May 2002. The joint expert's report shall be filed no later than 20 June 2002 and paid for initially by the Defendant.

Standard disclosure takes place.

The council do not agree to the use of Mr Bala's report and want another expert to be instructed jointly. They agree an expert with the Claimant's solicitor. The joint expert instructed is Carolyn Ellis. Ms Ellis's report generally agrees with Mr Bala's report. Negotiations to settle begin to take place but are not concluded by the time witness statements are due to be exchanged (see page 104). These are prepared and a listing questionnaire is completed (see page 83). The court is asked in a covering letter with the listing questionnaire to stay the proceedings so as to allow negotiations to settle to take place. The court grants the stay.

List of documents: standard disclosure

In the ANYWHERE COUNTY COURT

Claim No.	AN54321
Claimant (including ref)	Stephanie Povey
Defendant (including ref)	Anywhere Borough Council
Date	

Notes:

- The rules relating to standard disclosure are contained in Part 31 of the Civil Procedure Rules.
- Documents to be included under standard disclosure are contained in Rule 31.6
- A document has or will have been in your control if you have or have had possession, or a right of possession, of it **or** a right to inspect or take copies of it.

Disclosure Statement

I state that I have carried out a reasonable and proportionate search to locate all the documents which I am required to disclose under the order made by the court on *(insert date)*

(I did not search for documents -

1. pre-dating
   January 2000
2. located elsewhere than
   in the Claimant's possession
3. ~~in categories other than~~

)

I certify that I understand the duty of disclosure and to the best of my knowledge I have carried out that duty. I further certify that the list of documents set out in or attached to this form, is a complete list of all documents which are or have been in my control and which I am obliged under the order to disclose.

I understand that I must inform the court and the other parties immediately if any further document required to be disclosed by Rule 31.6 comes into my control at any time before the conclusion of the case.

(I have not permitted inspection of documents within the category or class of documents (as set out below) required to be disclosed under Rule 31(6)(b)or (c) on the grounds that to do so would be disproportionate to the issues in the case.)

Signed   **Date**

(Claimant)~~(Defendant)('s litigation friend)~~

Position or office held *(if signing on behalf of firm or company)*
Please state why you are the appropriate person to make the disclosure statement.

List of documents:
N265 - w3 standard disclosure (4.99)

continued overleaf
Printed on behalf of The Court Service

List and number here, in a convenient order, the documents (or bundles of documents if of the same nature, e.g. invoices) in your control, which you do not object to being inspected. Give a short description of each document or bundle so that it can be identified, and say if it is kept elsewhere i.e. with a bank or solicitor

I have control of the documents numbered and listed here. I do not object to you inspecting them/producing copies.

1. Tenancy agreement dated 12.01.00
2. Copy letter from Anywhere Law Centre to the Defendant dated 06.01.02
3. Copy letter from Anywhere Law Centre to the Defendant dated 27.01.02.

List and number here, as above, the documents in your control which you object to being inspected. (Rule 31.19)

I have control of the documents numbered and listed here, but I object to you inspecting them:

1. Instruction to Counsel, advice, opinion and drafts
2. Correspondence between the Claimant and her solicitors and advisers
3. Correspondence, reports, memoranda and statements made by the Claimant, her solicitors, her advisers, agents and others and written, obtained or received for the purposes of these proceedings.

Say what your objections are

I object to you inspecting these documents because:

they need not be disclosed due to legal professional privilege.

List and number here, the documents you once had in your control, but which you no longer have. For each document listed, say when it was last in your control and where it is now.

I have had the documents numbered and listed below, but they are no longer in my control.

1. The originals of copy letters set out in part 1 of this list
2. Originals were not kept of the following:
    i. Claimant's list of complaints given to Defendant undated
    ii. letter from Claimant to Defendant dated 06.06.01
3. Postcard from Defendant to Claimant dated 22.01.00. The Claimant threw this away.

Statement on behalf of the Claimant
Witness: Stephanie Povey
First statement
Exhibits: LSP1
Made this   day of   2002

IN THE ANYWHERE COUNTY COURT   **Claim No: AN54321**

BETWEEN:

STEPHANIE POVEY

Claimant

and

ANYWHERE BOROUGH COUNCIL

Defendant

WITNESS STATEMENT OF STEPHANIE POVEY

1. I am Stephanie Povey of 23 Old Street, Anywhere. I am the Claimant in this matter. I am currently unemployed and have lived at the property since 14 January 2000. I live at the property with my two daughters.

2. Anywhere Borough Council offered me the property in January 2000. I did not have a chance to look at the property, as I did not live in the area when it was offered to me. My sister who lives in the area inspected the property for me and told me that she pointed out various items of concern with the condition of the property, including the damp and the mouldy plaster of the walls in the bedrooms and bathroom to the man who showed her the property. She does not remember his name.

3. On 21 January 2000 I took a list of complaints to the estate office and gave them to my housing officer, Nigel Ford. This list was of all the repairs that have been mentioned in my Particulars of Claim. These have still not been rectified. In response to that visit, I was told that an order would be placed for workmen to re-plaster the walls affected by damp, confirmation of which came by postcard on 22 January 2000. This work has still not been done. I was also told that someone would inspect the property to assess the extent of the disrepair.

4. When I reported the dampness on that date, Nigel Ford responded by saying that I should open the windows whilst cooking.

5. In June 2000 I complained by telephone to Mr Ford that the re-plastering had still not been done and that no-one had visited the property. Mr Ford told me that he had put an order in for the works to be done and would chase this up.

6. I complained again by telephone in September 2000 and November 2000 as the damp seemed to be getting worse and the smell was becoming very bad. I also complained that mould was now appearing on our window frames all over the house and in other parts of the property.

7. In March 2001, I telephoned Mr Ford and reported that damp patches had appeared on the ceiling in my bedroom. He said that he would send someone round to inspect my house.

8. Someone from the council, whose name I cannot remember, came to look at the disrepair in April 2001. I showed him where the damp and mould was quite bad. I also remember that he commented on how bad the smell was and how awful it must be for me especially with young children. I also showed him the sash windows. He told me that they would not stay open because the cords in them had snapped. He said this was probably due to wear and tear as the windows were quite old. I told him where there were leaks in the roof but he did not see any water coming through as it was a sunny day. I heard nothing more from the council after this inspection.

9. I wrote to the head of Anywhere Borough Council in June 2001 about the dampness, the broken sash windows and the leaking roof. I also mentioned that Mr Ford had told me in January 2000 that workmen would re-plaster the walls but that this had still not been done. Unfortunately, I did not keep a copy of this letter. The response I got was again that I should open the windows. I was also offered a mould cleaning kit. I did not chase this up as I had already tried a similar kit and it had not prevented mould from reappearing.

10. I contacted Anywhere Law Centre for advice in January 2002. On 6 January 2002, my solicitor, Sarah Lund at Anywhere Law Centre, wrote a letter to Anywhere Borough Council on my behalf stating what the defects were and asking them to forward my housing file to me. A copy of the letter is attached as 'SP1' [not attached] which is a bundle of letters sent and received.

11. Anywhere Law Centre received nothing back from Anywhere Borough Council.

12. In January 2002 Anywhere Law Centre instructed Tushar Bala an Environmental Health Consultant for the Health and Housing group to inspect the property to prepare a report on the extent of disrepair.

13. Ms Lund wrote to Anywhere Borough Council again on 27 January 2002

requesting that they carry out repairs to my house. A copy of this letter is attached in the bundle marked 'SP1'. In response to this letter, Ms Lund told me that Mr Ford had telephoned her to inform her that the council's expert would also be attending on the same day as our expert.

14. Mr Bala inspected the property in February 2002. Mr Jones, the council's senior maintenance surveyor, also called on me at the same time. Mr Bala and Mr Jones disagreed about the various aspects of my disrepair and dampness problems. Mr Jones on that day said the problem would go away if I turned up the heating and opened the windows. Mr Bala's opinion was very different, believing that the council owed me a duty of repair in respect of the disrepair mentioned above.

15. I have lived in my house with my two children now for over two years. The state of the house has not improved. I have been unable to use one of my bedrooms throughout my tenancy because of damp. Additionally, I cannot use the other bedroom during the summer months because the smell of damp is too much to bear. The damp has ruined some of my belongings: my jacket and my boots. I do not enjoy being at home as the smell is quite bad. I feel that I cannot invite anyone over to my house because I do not want them to see what a mess I live in. My girls are also embarrassed to bring friends home and never do. The disrepair problem has only got worse over time and I have become more and more stressed by it because no one at the council seems to understand what I am going through.

16. I moved to Anywhere hoping to make a fresh start with my children but I have had a very difficult time trying to persuade the council to do something about the state of my house. I did not think that I would still be in this situation two years after moving into the house.

I believe that the contents of this witness statement are true.

Dated this   day of   2002

Signed:...

Stephanie Povey

Case update

After both parties have filed their listing questionnaires, they start negotiations to settle the claim. The council know that their case is much weaker now because of the joint expert's report stating that the council are responsible for the repairs.

The parties finally reach an agreement after various "without prejudice" communications lasting around three weeks. After this agreement has been reached, Ms Povey's solicitor agrees to draw up a consent order which is then signed by both parties. The original consent order plus two copies are sent to the court to file and seal. A copy is served on each of the parties.

The consent order has the same effect as if the court had made the order, ie. it will effectively bring the claim to an end (unless enforcement proceedings are necessary – see paragraph 12.2).

Listing questionnaire

In the ANYWHERE COUNTY COURT

Claim No. AN54321

Last date for filing with court office 27 November 2002

To

ANYWHERE LAW CENTRE

- The court will use the information which you and the other party(ies) provide to fix a date for trial (or to confirm the date and time if one has already been fixed), to confirm the estimated length of trial and to set a timetable for the trial itself. In multi-track cases the court will also decide whether to hold a pre-trial review.

- If you do not complete and return the questionnaire the procedural judge may
    - make an order which leads to your statement of case (claim or defence) being struck out.
    - decide to hold a listing hearing. You may be ordered to pay (immediately) the other parties' costs of attending.
    - if there is sufficient information, list the case for trial and give any appropriate directions.

A Directions complied with

1. Have you complied with all the previous directions given by the court? ☐ Yes ☑ No

2. If no, please explain which directions are outstanding and why

Directions outstanding	Reasons directions outstanding
EXCHANGE OF WITNESS STATEMENTS	POSSIBILTY OF SETTLEMENT, PARTIES WILL AGREE THE DATE FOR EXCHANGE IF NECESSARY

3. Are any further directions required to prepare the case for trial? ☐ Yes ☐ No
(If no go to section B)

4. If yes, please explain directions required and give reasons

Directions required	Reasons required

N170 - w3 Listing questionnaire (4. 99)   *Printed on behalf of The Court Service*

B Experts

1. Has the court already given permission for you to use written expert evidence?   ☑ Yes   ☐ No
(If no go to section B6)

2. If yes, please give name and field of expertise.

Name of expert	Whether joint expert *(please tick, if appropriate)*	Field of expertise
CAROLYN ELLIS 570 ST JOHNS ST ANYWHERE	✓	ENVIRONMENTAL HOUSING

3. Have the expert(s') report(s) been agreed with the other parties?   ☑ Yes   ☐ No

4. Have the experts met to discuss their reports?   N/A ☐ Yes   ☐ No

5. Has the court already given permission for the expert(s) to give oral evidence at the trial?   *(If yes go to Q7)* ☐ Yes   ☑ No

6. If no, are you seeking that permission?   ☐ Yes   ☑ No
(If no go to section C)

7. If yes, give your reasons for seeking permission.

8. If yes, what are the names, addresses and fields of expertise of your experts?

Expert 1	Expert 2	Expert 3	Expert 4

9. Please give details of any dates within the trial period when your expert(s) will not be available.

Name of expert	Dates not available

C Other witnesses

(If you are not calling other witnesses go to section D)

1. How many other witnesses (including yourself) will be giving evidence on your behalf at the trial? *(do not include experts - see section B above)*

1

(Give number)

2. What are the names and addresses of your witnesses?

Witness 1	Witness 2	Witness 3	Witness 4
STEPHANIE POVEY 23 OLD STREET ANYWHERE			

3. Please give details of any dates within the trial period when you or your witnesses will not be available?

Name of witness	Dates not available
N/A	

4. Are any of the witness statements agreed? ☐ Yes ☑ No

(If no go to question C6)

5. If yes, give the name of the witness and the date of his or her statement

Name of witness	Date of statement

6. Do you or any of your witnesses need any special facilities? ☐ Yes ☑ No

(If no go to question C8)

7. If yes, what are they?

8. Will any of your witnesses be provided with an interpreter? ☐ Yes ☑ No

(If no go to section D)

9. If yes, say what type of interpreter e.g. language (stating which), deaf/blind etc.

D Legal representation

1. Who will be presenting your case at the hearing or trial? ☐ You ☑ Solicitor ☐ Counsel

2. Please give details of any dates within the trial period when the person presenting your case will not be available.

Name	Dates not available
SARAH LUND	

E Other matters

	Minutes	Hours	Days
1. How long do you estimate the trial will take, including cross-examination and closing arguments?		4	

If your case is allocated to the fast track the maximum time allowed for the whole case will be no more than one day.

2. What is the estimated number of pages of evidence to be included in the trial bundle?

40

(please give number)

Fast track cases only

3. The court will normally give you 3 weeks notice in the fast track of the date fixed for a fast track trial unless, in exceptional circumstances, the court directs that shorter notice will be given. Would you be prepared to accept shorter notice of the date fixed for trial? ☑ Yes ☐ No

Signed

~~Claimant/defendant or Counsel~~/Solicitor for the claimant/~~defendant~~

Date

IN THE ANYWHERE COUNTY COURT   Claim No: AN54321

BETWEEN:

STEPHANIE POVEY

<u>Claimant</u>

and

ANYWHERE BOROUGH COUNCIL

<u>Defendant</u>

CONSENT ORDER

IT IS HEREBY ORDERED BY CONSENT:

1. The Claimant does accept the sum of £5,000 in full and final settlement of this action.

2. The Defendant do carry out the works listed in the Schedule of Works attached to the report of Tushar Bala by 31 August 2002.

3. Upon payment of £5,000 to the Claimant and upon completion of the works listed in the Schedule of works, the action be dismissed.

4. The Defendant do pay the Claimant's costs of the action, to be determined by detailed assessment if not agreed.

5. There be a detailed assessment in accordance with The Community Legal Services (Funding) Order 2000.

6. Permission for either party to apply to implement the terms of this order.

Dated 8 July 2002

....

Anywhere Borough Council   Anywhere Law Centre
Town Hall   City Street
Anywhere   Anywhere

Background

Robert Smith and Jim Reid entered into a tenancy agreement with John Gallagher in March 2001 to rent a two-bedroom flat at 5 Acacia Gardens, Anywhere, AN3 6AL. The agreement was a six-month assured shorthold tenancy. The rent agreed was £650 per month. Mr Gallagher collected the rent in person every month.

Just before the end of the six months in September 2001, Robert and Jim were asked to attend Mr Gallagher's office. Mr Gallagher told them that he was going to increase the rent to £800 the following month. He told Robert and Jim that if they did not want to pay this rent then he would allow them to stay on for just another six weeks so that they could find alternative accommodation. Both Robert and Jim signed an agreement to stay there for another six weeks.

Jim Reid left the property in November 2001 because of the proposed rent increase. He gave notice of this to Mr Gallagher. Jim's brother, William, moved in to replace him; Mr Gallagher was informed of this.

Robert Smith found another person, Ben Watt, to also move in so that he could afford the rent increase. Robert told Mr Gallagher about this arrangement.

On 20 January 2002 Robert arrived home to find the locks had been changed. He was unable to gain access to the flat. Robert contacted William who told him that Mr Gallagher had informed him that they were all being evicted.

Mr Gallagher then contacted Robert informing him that he had £650 rent arrears and that, if this was not paid immediately, he would remove Robert's belongings. He also told Robert to move out of the flat that day.

Robert went to Good Advice Law Centre who took on his case for unlawful eviction, and wrote a **letter before action** on his behalf.

Robert stays with friends who have told him that he can only remain for a few days.

25 January 2002

Mr John Gallagher
43 King Street
Anywhere

By fax and post: 0234 567890

URGENT

Dear Mr Gallagher

Re: Robert Smith, 5 Acacia Gardens, Anywhere AN3 6AL

We act on behalf of Mr Smith in respect of the above property.

We are instructed that Mr Smith holds a periodic tenancy in respect of these premises, to which access has been denied since 20 January 2002. We are informed that you attended the premises and changed the locks to the external gate.

In addition, Mr Smith has subsequently been refused access to the property to collect his belongings.

We have advised Mr Smith that you have acted unlawfully, as follows.

1. In respect of refusing Mr Smith access to the property to collect his goods

You, either directly or indirectly by your agents or employees, are guilty of the tort of conversion and interference with goods in denying Mr Smith access to his belongings which remain in the property.

2. In evicting Mr Smith by changing the locks to the premises

You, either directly or indirectly through your agents or employees, are guilty of unlawful eviction which is a criminal offence (section 1 of the Protection from Eviction Act 1977) and gives rise to a claim for damages in the county court. We understand that criminal proceedings are being considered by the local authority.

Under the implied terms of Mr Smith's tenancy, you are in breach of your covenant for quiet enjoyment. Mr Smith also has a claim for damages against you under section 27 of the Housing Act 1988.

In the circumstances, please confirm to us by **12 noon on Monday 28 January** that:

1. Mr Smith will be readmitted to 5 Acacia Gardens on **Monday 28 January** without interference;

2. His belongings will be returned to him when he attends the premises on Monday.

Any attempt to sell the goods currently held by you will be treated as theft and reported to the police accordingly.

Please note that if we do not hear from you by 12 noon on Monday, an application will be made to the county court for an injunction ordering you to allow our client access to the premises and delivery up of our client's goods. This will include a claim for costs. A copy of this letter will also be brought to the court's attention.

We trust this course of action will not prove necessary. A copy of this letter has been forwarded to the tenancy relations officer at Anywhere Borough Council.

Yours sincerely

Simon Gallup
Solicitor
Good Advice Law Centre

Case update

Good Advice Law Centre hears nothing from the landlord in response to the **letter before action**.

Simon Gallup, Robert Smith's solicitor at Good Advice Law Centre, rings the local court to inform them that an application for an **injunction** is going to be made. It is good practice to do this as the court will then try to make sure that a judge will be available.

Mr Gallup then drafts a **particulars of claim** and an application for an **injunction** with supporting statements. A draft order is also drawn up for the injunction application.

Claim Form

In the ANYWHERE COUNTY COURT
Claim No.

Claimant

ROBERT SMITH
53 WELLINGTON STREET
ANYWHERE
AN3 7BR

SEAL

Defendant(s)

JOHN GALLAGHER
43 KING STREET
ANYWHERE
TEL: 0987 543322

Brief details of claim

CLAIM IS FOR COMPENSATION FOR UNLAWFUL EVICTION AND AN INJUNCTION TO READMIT THE
CLAIMANT INTO 5 ACACIA GARDENS, ANYWHERE, AN3 6AL.

Value

LIMITED TO £15,000

Defendant's name and address			£
JOHN GALLAGHER 43 KING STREET ANYWHERE TEL: 0987 543322	Amount claimed	N/A
	Court fee	120.00
	Solicitor's costs	100.00
	Total amount	
	Issue date	

The court office at

is open between 10 am and 4 pm Monday to Friday. When corresponding with the court, please address forms or letters to the Court Manager and quote the claim number.
N1 Claim form (CPR Part 7) (10.00)   *Printed on behalf of The Court Service*

	Claim No.	

Does, or will, your claim include any issues under the Human Rights Act 1998?   ☐ Yes   ☑ No

Particulars of Claim (attached)(to follow)

SEE ATTACHED

Statement of Truth
*(I believe)(The Claimant believes) that the facts stated in these particulars of claim are true.
* I am duly authorised by the claimant to sign this statement

Full name   SIMON GALLUP

Name of claimant's solicitor's firm   GOOD ADVICE LAW CENTRE

signed _____   position or office held   SOLICITOR

*(Claimant)(Litigation friend)(Claimant's solicitor)   (if signing on behalf of firm or company)

*delete as appropriate

GOOD ADVICE LAW CENTRE
ANYTOWN ROAD
ANYWHERE

TEL: 0987 666555
FAX: 0987 666557

Claimant's or claimant's solicitor's address to which documents or payments should be sent if different from overleaf including (if appropriate) details of DX, fax or e-mail.

ANYWHERE COUNTY COURT   **Claim No:**

BETWEEN:

ROBERT SMITH

Claimant

and

JOHN GALLAGHER

Defendant

PARTICULARS OF CLAIM

---

1. At all material times, the Claimant was a joint assured shorthold tenant of the premises known as 5 Acacia Gardens, Anywhere, AN3 6AL. The Defendant was the landlord thereof.

2. The premises are a self-contained two bedroom flat ("the flat").

3. The said assured shorthold tenancy commenced on 23 March 2001 for a fixed term of six months. The rent for the flat was £650 per calendar month. As a term of the agreement, the Claimant and the other joint tenant, Jim Reid, paid a deposit of £650 to the Defendant to be held until the end of the tenancy.

4. Upon the expiry of the fixed term, the Claimant and Jim Reid continued to occupy the flat as statutory periodic tenants.

5. By agreement with the Defendant, Jim Reid left the flat on 18 November 2001 and was replaced by William Reid.

6. It was an implied term of the tenancy that the Defendant would allow the Claimant quiet enjoyment of the flat.

7. The Defendant has unlawfully deprived the Claimant of his occupation of the flat, thus entitling him to damages under section 27 of the Housing Act 1988.

8. By reasons of the matters hereinafter set out the Defendant has breached the said term and committed trespass to the Claimant's flat and property.

Particulars of breach

   a) On 20 January 2002, the Claimant returned to the flat to find that he was unable to gain access as the locks had been changed.

   b) The Claimant then received a telephone call from the Defendant and was informed that he owed £650 to the Defendant and that if the same was not paid immediately, the Claimant's goods would be removed. In addition, the Claimant was told that he had to move out of the flat that day.

c)   The Claimant has been unable to gain access to the flat.

9.   By reason of the matters aforesaid, the Claimant has suffered loss, damage, distress, discomfort and inconvenience.

Particulars of general damage

a)   The Claimant has been denied access to all his personal property, save for the clothes he was wearing on 20 January.

b)   The Claimant has had to arrange to stay temporarily with a friend and has had to take time off work.

Particulars of special damage

	£
Loss of earnings (6 days at £52 per day)	312.00
Additional telephone costs incurred	67.00

The following items have not been returned to the Claimant:

	£
Clothes	300.00
Sofa	45.00
Desk	100.00
2 mattresses	100.00
Computer, monitor, scanner and printer	1,000.00
2 hi-fi systems	200.00
Microwave	25.00
Video player and cassettes	230.00
CDs and tapes	450.00
Cash	300.00
Chest of drawers	50.00
Kitchen utensils and pans	100.00
Books	150.00
Camera	20.00
Shelving	10.00
Passport and birth certificate	25.00
Total	**3,484.00**

In addition other items too numerous to list have not been returned to the Claimant.

10.   The Claimant claims to be entitled to exemplary and/or aggravated damages.

Particulars of exemplary and/or aggravated damages

a)   The Claimant's solicitors wrote to the Defendant by letter dated 25 January 2002 advising him that he was acting illegally. The Defendant ignored this advice and proceeded in unlawfully evicting the Claimant while knowing that he was acting illegally. As a result, the Claimant claims exemplary damages.

b)   The Claimant was very distressed by the way the eviction was carried out. He had no warning from the Defendant that he was to be evicted and has been unable to collect any of his belongings since the unlawful eviction. In the circumstances, the Claimant claims aggravated damages.

11.   Further, or in the alternative, by reason of the matters set out in paragraph 7 herein, the Defendant has unlawfully deprived the Claimant of his occupation of the flat and the Claimant seeks damages to be assessed in accordance with sections 27 and 28 Housing Act 1988.

AND the Claimant claims:

(1)   An injunction requiring the Defendant forthwith to readmit the Claimant to the premises and restraining the Defendant by himself, his servants or agents, from further interfering with the Claimant's quiet enjoyment of the premises or further trespassing on the Claimant's premises or goods, or in any way harassing the Claimant.

(2)   Damages limited to £15,000.

(3)   Aggravated and/or exemplary damages.

(4)   Interest pursuant to section 69 County Courts Act 1984 at such rate and for such period as the court thinks fit.

(5)   Costs.

Statement of truth

The Claimant believes that the facts stated in these particulars of claim are true.

Signed:...

Simon Gallup
Solicitor to the Claimant
Good Advice Law Centre
Anywhere
Dated 28 January 2002

Application for Injunction (General Form)

Between ROBERT SMITH

☑ Claimant
☐ Applicant
☐ Petitioner
(Tick whichever applies)

and JOHN GALLAGHER

☑ Defendant
☐ Respondent

In the

ANYWHERE

County Court

Claim No.

Claimant's Ref.

Defendant's Ref.

Notes on completion

Tick whichever box applies and specify legislation where appropriate

(1) Enter the full name of the person making the application

(2) Enter the full name of the person the injunction is to be directed to

(3) Set out here the proposed restraining orders (if the defendant is a limited company delete the wording in brackets and insert "whether by its servants, agents, officers or otherwise")

(4) Set out here any proposed mandatory orders requiring acts to be done

(5) Set out here any further terms asked for including provision for costs

(6) Enter the names of all persons who have sworn affidavits or signed statement in support of this application

(7) Enter the names and addresses of all persons upon whom it is intended to serve this application

(8) Enter the full name and address for service and delete as required

☑ By application in pending proceedings
☐ Under Statutory provision _____

Seal

This application raises issues under the Human Rights Act 1998   ☐ Yes   ☑ No

The Claimant ~~(Applicant/Petitioner)~~[1] Robert Smith

applies to the court for an injunction order in the following terms:

That the Defendant ~~(Respondent)~~[2] John Gallagher

be forbidden (whether by himself or by instructing or encouraging any other person[3]

disposing of or further interfering with the Claimant's goods, a list of which is annexed hereto. [This would be similar list to that outlined in the Particulars of Special Damages.]

And that the Defendant~~(Respondent)~~[4]

1. Forthwith readmit the Claimant to 5 Acacia Gardens, Anywhere, AN3 6AL ('the premises').
2. Forthwith provide the Claimant with keys to the premises.
3. Forthwith return the Claimant's goods to him.

And that[5]

Costs are reserved.

The grounds of this application are set out in the written evidence

of[6] Robert Smith   ~~sworn~~ (signed) on

This written evidence is served with this application.

This application is to be served upon[7]

John Gallagher of 43 King Street, Anywhere

This application is filed by[8] Good Advice Law Centre

(the Solicitors for) the Claimant ~~(Applicant/Petitioner)~~

whose address for service is Anytown Road, Anywhere

Signed   Dated 28 January 2002

This section to be completed by the court

* Name and address of the person application is directed to

To*
of
This application will be heard by the (District) Judge
at
on   the   day of   [20   ]   at   o'clock
If you do not attend at the time shown the court may make an injunction order in your absence

If you do not fully understand this application you should go to a Solicitor, Legal Advice Centre or a Citizens' Advice Bureau

The court office at

is open between 10am and 4pm Mon - Fri. When corresponding with the court, please address all forms and letters to the Court Manager and quote the claim number.

N16A General form of application for injunction (10.00)   *The Court Service Publications Unit*

Statement on behalf of the Claimant
First statement of Robert Smith
Exhibits: RS1, RS2, RS3 and RS4
Dated: 29 January 2002

ANYWHERE COUNTY COURT

Claim No: AN0198765

BETWEEN:

ROBERT SMITH

<u>**Claimant**</u>

and

JOHN GALLAGHER

<u>**Defendant**</u>

STATEMENT OF ROBERT SMITH

I, Robert Smith, currently of 53 Wellington Street, Anywhere, AN3 7BR, will say as follows:

1. I make this statement in support of my application for an injunction to readmit me to 5 Acacia Gardens, Anywhere, AN3 6AL.

2. The application is being made without notice because I have been asked to leave the premises where I have been temporarily staying with friends. I have nowhere to stay tonight. My landlord, John Gallagher, has been warned by letter dated 25 January 2002 that I have applied for this injunction. This letter is exhibited to this statement and marked RS1.

3. In March 2001, Jim Reid and I entered into a joint, six-month, assured shorthold tenancy of 5 Acacia Gardens, Anywhere, AN3 6AL. The property is owned and let by John Gallagher. The rent was £650 per calendar month and we paid a deposit of £650. The property is a two-bedroom flat.

4. The tenancy agreement was in John Gallagher's name. All payments were made to him and he attended the property each month, without prior notice, to collect the rent.

5. When the tenancy expired in September 2001, John Gallagher asked me to attend his office at 43 King Street, Anywhere. At his office, he told me that he wanted to increase the rent to £800 per calendar month. I was told that if I did not accept the increase, I could sign a further agreement to continue living at the property for six weeks, paying the existing rent and then decide what to do at the end of that period. I signed an agreement to this effect.

6. Jim left the property in November 2001 because of the proposed rent increase. I understand that he gave notice to John Gallagher and arranged for his brother, William, to take his place.

7. I was also arranging for another tenant to move in as well, to share the increased rent, which was due to come into force in January. Towards the end of December, I informed John Gallagher verbally that I had found another person, Ben Watt, to move in with William and me. At no time did he raise any objections to my course of action. A few days later, Ben Watt moved in.

8. On 20 January 2002, I returned home to find that I could not get in because the locks had been changed. I contacted William who told me that he had arrived home to find John Gallagher in the property. He told me that he was told by John Gallagher that we were all being evicted and some of my belongings were being seized. John Gallagher allowed William into the property to remove his own belongings.

9. After speaking to William, John Gallagher himself called me on my mobile telephone and informed me that if I did not pay £650 immediately, he would remove my belongings. He also told me that I had to move out of the flat that day.

10. I then telephoned Anywhere police who confirmed that they had been asked to attend the property to safeguard against any breach of the peace. I also telephoned my family and friends to arrange alternative accommodation.

11. Since I was evicted, I have been staying in a friend's spare room.

12. John Gallagher claims that I owe £650 in unpaid rent, which fell to be paid on 14 January 2002. I never refused to pay the rent and was waiting for John Gallagher to collect it as usual. However, he had contacted me and told me to take the rent to his office. I refused and asked him to collect it from me at the flat, as he has done every month since the tenancy commenced. I have always paid my share of the rent when demanded and am shocked by John Gallagher's actions.

13. I do not know what belongings have been removed from the flat and what items are still there. All I have are the clothes I was wearing on 20 January.

14. I reported the eviction to Anywhere Borough Council. I understand that the council are considering whether to bring a criminal prosecution against John Gallagher.

15. I am now being assisted by Good Advice Law Centre who wrote to my landlord on 25 January. This letter is exhibited with this statement and

marked RS3. I had previously written on 24 January (Exhibit RS4) asking John Gallagher not to dispose of any of my belongings as I was seeking legal advice. I am advised that I cannot be lawfully evicted without a court order and confirm that I have never received a notice to quit the property or notice of court proceedings. In addition, I am informed that my landlord cannot lawfully refuse me access to the flat and cannot lawfully hold all my belongings.

16. This whole incident has shocked me and, but for the generosity of my friends, I would have been homeless. I had to take the rest of the week following the eviction off from work, which caused a lot of disruption both to myself and my colleagues.

17. I ask that the court make an order requiring John Gallagher to readmit me to the flat and to return all my goods. I intend to pursue John Gallagher for compensation to me.

I believe that the facts stated in this witness statement are true.

Signed: *Robert Smith*

Robert Smith

Dated: 28 January 2002

ANYWHERE COUNTY COURT   **Claim No:**

BETWEEN:

ROBERT SMITH

<u>**Claimant**</u>

and

JOHN GALLAGHER

<u>**Defendant**</u>

DRAFT ORDER

If you do not obey this order you will be guilty of contempt of court and you may be sent to prison.

On   January 2002, the court considered an application by the Claimant for an injunction.

The court ordered that John Gallagher is forbidden whether by himself or by instructing or encouraging any other person from:

1.   Disposing or further interfering with the Claimant's goods, a list of which is annexed hereto.

And it was ordered that John Gallagher shall:

1.   Forthwith readmit the Claimant to 5 Acacia Gardens, Anywhere, AN3 6AL ("the premises").

2.   Forthwith provide the Claimant with keys to the premises.

It is further ordered that costs are reserved.

This order will remain in force until   2002 at

        o'clock unless before then it is revoked by a further order of the court.

Notice of further hearing

The court will consider the application and whether the order should continue at a further hearing at the Anywhere County Court on
     2002 at   o'clock.

If you do not attend at the time shown, the court may make an injunction order in your absence.

You are entitled to apply to the court to re-consider the order before that day.

The Claimant gave an undertaking promising to pay any damages ordered by the court if it later decides that the Defendant has suffered loss or damage as a result of this order and to serve on the Defendant the application notice, evidence in support and this order as soon as practicable.

Case update

The court hears the application for the **injunction** and grants the order in the terms outlined in the draft order. It orders that the injunction is to remain in force until 4 February 2002 when the injunction application is to be heard again with John Gallagher present. Mr Gallagher will then have been served with the injunction, and will have an opportunity to put forward his case for resisting the injunction.

On 4 February 2002, the hearing for the injunction application takes place. The court decides that Robert Smith should be allowed to remain in the premises until the trial.

ANYWHERE COUNTY COURT   Claim No: AN0198765

BETWEEN:

ROBERT SMITH

<u>Claimant</u>

and

JOHN GALLAGHER

<u>Defendant</u>

DEFENCE

---

1.   Paragraph 1 of the Particulars of Claim is admitted.

2.   Paragraph 2 is admitted.

3.   Paragraph 3 is admitted.

4.   Paragraph 4 is admitted.

5.   Paragraph 5 is denied. At no time was the Defendant informed that Jim Reid would be moving out. The Defendant is only aware that the Claimant and Jim Reid occupied the flat.

6.   Paragraph 6 is admitted.

7.   Paragraph 7 is denied. It is the Defendant's case that the Claimant and Jim Reid moved out of the flat on 14 January 2002 after giving the Defendant two months' notice of this.

8.   Paragraph 8a is denied. It is the Defendant's case that the Claimant and Jim Reid moved out of the flat on 14 January 2002 after giving the Defendant two months' notice of this. The flat was left empty on this date and the Defendant made arrangements to re-let it.

9.   Paragraph 8b is denied. The Defendant did not make such a call. The Defendant repeats that the Claimant and Jim Reid moved out of the flat on 14 January 2002 leaving it empty.

10. Paragraph 8c is admitted but the Defendant claims that the Claimant is no longer entitled to access to the flat since he moved out and ended the tenancy.

11. As to paragraph 9, no admissions are made as to any loss, damage, distress, discomfort and inconvenience suffered by the Claimant as these are matters outside the Defendant's knowledge. The Claimant is put to strict proof.

12. Paragraph 10 is denied. The Defendant did not unlawfully evict the Claimant. The Claimant and Jim Reid moved out of the flat on 14 January 2002 after giving the Defendant two months' notice of this. The flat was left empty on this date and the Defendant made arrangements to re-let it.

13. Paragraph 11 is denied.

14. It is denied that the Claimant is entitled to the relief claimed, or any relief.

Statement of truth

The Defendant believes that the facts stated in this Defence are true.

Signed:..

Full Name: Susan Banshee
Position held: Solicitor to the Defendant
Dated 19 February 2002

TO the court
AND to the Claimant

Case update

After the Defence is filed, allocation questionnaires are sent out to the parties to be completed by them. Once completed and returned to court, a **directions hearing** is listed. At this hearing, the court decides the case should be allocated to the **fast track** as it is unlikely that the trial will last longer than a day and the value of the claim is limited to £15,000. Directions are given for the **disclosure** and exchange of **witness statements.**

Following the exchange of witness statements, the parties prepare for trial (see paragraph 10.1). The trial takes place 26 weeks after allocation to the fast track. The court decides that, on balance, Robert Smith's evidence is more believable than that of John Gallagher. The court orders that Robert Smith be allowed to remain in the property and awards **damages** to him. Additionally, it is ordered that John Gallagher is to pay Robert Smith's costs.

Background

Andrea Miller moved into 17 Jacob Way, Anywhere, AN2 4DK on 17 August 2001. She had an assured shorthold tenancy for six months. Her rent was £450 per month and she paid a deposit of £450. Ms Miller moved out at the end of this six months on 16 February 2002. She told her landlord, Ben Theodopollis, that she was moving out then. He agreed that he would come to the flat on the 16 February to pay back her deposit.

On the 16 February, Mr Theodopollis told Ms Miller that he would not pay her deposit back that day as he had to check all the bills had been paid. Once he had done this, he said he would send her a cheque for her deposit. He told her it would only take one to two weeks for this. Ms Miller agreed to this and gave him her forwarding address.

While at the property, Mr Theodopollis checked that it was in a good state. He agreed that it was and said that he would only deduct money from the deposit if there were any outstanding bills.

Two weeks later, Ms Miller had still not received back her deposit. She called Mr Theodopollis. He told her that he would be sending the cheque immediately as it had just been agreed that there were no outstanding bills.

Ms Miller did not receive the cheque and called Mr Theodopollis again. He told her he had sent a cheque and that she should contact him once she received it. Ms Miller again did not receive the cheque. She called Mr Theodopollis about six or seven times after this but each time was told that he was not in.

Ms Miller went to her local advice centre to get advice on how to get back her deposit. She was advised to write a **letter before action** and, if necessary, start a claim in the small claims court.

28 March 2002

Ben Theodopollis
52 Windmill Avenue
Anywhere
AN4 7TR

Dear Mr Theodopollis

Re: The return of my deposit for 17 Jacob Way, Anywhere AN2 4DK

As you are aware, my tenancy for 17 Jacob Way ended on 16 February 2002. I
moved out on that day. You told me then that you would send me a cheque for
the return of my deposit of £450. As yet, I have not received this money
despite numerous telephone calls to you requesting the return of my deposit.

Unless I receive the repayment of my deposit within 14 days of the date of this
letter, I will be starting a claim in the county court to recover my deposit. I
would prefer not to take this course of action and hope to hear from you as
requested. If I need to go to court to claim my deposit money back, I will be
applying for my costs to be paid by you.

Yours sincerely

Andrea Miller

Case update

Mr Theodopollis does not reply to Ms Miller's **letter before action**. She completes a claim form to issue proceedings to recover her deposit. She also drafts a **witness statement** to put in as evidence before the court.

Claim Form

In the ANYWHERE COUNTY COURT

Claim No.

Claimant

MS ANDREA MILLER
2 ACACIA GARDENS
ANYWHERE
AN7 3BF
TEL: 0234 953764

SEAL

Defendant(s)

MR BEN THEODOPOLLIS
52 WINDMILL AVENUE
ANYWHERE
AN4 7TR
TEL: 0234 953222

Brief details of claim

THE DEFENDANT IS THE CLAIMANT'S EX-LANDLORD. THE CLAIMANT CLAIMS REPAYMENT OF HER DEPOSIT. THE DEFENDANT HAS UNLAWFULLY RETAINED IT.

Value
£450

Defendant's name and address			£
MR BEN THEODOPOLLIS 52 WINDMILL AVENUE ANYWHERE AN4 7TR	Amount claimed		450.00
	Court fee		60.00
	Solicitor's costs		NIL
	Total amount		510.00
	Issue date		

The court office at

is open between 10 am and 4 pm Monday to Friday. When corresponding with the court, please address forms or letters to the Court Manager and quote the claim number.
N1 Claim form (CPR Part 7) (10.00)   *Printed on behalf of The Court Service*

Claim No.	

Does, or will, your claim include any issues under the Human Rights Act 1998?　　☐ Yes　　☑ No

Particulars of Claim (attached)(to follow)

1. I moved into 17 Jacob Way on 17 August 2001. My landlord for this accommodation is the Defendant.

2. On the 12 August 2001, before moving in, I gave the Defendant £900 in cash. This included £450 for the first month's rent and £450 for the deposit. I also signed a six-month assured shorthold tenancy agreement.

3. I moved out of 17 Jacob Way on 16 February 2002. My landlord came to the flat to check the condition of the flat and to pay back my deposit.

4. After checking the flat, he told me that he was happy with its condition but that he would not pay back my deposit until he had checked that all the bills had been paid for the flat.

5. There were no outstanding bills when I left the flat. My landlord agreed that there were no outstanding bills and promised to return my deposit in full.

6. I have still not received my deposit money back from my landlord.

7. Further details of the facts are contained in my witness statement attached to this claim form.

8. I claim the return of my £450 plus interest pursuant to section 69 of the County Court Act 1984 and costs.

DATED: 16.04.02

Statement of Truth
*(I believe)(The Claimant believes) that the facts stated in these particulars of claim are true.
* I am duly authorised by the claimant to sign this statement

Full name _____ANDREA MILLER_____

Name of claimant's solicitor's firm _N/A_____

signed _____　　position or office held _____
*(Claimant)(Litigation friend)(Claimant's solicitor)　　(if signing on behalf of firm or company)

*delete as appropriate

Claimant's or claimant's solicitor's address to which documents or payments should be sent if different from overleaf including (if appropriate) details of DX, fax or e-mail.

Statement on behalf of the Claimant
Witness: Andrea Miller
First statement
Dated: 16.04.02
Exhibits: AM1, AM2 and AM3

ANYWHERE COUNTY COURT   **Claim No:**

BETWEEN:

ANDREA MILLER

Claimant

and

BEN THEODOPOLLIS

Defendant

WITNESS STATEMENT OF ANDREA MILLER

1. I, Andrea Miller, of 2 Acacia Gardens, Anywhere, AN7 3BF, make this statement in support of my claim for repayment of my deposit for my tenancy at 17 Jacob Way, Anywhere, AN2 4DK.

2. In early August 2001, Ben Theodopollis showed me around a one-bedroom flat at 17 Jacob Way with a view to renting it. I liked the flat immediately and decided I wanted to live there. Ben Theodopollis told me that he was the landlord and that he would require £450 for the deposit and £450 for the first month's rent before I moved in. He wanted this money in cash. I agreed to this. He told me that he would draw up an assured shorthold tenancy agreement for six months and that I should sign it before I moved in.

3. On 12.08.01, I signed the tenancy agreement and paid Ben Theodopollis £900 in cash. He gave me a receipt for this that is attached to this statement marked 'Exhibit AM1'. [not attached]

4. I moved into the one-bedroom flat at 17 Jacob Way on 17.08.01.

5. My rent was paid one month in advance in cash on the 17th of each month. Ben Theodopollis did not give me any receipts for these payments. However, I have attached my bank statements to this witness statement to show that I withdrew £450 each month in cash from my account. This was to pay my rent. These bank statements are attached to this statement and marked 'Exhibit AM2'. [not attached]

6. I had no problems whilst I lived in the property and always paid my rent on time. I remember Ben Theodopollis saying how pleased he was to have me as a tenant because I always paid my rent on time and kept the flat clean.

7. In January 2002, I told my landlord that I did not want to renew the tenancy at the end of the six months as I was going to move in with my boyfriend. I told him I would be moving out on 16 February 2002. He accepted this and told me that he would be showing people around the flat during the next month. I agreed to this.

8. On 16.02.02, Ben Theodopollis came to the flat as arranged to give me back my deposit. He checked that the flat was in good condition. He told me that it was but that he would not pay back my deposit until he had confirmed that I had paid all my bills. He told me that this would only take one to two weeks.

9. I gave him the details of the address I was moving to and he said he would send me a cheque once he had sorted out the business with the bills.

10. Two weeks later, I had still not heard from him. I decided to call him to find out what was going on. I knew that I had paid all my bills and did not see what the problem could be. When I spoke to Ben Theodopollis, he told me that there had been no problems with the bills and that he would send me a cheque for £450 immediately.

11. A week later, I had still not received the cheque so I called Ben Theodopollis again. He told me that he had sent the cheque and that I should call him once I received it.

12. I waited another week but did not receive the cheque. I called Ben Theodopollis again. A woman answered the telephone. I do not know who this was. She told me that Ben Theodopollis was not in and that I should try calling again later. I telephoned around six or seven times after this over the next week. I think it was the same woman who answered each time. She told me that Ben Theodopollis was not in. I felt more and more frustrated and decided to get legal advice on how to get my deposit back.

13. I went to Anywhere Citizens Advice Bureau (CAB) some time in March 2002. An adviser there told me about writing a letter before action and how to start court proceedings if Ben Theodopollis did not pay back my money.

14. I wrote a letter before action on 28 March 2002. This is exhibited to my witness statement and marked 'Exhibit AM3'. [not attached] Ben Theodopollis has still not responded to this.

I believe the facts stated in this witness statement are true.

Dated 16 April 2002

Signed:..

Andrea Miller

Defence and Counterclaim (specified amount)

- Fill in this form if you wish to dispute all or part of the claim and/or make a claim against the claimant (counterclaim).
- You have a limited number of days to complete and return this form to the court.
- Before completing this form, please read the notes for guidance attached to the claim form.
- Please ensure that all boxes at the top right of this form are completed. You can obtain the correct names and number from the claim form. The court cannot trace your case without this information.

How to fill in this form

- Complete sections 1 and 2. Tick the correct boxes and give the other details asked for.
- Set out your defence in section 3. If necessary continue on a separate piece of paper making sure that the claim number is clearly shown on it. In your defence you must state which allegations in the particulars of claim you deny and your reasons for doing so. **If you fail to deny an allegation it may be taken that you admit it.**
- If you dispute only some of the allegations you must
  - specify which you admit and which you deny; and
  - give your own version of events if different from the claimant's.

In the	ANYWHERE COUNTY COURT
Claim No.	AN2468
Claimant (including ref.)	ANDREA MILLER
Defendant	BEN THEODOPOLLIS

- If you wish to make a claim against the claimant (a counterclaim) complete section 4.
- Complete and sign section 5 before sending this form to the court. Keep a copy of the claim form and this form.

Legal Aid

- You may be entitled to legal aid. Ask about the legal aid scheme at any county court office, Citizens Advice Bureau, legal advice centre or firm of solicitors displaying the legal aid sign.

1. How much of the claim do you dispute?

☑ I dispute the full amount claimed as shown on the claim form

or

☐ I admit the amount of £

If you dispute only part of the claim you must **either**:

- pay the amount admitted to the person named at the address for payment on the claim form (see How to Pay in the notes on the back of, or attached to, the claim form). Then send this defence to the court.

  or

- complete the admission form **and** this defence form and send them to the court.

☐ I paid the amount admitted on (*date*) [   ]
  or
☐ I enclose the completed form of admission
  (go to section 2)

2. Do you dispute this claim because you have already paid it? *Tick whichever applies*

☑ **No** (*go to section 3*)

☐ **Yes** I paid £ [   ] to the claimant
on [   ] *(before the claim form was issued)*

Give details of where and how you paid it in the box below *(then go to section 5)*

3. Defence

1. I do not owe the Claimant £450 as she claims.

2. I admit that she paid £450 for me to hold as a deposit whilst she was a tenant of 17 Jacob Way, Anywhere, AN2 4DK. She moved in on 17 August 2001.

3. In January 2002, the Claimant told me she did not want to renew the tenancy.

4. On 17 January 2002, I went to 17 Jacob Way to collect the rent. The Claimant did not answer the door so I went away. I tried collecting this rent again on 18, 19, 20, 21 and 22 January by turning up at her flat. On 22 January, I put a note through her door requesting that she pay the rent for the final month of her tenancy.

5. I heard nothing further from her.

6. I went to the flat on 16 February 2002 to check that it was in good condition as the Claimant was due to move out that day. She was in and handed the keys back to me. The flat was in good condition so I was happy and did not request that she pay the last month's rent as I would only have returned it to her for repayment of the deposit I was holding.

N9B - w3 Defence and Counterclaim (specified amount)(4.99)   *Printed on behalf of The Court Service*

Defence (continued)   Claim No. | AN2468 |

7. There was no conversation about outstanding bills.

8. I do not recollect any telephone calls from the Claimant after she moved out.

9. I was abroad from 21.03.02 until 22.04.02. On my return, I received the letter from the Claimant asking for the repayment of the deposit and the Claim Form.

10. I do not owe the Claimant £450 as she states.

4. If you wish to make a claim against the claimant (a counterclaim)

If your claim is for a specific sum of money, how much are you claiming? £ [   ]

My claim is for *(please specify nature of claim)*

[   ]

- To start your counterclaim, you will have to pay a fee. Court staff will tell you how much you have to pay

- You may not be able to make a counterclaim where the claimant is the Crown (e.g. a Government Department). Ask at your local county court office for further information.

What are your reasons for making the counterclaim?
If you need to continue on a separate sheet put the claim number in the top right hand corner

[   ]

5. Signed
(To be signed by you or by your solicitor or litigation friend)

*(I believe)~~(The defendant believes)~~ that the facts stated in this form are true. ~~*I am duly authorised by the defendant to sign this statement~~

delete as appropriate

Position or office held
(if signing on behalf of firm or company)

[   ]

Date 28.04.02

Give an address to which notices about this case can be sent to you

52 WINDMILL AVENUE
ANYWHERE

Postcode AN4 7TR

Tel. no. 0234 953222

	if applicable
fax no.	
DX no.	
e-mail	

Case update

On receiving the Defence from Ben Theodopollis, the court lists the claim for a hearing giving both parties 21 days' notice, and informing them that 30 minutes will be allowed by for the hearing as required by CPR 27.4(2).

The Practice Direction to CPR 27 lists standard directions for various proceedings in the small claims court. The standard directions for the tenants' claims for the return of deposits is listed at Form D in the Practice Direction. The court directs that these standard directions should be followed.

General Form of Judgment or Order

To [Claimant] [Defendant] ['s Solicitor]

Andrea Miller
17 Jacob Way
Anywhere
AN2 4DK

In the	
	ANYWHERE COUNTY COURT
Claim No.	AN2468
Claimant (including ref)	ANDREA MILLER
Defendant (including ref)	BEN THEODOPOLLIS

SEAL

THE COURT DIRECTS

1. Each party shall deliver to every other party and to the court office copies of all documents on which he intends to rely at the hearing. These may include:
  -the tenancy agreement and any inventory,
  -the rent book or other evidence of rent and other payments made by the claimant to the defendant,
  -witness statements.

2. The copies shall be delivered no later than 14 days before the hearing.

3. The original documents shall be brought to the hearing.

4. Signed statements setting out evidence of all witnesses on whom each party intends to rely shall be prepared and included in the documents mentioned in paragraph 1. This includes the evidence of the parties themselves and of any other witness whether or not s/he is going to come to court to give evidence.

5. The parties should note that the judge may decide not to take into account a document or the evidence of a witness if no copy of that document or no copy of a statement or report by that witness has been supplied to the other parties.

6. TAKE NOTICE that the HEARING will take place on 31 May 2002 at 10.30am at Anywhere County Court, Anywhere. 30 minutes have been allowed for the hearing.

7. The court must be informed immediately if the case is settled by agreement before the hearing date.

DATED: 11 May 2002

Note: If judgment is for £5,000 or more, or is in respect of a debt which attracts contractual or statutory interest for late payment, the claimant may be entitled to further interest

The court office at

is open between 10 am and 4 pm [4.30pm]Monday to Friday. When corresponding with the court, please address forms or letters to the Court Manager and quote the case number.

N24 -w3 General form of judgment or order (4.99)

Case update

When Andrea Miller arrives at the court for the hearing, she tells the usher that she is there. The usher tells her District Judge Jones will be hearing her case. She then waits to be called into court.

The hearing takes place in a room in court. The judge, Ms Miller and Mr Theodopollis sit around a table. At the hearing, the judge first listens to evidence from Ms Miller. She refers the judge to her **witness statement**. The judge invites Mr Theodopollis to ask Ms Miller questions about her statement. He asks Ms Miller if she paid her rent for the last month that she lived in the flat. Ms Miller replies that she did and shows Mr Theodopollis and the judge her bank statement; it states that £450 was withdrawn from her account in her last month of living at the flat. The judge then asks her a few questions.

Next, the judge asks Mr Theodopollis to tell his side of the story. Mr Theodopollis expands on what he has written in his defence. The judge asks Ms Miller if she would like to ask Mr Theodopollis any questions. Ms Miller shows the judge and Mr Theodopollis a breakdown of calls from BT that she received yesterday. It shows that calls were made to Mr Theodopollis's house. Mr Theodopollis states again that he does not remember getting any calls from Ms Miller. The judge asks him questions. This includes a question about who else lives with him and whether this person would have passed on messages to him. Mr Theodopollis answers that his wife lives with him and that she would pass on messages.

The judge then invites Ms Miller and Mr Theodopollis in turn to make any closing remarks. Neither of them make any.

Judgment is given. The judge decides in favour of Ms Miller. This is mainly because she has proved that calls were made to Mr Theodopollis's house and that Mr Theodopollis had still denied these, even though he claimed that his wife always passes on messages. The judge awards Ms Miller £450 plus interest and costs of £60 for the court fee of issuing the claim.

Interest is calculated at 8 per cent per annum from the date of issue of the claim to the date of judgment. In this case, there are 46 days from the date of issue to the date of judgment and so the interest amounts to £4.54.

General Form of Judgment or Order

In the	
	ANYWHERE COUNTY COURT
Claim No.	AN2468
Claimant (including ref)	ANDREA MILLER
Defendant (including ref)	BEN THEODOPOLLIS

To [Claimant] [Defendant] ['s Solicitor]

> Andrea Miller
> 17 Jacob Way
> Anywhere
> AN2 4DK

SEAL

Before DISTRICT JUDGE JONES sitting at Anywhere County Court, Anywhere

Upon hearing both parties in person

IT IS ORDERED that the Defendant pay the Claimant the sum of £450.00 in respect of her claim, interest of £4.54 and £60 for costs amounting in total to the sum of £514.54 to the Claimant on or before 28 June 2002.

DATED: 31 May 2002

Note: If judgment is for £5,000 or more, or is in respect of a debt which attracts contractual or statutory interest for late payment, the claimant may be entitled to further interest

The court office at

is open between 10 am and 4 pm [4.30pm]Monday to Friday. When corresponding with the court, please address forms or letters to the Court Manager and quote the case number.

N24 -w3 General form of judgment or order (4.99)

A

D

E